# MEN OF COLOR

## by
## William A. Gladstone

**THOMAS PUBLICATIONS**
Gettysburg PA 17325

Copyright © 1993 William A. Gladstone

Printed in the United States of America

Published by  THOMAS PUBLICATIONS
P.O. Box 3031
Gettysburg, Pa. 17325

ISBN-1-57747-010-9

Front cover illustration "Soldier of the 1st South Carolina Infantry" by Don Troiani is courtesy of Historical Art Prints, Ltd., P.O. Box 660, Southbury, CT 06488.

**Photo Credits**

Howard University - p. 154

Roger D. Hunt - p. 48

Library Company of Philadelphia - pp. 109, 110, 138, 157

Library of Congress - p. 146

Rob Lyon - p. 147 (right)

Museum of the U.S. Military Academy - pp. 10, 164

Carlo Pappolla - p. 172

Union League of Philadelphia - p. 21

U.S. Army Military History Institute - pp. 19 (left), 20, 25, 33, 51, 53, 54, 78 (right), 117, 131, 147 (left), 167 (bottom), 175

Wadsworth Antheneum, photo by Joseph Szasfai - p. 112

# Contents

# Acknowledgments

Information is gathered from different sources and with the help of many. Very often the writer does not have an awareness of additional available information. It is because of the professional approach taken by many of these librarians and staff historians who offered their help that made this book possible. I appreciate it very much.

Special thanks goes out to Mike McAfee, Museum Curator, and Alan Aimone, Special Collections Section, Cadet Library of the U.S. Military Academy. I would also like to thank Mike Winey, Curator of Photos and Prints, and Randy Hackenburry, his assistant; Dr. Richard Sommers, Archivist and Historian; and John Sloanaker, Librarian; along with the other historians at the U.S. Army Military History Institute. They have been most helpful.

I must also extend a very special and particular thanks to John Graham of Alexandria, Virginia, for the courtesy he has given me in my research, and to Gregory J.W. Urwin, Ph.D., University of Central Arkansas, who reviewed the entire manuscript. He was kind enough to give me the benefit of his knowledge and I owe him a great deal. The accuracy of the book may be credited to him, and any errors are entirely my own.

Furthermore, it is necessary to offer my thanks to all those who have supplied me with material over the years. It is impossible to name them all and give equal recognition, so I will allow this statement to suffice. It was through the help and assistance of all these people that this project became a reality. They added to my motivation to continue to search for the stories associated with the images that I have acquired. Even though the storytellers have long since passed, the photos remain, which allow the stories to be rejuvenated and preserved.

The librarians of the Westport Public Library and the neighboring Pequot Library also aided me a great deal in my quest for information, and simultaneously saved me from hundreds of miles of travel. These two libraries are within easy access to my home community of Westport, Connecticut.

Thanks also goes to my sister and brother-in-law, Bernice and Bernard Maltz, who aided in the success of this project.

# Introduction

*Men of Color* is being presented as an extended and further examination of the role of blacks in the Civil War. Rather than serving as a supplement or an extension of *United States Colored Troops, 1863-1867*, it has become a greater necessity to expand the initial text and more closely examine other photos and documents that have been preserved. It would be impossible to attempt to record the entire history of black soldiers of the Civil War era, therefore, this text focuses on providing a general perspective based on the author's personal collection of materials.

Although much has been documented about the negative aspects of black men who served in the Civil War, this book concentrates mostly on the positive side of their participation. It is obvious that prejudices existed throughout the ranks of servicemen and elsewhere, but often these elements are exaggerated and inaccurate. It was not only the black men who suffered a shortage of food, clothing, shelter, weapons, and other things; white soldiers experienced these problems as well. However, black men also contributed a great deal to the success of the Union armies. It cannot be denied that their participation in the war was highly valuable.

There is actually a tremendous amount of information on black soldiers who were active in the War of the Rebellion. Sometimes this information is not easily obtained, and many times things are lost or misinterpreted; nevertheless, the information does exist. It is important for it to be passed on to future generations because the black soldiers must not be forgotten. Their participation is of notable significance because they were literally fighting for freedom and acceptance in their country.

# In the Beginning

The first official authorization to use black men (described as men of "African Descent") in the military for the North was in the Second Confiscation Act, Section 11, July 17, 1862 and Sections 12, 13, and 15 of the Militia Act of July 17, 1862. Section 11 of the Second Confiscation Act "authorized the President to receive into the service of the United States, for the purpose of constructing entrenchments or performing camp duty, or any labor, or any military or naval service for which they were found to be competent, persons of African descent, and provided that such persons should be enrolled and organized, under such regulations nor inconsistent with the Constitutions and laws as the President might prescribe."

Section 15 of the Militia Act was the cause of the problem for paying these soldiers when they first entered the service. The Act provided that "persons of African descent who under this law shall be employed, shall receive $10.00 a month, one ration, $3.00 of which monthly pay may be in clothes."

These two Acts authorized President Lincoln to receive black men into military service as soldiers, but on August 6, 1862, President Lincoln announced that he was still unready to enroll blacks as soldiers in the Union Army; that would have to wait for his Emancipation Proclamation.

Before the Emancipation Proclamation, five black regiments were in uniform. They were the 1st Regiment of the South Carolina Volunteer Infantry (African Descent), mustered in federal service on January 31, 1863; the 1st, 2d, and 3d Regiments of the Louisiana Native Guard, mustered into federal service in September and November of 1862; and the 1st Regiment of the Kansas Colored Infantry, mustered into federal service on January 13, 1863. These initial regiments, in the experiment of arming the black man, had most of their promises broken and a very difficult time getting recognized as a military force.

These five regiments were eventually redesignated and amalgamated into the United States Colored Troops. The 1st South Carolina and the 1st Kansas Colored were redesignated the 33d and 79th (new) Regiment Infantry, United States Colored Troops. The 1st, 2d, and 3d Louisiana Native Guard were redesignated into the Corps d'Afrique first, and then into the 73d, 74th, and 75th Regiments of Infantry, United States Colored Troops.

Ironically, in order for black men to fight for their freedom, they first had to fight for their right to join the military. The leading black abolitionist of the period, Frederick Douglass, felt that by fighting for the Northern cause the black man would earn his right to the citizenship that was denied to him: "Once let the black man get upon his person the brass letters 'U.S.,' let him get an eagle on his button, and a musket on his shoulder and bullets in his pocket, and there is no power on earth which can deny that he has earned the right to citizenship in the United States." Most black men did not enjoy the right of citizenship at this time. Douglass

1

"Once let the black man get upon his person the brass letters 'US,' let him get an eagle on his button and a musket on his shoulder and bullets in his pockets and there is no power on earth which can deny that he has earned the right to citizenship in the United States."

— **Frederick Douglass**

*Frederick Douglass*

knew that the problems of unequal pay, prejudice, and acceptance by the North, as well as the problems they would have in fighting the Confederates could not stand in the way of black soldiers who were fighting for their freedom and citizenship.

Douglass also said, "The decision of our destiny is now as never before in our own hands. We may lie low in the dust, despised and spit upon by every passer-by, or we may, like brave men, rise and unlock to ourselves the golden gates of a glorious future. To hold back is to incite infamy upon ourselves, and upon our children. The chance is now given us. We must improve it, or sink deeper than ever in the pit of social and political degradation, from which we have been struggling for years to extricate ourselves."

General Order No. 1, issued on January 2, 1863, from the War Department, was President Lincoln's Proclamation of Emancipation. The seventh paragraph gave the military the authority to "such persons of suitable condition, will be received into the armed service of the United States, to garrison Forts, positions, stations, and other places, and to man vessels of all sorts in said service."

Permission was given to the Governor of Rhode Island on January 15, 1863, to raise an infantry regiment of volunteers of African descent. This became the 14th Regiment Rhode Island Volunteer Heavy Artillery. This was redesignated the 8th Regiment U.S. Colored Heavy Artillery and then the 11th Regiment U.S. Colored Heavy Artillery. Next, permission was given, on January 26, 1863, to the Governor of Massachusetts to raise "a special corps of men of African descent." This became the Fifty-Fourth Regiment Massachusetts Volunteer Infantry (colored). Recruiting began on February 9, 1863, with the first squad of recruits going into Camp Meigs, Reidville, Massachusetts, on February 21st. Frederick Douglass had two sons in this regiment. One of them, Lewis H. Douglass, was a Sergeant Major. He served under Colonel Robert Gould Shaw. This regiment maintained its state identity throughout its time of service.

Secretary of War Edwin Stanton authorized Brigadier General Daniel Ullman to raise a brigade of four regiments, later changed to six regiments, of Louisiana Volunteer Infantry to serve three years. This became part of the Corps d'Afrique under Major General Nathaniel Banks, who commanded the Department of the Gulf. General Banks had proposed the organization of a Corps d'Armee of colored troops to be designated as the Corps d'Afrique on May 1, 1863. This branch of the military was the first recognized branch for black soldiers in the Civil War. This was before the formation of the United States Colored Troops. The Corps d'Afrique was redesignated into the United States Colored Troops.

On May 22, 1863, the War Department issued General Orders No. 143, which established the Bureau of Colored Troops. This bureau was directly under the Adjutant General's Office, with Major Charles W. Foster appointed Chief with the title of Assistant Adjutant General.

The Bureau was responsible for recruiting black soldiers, commissioning officers to command them, organizing regiments, and maintaining their records. The first regiment of the U.S. Colored Troops (U.S.C.T.) was the 1st U.S. Colored Infantry mustered into federal service at Washington, D.C., on June 30, 1863. They were put in a good state of drill and discipline and ordered to the field within 60 days.

Fifteen states raised volunteer regiments under their state designations only to have them eventually redesignated as U.S. Colored Troops. (See Appendix IV.) A number of states raised black soldiers whose identity remained with state designations.

Black men became part of the United States Colored Troops in four ways: 1) They may have enlisted into a regiment which was initially redesignated into the Corps d'Afrique, and then into the United States Colored Troops (i.e. Ullman Brigade, Louisiana Native Guards); 2) They could have enlisted into the Corps d'Afrique which was later redesignated into the United States Colored Troops; 3) They could have enlisted, drafted, or substituted into a state volunteer regiment which was later redesignated into the United States Colored Troops; or 4) They could have enlisted, drafted, or substituted directly into the United States Colored Troops.

Nine U.S.C.T. regiments were at the surrender of the Army of Northern Virginia to Major General U.S. Grant by General Robert E. Lee. Six black regiments were also at the surrender of the Confederate Army under General Joseph E. Johnston to General William T. Sherman. The 62d U.S.C.T. participated in the last engagement of the Civil War at Palmetto Ranch, Texas, on May 15, 1865.

By the end of the war, 178,975 black men served in the U.S. Colored Troops. These men served their country in 135 infantry regiments, six cavalry regiments, 12 regiments of heavy artillery, and 10 batteries of light artillery (see Appendix I). They fought in 39 major engagements and 410 lesser actions. Another 9,695 served in the U.S. Navy, many of which had been transferred from the U.S. Colored Troops into the U.S. Navy. Their record is one of valor, determination, and sacrifice.

The history of the black soldier in the Civil War involves more than the plight of the soldier alone, although he certainly is the key figure. The black soldier's participation was due to the efforts of both the white and black men, politicians, abolitionists, military and religious leaders, and simple concerned citizens of the nation.

As the number of black soldiers increased, their participation expanded in the war. There were problems of pay, bounty, fatigue, education, health, cooperation with white soldiers, family considerations, and a number of other problems. These problems could not have existed unless the black man came into the military and by the time the black soldier of this period was discharged, most of them had been rectified. The prejudice many whites felt towards the black man did not go away, but it is true that black participation in this war helped to shed light on these problems.

By March of 1865, the Government rectified the problem of unequal pay, and retroactively paid them an amount equal to that of white soldiers. The problem of prejudice, for many, still existed at the end of the war, but those soldiers having experienced the "fighting black soldier" usually changed their mind; their prejudice disappeared when they found themselves fighting and dying alongside black men.

For most soldiers, both North and South, the war was over with the surrenders of Confederate Generals Lee and Johnston. However, it was far from over for the members of the U.S. Colored Troops. By the end of the war, 11% of the U.S. Army consisted of black men. By the fall of 1865, most white regiments had been disbanded, and black soldiers made up 36% of the military. At this time, the majority of black units belonged to the 25th Army Corps, which was the only all black Army Corps. They were sent to Texas because of the threat of the French influence in Mexico. If the Government would have released these black veterans in Union blue, a problem would have developed when the 144,000 who had come from slave and border states were confronted by defeated Confederate soldiers returning to their homes. These victorious black soldiers in Union blue, walking the streets of Confederate cities would have caused another war because there are many recorded instances of violent acts committed by rebels on black soldiers stationed in the south. For example, an officer in the 33rd U.S.C.T. caught a former Confederate soldier who had knifed an enlisted man in his regiment; the rebel was executed the next day. There was also a race riot in Memphis caused by similar situations (Glatthaar, p. 215), and now that the black soldier was able to fight, the military could not allow these actions to go unnoticed.

In general, the Civil War lasted from 1861-1865 but this was not the case for black soldiers. However, black soldiers in several regiments continued to serve their country. In December 1867, the last U.S.C.T. regiment, the 125th Infantry was mustered out one and one-half years after the war was over.

Their deeds of valor are a matter of public record. Sixteen black soldiers were recipients of the Medal of Honor. Eight men in the U.S. Navy were awarded the Medal of Honor. Thirteen white officers received the Medal of Honor leading black soldiers in battle. These figures represent a higher proportion of men than the other branches of the U.S. military service.

The Civil War established a permanent black presence in the American military. At first the victims of segregation and substandard treatment, African-Americans went on to make the military their vehicle for attaining equality and opportunity. After nearly a century of injustice, black men attained the ranks of general and admiral in the Army and Navy. One African-American has served as Commandant of the U.S. Military Academy at West Point and another presided over Operation Desert Storm as Chairman of the Joint Chiefs of Staff.

# Before the Emancipation

## To Arms! Freemen To Arms!

With the firing of the first shot on Fort Sumter, black men wanted to fight for their cause—volunteering to fight for the South as well as the North. Neither the Federal nor Confederate governments felt that they wanted the colored man to be uniformed and armed. The initial thinking of this "White Man's War" was that it would be over in a short time. Each side thought that they would win and not need the aid of the black man.

By 1862, when this painting by W.M. Hunt was copyrighted in Massachusetts, active efforts to incorporate the black men into the war are easily seen. Movements such as the unauthorized formation of the 1st South Carolina Volunteers (African Descent), the Second Confiscation and Militia Act, and the forming of the 1st Kansas Colored, and the drafting of the Emancipation Proclamation clearly illustrate the interest of the black man in the cause.

The call of "To Arms! Freemen to Arms!" did not refer to the slave or former slave since it was dated 1862. Black leaders, such as Frederick Douglass, had always felt the necessity of the black man to answer the call to arms. Before the end of the war, both the Federal and the Confederate governments had authorized the black man to be uniformed and armed.

TO ARMS! FREEMEN TO ARMS!

Entered according to Act of Congress in the year 1862 by W.M. Hunt, in the Clerks Office of the District Court of Mass

# The 1st Regiment South Carolina Volunteer Infantry (African Descent)

There had been slight hints from the Government's action about the changing view towards the black man during the early part of the Civil War. General Fremont issued a proclamation on August 30, 1861 declaring "free any slave, in the state of Missouri, whose master took up arms against the United States." On September 11, 1861, President Lincoln had Fremont change this order.

Brigadier General T.W. Sherman was authorized to employ fugitive slaves as Union soldiers in South Carolina. This was from orders dated October 14, 1861, from the Secretary of War, Simon Cameron but the authorization was not implemented by General T.W. Sherman, nor was the document rescinded.

One of the abolitionist generals, Major General David Hunter, USMA 1822, was appointed commander of the Department of the South in March of 1862. Hunter wanted to recruit all able-bodied Negroes capable of bearing arms within the limits of his Department (O.R. S III, Vol. III, p. 31). This was done without the official sanction of the War Department. Hunter was using the excuse of the orders given to his predecessor, General T.W. Sherman, by the Secretary of War as being valid. He concluded that he was authorized to enlist "fugitive slaves" found in his Department as soldiers (O.R. S III, Vol. III, p. 197).

General Hunter wrote to Cameron's successor as Secretary of War, Edwin M. Stanton, from his headquarters at Hilton Head, South Carolina on April 3, 1862. Hunter requested 50,000 muskets with all the necessary accouterments, and 200 rounds for each piece. He asked for this to be sent to him at once with the authority to arm such loyal men as he can find in the country, whenever, in his opinion, they could be used advantageously against the enemy.

He further stated that it was important that he should be able to know and distinguish these men at once, and for this purpose he requested that 50,000 pairs of scarlet pantaloons be sent to him. This is all the clothing he required for these people (O.R. S I, Vol. VI, P. 264).

Martial law was declared on April 25, 1862 by General Hunter. He felt that he was authorized by the War Department to form the Negroes into "Squads, companies, or otherwise as he sees fit." It was his intention to enlist two regiments. The first company was to be raised at Beaufort, South Carolina, and he appointed Captain Charles Trowbridge and two lieutenants to oversee the organization of this group.

General Hunter issued General Order No. 11 on May 9, 1862 from the Department of the South, Hilton Head, South Carolina. An excerpt from the orders reads: "Slaves and martial law in a free country are altogether incompatible: the persons in these three states—Georgia, Florida, and South Carolina—heretofore held as slaves are therefore declared forever free" (O.R. S I, Vol. XIV, p. 341).

Hunter issued a circular, dated May 11, 1862, from Beaufort, South Carolina, stating "that agents and overseers of plantations must send to Beaufort, the next day, every able-bodied negro between the ages of 15-45 years of age capable of bearing arms" (O.R. S III, Vol. III, p. 50).

On May 19, 1862, the President replied to General Hunter's actions. "Neither General Hunter nor any commanders or person has been authorized by the Government of the United States to make Proclamations declaring the slaves of any state free, and the supposed proclamation now in question whether genuine

7

*Private, 1st South Carolina Vol. Inf. (African descent).*

or false is altogether void so far as respects such declarations." The President further expressed himself when he said that "The changes contemplated could come as gently as the dews of Heaven not rendering or wrecking anything" (O.R. S II, Vol. I, pp. 818-819).

The men raised for the 1st South Carolina were mostly impressed into service (i.e. taken without their approval, often at bayonet point). This forced conscription created a problem to the plantation superintendents, depleting them of their labor force. They complained of the violent seizure of these men, stating that "They were taken from the field without being allowed to go to their houses even to get a jacket" (O.R. S III, Vol. III, pp. 55-60). This also created a problem for the families that did not know what had happened to the men who didn't come home.

As of August 4, 1862, General Hunter was still building up his force and still asking Secretary Stanton for arrangements to be made for paying the men, either by an order from the President or an order to the Chief Quartermaster. Although he stopped, in a great measure, all formal recruiting, Hunter kept his agents busy accumulating able-bodied Negroes at central depots from which they could be rapidly absorbed into regimental organizations. He asked the Secretary of War for authority to issue commissions to his officers in the 1st South Carolina Regiment, but no answer came from Stanton.

On August 10, 1862, Major General David Hunter failed to receive authority from the Secretary of War to muster the 1st Regiment South Carolina Volunteers, and therefore disbanded the men. Hunter had hoped not only to have this regiment accepted by but to also gain the authorization to raise other regiments of black soldiers to help fill the decimated Army (O.R. S I, Vol. III, P. 346).

On August 16, 1862, Brigadier General Rufus Saxton, USMA 1849, wrote to the Secretary of War requesting authority to enroll as laborers in the employ of the Quartermaster Department, a force not exceeding 5,000 able-bodied men from among the contrabands in his Department. The common laborers were to be paid, furnished with soldier's rations, uniformed, armed, and officered by men detailed from the Army (O.R. S I, Vol. XIV, pp. 374-376).

Stanton replied to this letter on August 25, 1862:

> It is considered by the department that the instructions given at the time of your appointment was sufficient to enable you to do what you have now requested authority for doing. But in order to place your authority beyond all doubt you are hereby authorized and instructed: 1. To enroll and organize, in any convenient organization, by squads, companies, battalions, regiments, and brigades, or otherwise, colored persons of African descent for volunteer laborers to a number not to exceed 5,000, and muster them into the service of the United States for the term of the war, at a rate of compensation not exceeding $5 per month for common laborers and $8 per month for mechanical or skilled laborers, and assign them to the quartermaster's department, to do and perform such laborers' duty as may be required during the present war, and to be subject to the Rules and Articles of War.
>
> 3d...you are authorized to arm, uniform, equip, and receive into the service of the United States such number of volunteers of African descent as you may deem expedient, not exceeding 5,000, and may detail officers to instruct them in military drill, discipline, and duty, and to command them. The persons so received into service and their officers are to be entitled to and receive the same pay and rations as are allowed by law to volunteers in the service.
>
> 6th. You may turn over to the Navy any number of colored volunteers that may be required for the naval service.
>
> 7th. By recent Act of Congress all men and boys received into the service of the United States who may have been the slaves of rebel masters are, with their wives, mothers, and children, declared forever free. You and all in your command will so treat and regard them.

Six weeks later, Saxton, reported to the Secretary of War that he was organizing the 1st South Carolina as rapidly as possible. They were organized with Hunter's disbanded troops (one company was still intact) as a nucleus, and were mustered in as Company A. Saxton knew he was going to have a hard time recruiting men. Most of the available men were working for the Engineer and Quartermaster Departments, and on the plantations. He also had to overcome the fact that those organized by Hunter had not been not paid and the men received no money after being discharged several months later.

Captain Thomas Wentworth Higginson of the 51st Massachusetts was appointed Colonel of Saxton's 1st Carolina Regiment. Higginson, like Major George L. Stearns, was one of the "Secret Six" who backed John Brown in his movement. Colonel Higginson found the scarlet pants worn by the men of Hunter's old regiment "intolerable to [his] eyes." On January 21, 1863 he noted that the regiment had been promised "pay when the funds arrive, [and] Springfield rifled muskets." They were issued red pants, fatigue blouse and probably a black felt hat. The Colonel referred to his men as his "Gospel Army" (Smith, p. 310).

By January 25, 1863, Saxton reported the 1st Regiment of South Carolina Volunteers as completed. The regiment was light infantry, composed of ten companies of about eighty-six men, each armed with muskets, and officered by white men. He was proud of the fact that given the length of time it was in service, discipline and morale had not been surpassed by any white regiment in that department. He reported to the Secretary of War that on this date he began the organization of the 2d Regiment South Carolina Volunteers, which was commanded by Colonel James Montgomery.

The 1st South Carolina was mustered into the service of the United States on January 31, 1863. It was the fifth black regiment in federal service. Its designation was changed to the 33d Regiment, U.S. Colored Troops, on February 8, 1864. It was mustered out of service on January 31, 1866.

The 1st South Carolina participated in the following battles: Township, Milltown Bluff, Hall Island, Jacksonville, and James Island.


**Presentation Plaques for the Flags of the 1st South Carolina**

Rally around the flag. The flag was the symbol representing a regiment's cause and the cause for which the soliders fought. In the Civil War, more men received the Medal of Honor in the name of Congress for protecting the flag or for capturing the enemy than for any other reason.

Colonel Higginson's regiment, the 1st South Carolina Volunteer Infantry Regiment (African Descent) took pride in their flags. The flags that these presentation plaques were attached to were presented on January 1, 1863, the day of Emancipation. The flags were presented by Reverand Mansfield French and his congregation, of New York. These presentation plaques may be the only artifacts of the regiment known to exist.

The plaques are inscribed as follows:

> Presented by Rev. Geo. B. Cheever D.D in the Church of the Puritans, N.Y. on Thanksgiving day November 27, 1862 to the 1st Reg. S.C.V. through Rev. Mansfield French Then Representing them and procured with the proceeds of a collection before taken up in that Church. Committee Edgar Ketchum Dexter Fairbanks Charles C. Leigh

This plaque is 5 5/8 inches long and has a diameter of 1 1/2 inches. The plaque is crafted out of brass.

The Church of the Puritans was a Congregational Church located on East 15th Street and Union place, New York City. Rev. Cheever was the Minister. Rev. French also lived in New York City.

The other plaque reads:

> Presented to the 1st Reg. South Carolina Vol. By a daughter of Connecticut November 1862.

This plaque is 5 1/2 inches long with a diameter of 1 1/2 inches. It was manufactured out of brass with a silver wash.

The flag was made of silk with 34 embroidered stars and inscribed: "God Gives Liberty."

Colonel T.W. Higginson described the presentation in his book *Army Life in a Black Regiment*, as follows:

> Receiving the flags, I gave them into the hands of two fine-looking men, jet black, as color-guard, and they also spoke, and very effectively,—Sergeant Prince Rivers and Corporal Robert Sutton. The regiment sang 'Marching Along.' General Saxton spoke next, as did two other speakers.... [T]he regiment sang next the John Brown song and they went to their beef and molasses.

The farewell address of Lieutenant Colonel Charles T. Trowbridge, commanding the 33rd U.S. Colored Troops (the next designation of this regiment), described their final destination: "The flags...which you have borne so nobly through the war, [are] now rolled up forever, and deposited in our nation's capital. And while there it shall rest, with the battles in which you have participated inscribed upon its folds, it will be a source of pride to us to all remember that it has never been disgraced by a cowardly faltering in the hour of danger or polluted by a traitor's touch" (Higgenson, pp. 193-194).

## Louisiana Native Guards

The story of Louisiana's black soldiers was unique and began long before the Civil War. As early as 1727, armed slaves and free black men fought for the French against the Choctaw Indians. When France transferred this territory to Spain, blacks also fought for the Spanish at Natchez and Baton Rouge in 1779. They participated in the capture of Pensacola in 1780, and black men served continuously in the Louisiana militia right up through the time of the Louisiana Purchase in 1803.

Louisiana in 1803 was the only area under the jurisdiction of the United States Government where black men were included in the militia. After Louisiana was admitted into the Union in 1812, Andrew Jackson utilized two companies of this colored militia of New Orleans in the Battle of Chalmette.

There is evidence of descendants of these men participating in the Mexican War. Jordan Noble, a drummer boy at Chalmette helped raise the Black Regiment of New Orleans at the beginning of the Civil War.

The Louisiana Native Guards began as the state militia of Louisiana, Confederate States of America, on April 23, 1861. The unit was known as the "Native Guards," composed of the free colored population of the city of New Orleans. This regiment had 440 enlisted men with their own black officers. By early 1862, there were more than 3,000 members of colored military organizations in Louisiana (Berry, p. 165). When New Orleans was evacuated by the Confederate authorities, in March of 1862, the Native Guards did not leave, even though they

Capt. Charles Sentmanat, Co. D.      1st Lieut. L. D. Larrieu, Co. A.      2d Lieut. J. L. Montieu, Co. A.      Capt. E. Davis, Co. A.
2d Lieut. V. Lavigne, Co. D.

*Our colored troops—the line officers of the First Louisiana Native Guards. (Harper's Weekly, Feb. 28, 1863).*

were ordered to report to Major General John Lewis, who commanded the State Militia under the orders of Governor Thomas O. Moore.

Major General Benjamin Butler, the Union commander at New Orleans, issued General Order No. 63 from his headquarters at the Department of the Gulf in New Orleans on August 22, 1862. This pertained to all members of the "Native Guards" and all other free colored citizens who intended to enlist in the Volunteer Service of the United States. It stipulated that they would be organized by the appointment of proper officers, and accepted, paid, equipped, armed, and rationed as the other volunteer troops of the United States, and were subject to the approval of the President of the United States.

As a result of this General Order, there were four regiments of the Louisiana Native Guards. Three of these regiments had black officers.

On June 6, 1863, the four regiments of the Louisiana Native Guards were transferred into the Corps d'Afrique, per G.O. No. 47, from the headquarters of the Department of the Gulf. The 1st, 2d, 3d, and 4th Regiments of Louisiana Native Guards became the 1st through 4th Regiments of Infantry, Corps d'Afrique. On April 4, 1864, these four regiments were designated 73d, 74th, 75th and 76th Regiments of Infantry, United States Colored Troops, respectively. They maintained this designation for the rest of the Civil War.

*Our colored troops at work—the First Louisiana Native Guards disembarking at Fort Macombe, Louisiana.* (Harper's Weekly, Feb. 28, 1863.)

OUR Artist has sent us some sketches which illustrate, in a striking degree, the novel phases of life, both military and civil, which the present struggle is evolving. The fact of black regiments being actively employed is not a novelty, since they have been for some time part of the British military system, which, with its usual common sense, avails itself of every aid in the pursuit of its objects. Our Artist says that among the cypress swamps of Louisiana negro soldiers are invaluable, and accompanies his sketch of the pickets of the First Louisiana native troops, guarding the New Orleans, Opelousas and Great Western Railroad, with some remarks which we quote:

"In this swamp in the wilderness the 'nigger soldiers' are eminently useful. The melancholy solitude, with the spectral cypress trees, which seem to stand in silent despair, like nature's sentinels waving in the air wreaths of gray funereal moss, to warn all human beings of the latent pestilence around, though unendurable to our soldiers of the North, seems an elysium to these sable soldiers, for the swampy forest has no horrors to them. Impervious to miasma, they see only the home of the coon, the possum and the copperhead, so that with 'de gun dat Massa Sam gib 'em,' they have around them all the essential elements of colored happiness, except ladies' society."
(Frank Leslie's Illustrated Newspaper, March 7, 1863.)

## First Regiment Kansas Colored Infantry

Senator James Lane, a general in the state militia of Kansas, became Commissioner of Recruiting in Leavenworth City, Kansas. He issued General Order No. 2 on August 6, 1862 from the Department of Kansas in Leavenworth. This order gave authority to the recruiting officers to make sure that persons of African descent who entered the service of the United States in that Department fully understood the terms and conditions upon which they would be received in the service. This referral to the $10.00 per month pay, from which $3.00 for clothing would be deducted (O.R. S III, Vol. II, p. 312).

Secretary of War Stanton directed correspondence to General Lane which stated that "raising the two regiments of persons of African descent can only be raised upon express and special authority from the President. The President has not given this authority. Such Regiments cannot be accepted into the service" (O.R. S III, Vol. II, p. 445). Lane went ahead with raising black troops without War Department Approval.

*Senator James Lane, Kansas Abolitionist.*

The First Kansas Colored was raised at Fort Scott, Kansas in August of 1862. It was largely comprised of fugitive slaves from Arkansas and Missouri, of battalion strength, and was without official sanction. The men were initially issued blue jackets, gray pants, and forage caps. In May of 1864, they were finally issued U.S. Regulation clothing (Todd, p. 812).

The First Kansas have the distinction of being the first black regiment to engage the enemy. This occurred in a skirmish at Island Mound, Missouri, on October 29, 1862. This resulted in the first combat deaths of black soldiers.

On January 13, 1863, the 1st Regiment Kansas Colored Volunteers (6 companies) was mustered into federal service. This was the fourth Union Army black regiment in the military, and was commanded by Lieutenant Colonel James M. Williams.

On December 13, 1864 the regiment changed its designation to the 79th (new) U.S. Colored Troops.

The 79th U.S.C.T. participated in the following engagements: Sherwood, Bush Creek, Cabin Creek, Honey Springs, Prairie d'Ann, Poison Spring, Jenkins' Ferry, Joy's Ford, Clarksville, Horse Head Creek, Roseville Creek, Timber Hill,

Lawrence, Island Mound, and Fort Gibson. The regiment ranked 21st among all Union Regiments in the percentage of total enrollment killed in battle.

Many of us are familiar with the massacre of black soldiers at Fort Pillow, Tennessee. Six days following this battle, on April 18, 1864, there was another massacre of black soldiers; the 1st Kansas Colored at Poison Spring, Arkansas.

There was also another regiment formed in Kansas, the 2d Regiment Kansas Colored Infantry, which was redesignated the 83d (new) U.S. Colored Infantry. This regiment avenged its sister regiment, the 1st Kansas on April 30, 1864, when it engaged the enemy for over two hours at the Battle of Jenkins' Ferry, Arkansas. When they charged with fixed bayonets they shouted, "Remember Poison Spring," silencing three rebel guns (Cornish, p. 177). They remained in the field for some time until they exhausted their ammunition and then they resupplied their weapons and returned to face the enemy for another hour until the rebels retreated. Colonel Samuel J. Crawford, commanding the 2nd Kansas Infantry, wrote in his report, "...although it was the first engagement...I have not seen troops who displayed a greater degree of coolness, courage and daring that was displayed by the colored troops under my command..." Crawford went on to say that "although worn out with fatigue and hunger at the close of the engagement, [his men] were 10th to leave the field" (O.R. S I, Vol. XXXIV, Part 1, pp. 757-759).

The rebels were vicious when they were fighting black soldiers. They gave "no quarter" and took as few prisoners as they could, and black soldiers knew this, and therefore, fought with ferocity.

Although the Confederates were well known for their "Rebel Yell" when going into a charge, the black soldiers had their own battle cry. East of the Mississippi it was "Remember Fort Pillow," and in the west it was "Remember Poison Spring" (Cornish, p. 177).

### The Black Brigade of Cincinnati

The raid by Confederate General John Hunt Morgan in July of 1862 and the defeat of the Union forces at Richmond, Kentucky, on August 20, 1862, gave warning to citizens of Cincinnati and the state of Ohio of a possible Confederate attack.

The colored people of Cincinnati did not take heed of this directive. At the time of the Fort Sumter attack, a meeting of colored citizens had been held to organize a company of "Home Guards." This idea encountered staunch opposition from the city's pro-slavery elements, who cried that this was a "white man's war."

Nevertheless, the city police rounded up black males wherever they could be found, including at home, at work, and on the farm, and placed them in a holding area. The greater part of the colored male population was dragged from their homes not knowing what was in store for them. They could not return home,

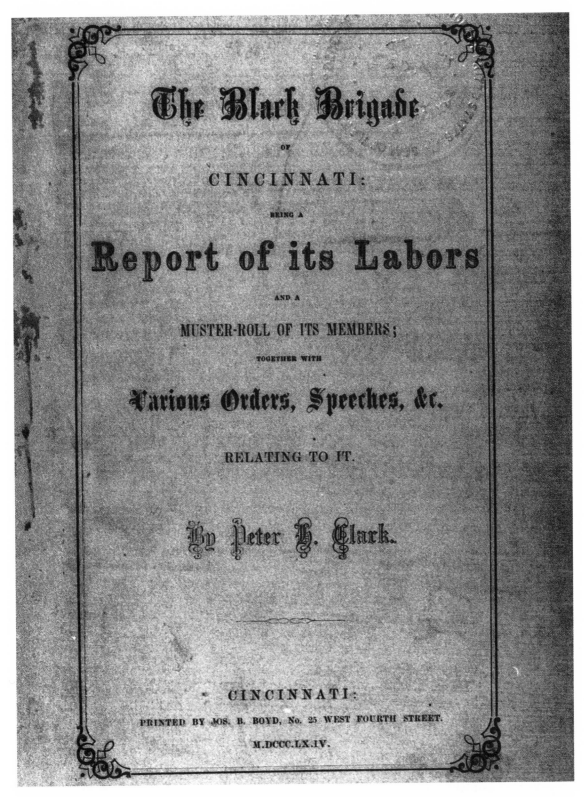

# The Black Brigade

OF

## CINCINNATI:

BEING A

# Report of its Labors

AND A

## MUSTER-ROLL OF ITS MEMBERS;

TOGETHER WITH

## Various Orders, Speeches, &c.

RELATING TO IT.

## By Peter H. Clark.

CINCINNATI:

PRINTED BY JOS. B. BOYD, No. 25 WEST FOURTH STREET.

M.DCCC.LX.IV.

*The first appearance of the Negro in military operations occurred in September 1862 in Cincinnati, Ohio, at the time of the threatened invasion by Confederate General John Hunt Morgan. A so-called Black Brigade of three regiments was then organized, and assigned to duty in constructing the fortifications and earthworks about Cincinnati. These men gave their services voluntarily, but were unarmed and without uniforms. Their organization, such as it was, existed for only three weeks, and had no connections with the movement for enlisting colored troops.*

nor inform their loved ones as to what had happened to them. This activity reflected the general attitude of the police force towards blacks in this city.

These instances of detention were brought to the attention of General Wallace. In order to eliminate any further problems in protecting the colored men and organizing them for fatigue work, he issued a circular from his headquarters on September 4, 1862. He assigned Judge William M. Dickson to command the Negro forces from Cincinnati to work on the fortifications near Newport and Covington. Colonel Dickson allowed his men to go home and prepare for their forthcoming work assignment.

These colored men worked on the rifle pits and trenches surrounding Fort Michael, near Covington, Kentucky. They worked all night on these fortifications to the praise of the engineer in charge, and most of the other work that they performed was noteworthy as well.

The men were presented with a handsome national flag by Captain James Lupton, a volunteer and acting camp commandant. The broad folds of the flag, contained the inscription: "The Black Brigade of Cincinnati." During the presentation ceremony, the men marched to the strains of martial music played by a band from their ranks, and they rallied around their flag. They later chose to name their camp after their commandant, and called it Camp Lupton.

In the beginning, there was no compensation for the men who answered General Wallace's call to fortify the city. Neither white nor black laborers received any pay until their second week of work. At this point, they were given $1.00 per day, and the following week this was increased to $1.50 per day.

At one point, the Black Brigade was working nearly a mile in front of the line of battle. The men were not armed, and only the cavalry scouts stood between them and the enemy. When the colonel of the 15th Ohio Volunteer Infantry saw troops in front of the line of battle, he ordered his men to fire on them. It took the persuasion of another officer and a flag of truce to convince the colonel that the troops were friendly.

On September 20, 1862, the restrictions on the black men of Cincinnati were raised. The Black Brigade of Cincinnati had been disbanded. Only one man lost his life during its efforts to protect the city, and his death was an accident which occurred while chopping trees.

Before the brigade disbanded, the men and the officers presented Colonel Dickson with a sword. The Colonel accepted the gift, and made an appropriate acknowledgment speech. The brigade was led by its commander as they proudly marched through the streets of Covington and Cincinnati with music playing and banners flying.

The Black Brigade of Cincinnati was comprised of approximately 700 men. This included some 300 men who were assigned to various duties in camps, on gunboats, and inside the city, whose names were never recorded. They had three regiments composed of different numbers of companies. The first regiment had seven companies and 317 men; the second had five companies and 192 men; and the third regiment had five companies and 197 men. This made a total of 706 men who were listed on the muster rolls.

After this initial taste of action in the Civil War, many of these men went on to become part of the Massachusetts regiments of color, and others joined the various regiments which were stationed in the Mississippi Valley.

*Major General David Hunter.*

*Major General Rufus Saxton.*

*Major General Benjamin Butler.*

*The Emancipation Proclamation not only freed the slaves in rebellious states, but allowed them to serve in the armed services of the United States: "such person, of suitable condition, will be received into the armed service of the United States, to garrison forts, positions, stations, and other places, and to man vessels of all sorts in said service."*

# BY THE PRESIDENT OF THE UNITED STATES OF AMERICA.

# A Proclamation.

......

**Whereas,** on the twenty-second day of September, in the year of our Lord one thousand eight hundred and sixty-two, a proclamation was issued by the President of the United States, containing, among other things, the following, to wit:

" That on the first day of January, in the year of our Lord one thousand eight hundred and sixty-three, all persons held as slaves within any State or designated part of a State, the people whereof shall then be in rebellion against the United States, shall be then, thenceforward, and forever, free; and the Executive government of the United States, including the military and naval authority thereof, will recognize and maintain the freedom of such persons, and will do no act or acts to repress such persons, or any of them, in any efforts they may make for their actual freedom.

" That the Executive will, on the first day of January aforesaid, by proclamation, designate the States and parts of States, if any, in which the people thereof, respectively, shall then be in rebellion against the United States; and the fact that any State, or the people thereof, shall on that day be in good faith represented in the Congress of the United States, by members chosen thereto at elections wherein a majority of the qualified voters of such State shall have participated, shall, in the absence of strong countervailing testimony, be deemed conclusive evidence that such State, and the people thereof, are not then in rebellion against the United States."

**Now, therefore,** I, ABRAHAM LINCOLN, PRESIDENT OF THE UNITED STATES, by virtue of the power in me vested as commander-in-chief of the army and navy of the United States, in time of actual armed rebellion against the authority and government of the United States, and as a fit and necessary war measure for suppressing said rebellion, do, on this first day of January, in the year of our Lord one thousand eight hundred and sixty-three, and in accordance with my purpose so to do, publicly proclaimed for the full period of one hundred days from the day first above mentioned, order and designate as the States and parts of States wherein the people thereof, respectively, are this day in rebellion against the United States, the following, to wit: ARKANSAS, TEXAS, LOUISIANA, (except the Parishes of St. Bernard, Plaquemines, Jefferson, St. John, St. Charles, St. James, Ascension, Assumption, Terre Bonne, Lafourche, St. Mary, St. Martin, and Orleans, including the City of New Orleans,) MISSISSIPPI, ALABAMA, FLORIDA, GEORGIA, SOUTH CAROLINA, NORTH CAROLINA, AND VIRGINIA, (except the forty-eight counties designated as West Virginia, and also the counties of Berkeley, Accomac, Northampton, Elizabeth City, York, Princess Ann, and Norfolk, including the cities of Norfolk and Portsmouth,) and which excepted parts are for the present left precisely as if this proclamation were not issued.

And by virtue of the power and for the purpose aforesaid, I do order and declare that all persons held as slaves within said designated States and parts of States are and henceforward shall be free; and that the Executive government of the United States, including the military and naval authorities thereof, will recognize and maintain the freedom of said persons.

And I hereby enjoin upon the people so declared to be free to abstain from all violence, unless in necessary self-defence; and I recommend to them that, in all cases when allowed, they labor faithfully for reasonable wages.

And I further declare and make known that such persons, of suitable condition, will be received into the armed service of the United States, to garrison forts, positions, stations, and other places, and to man vessels of all sorts in said service.

And upon this act, sincerely believed to be an act of justice warranted by the Constitution upon military necessity, I invoke the considerate judgment of mankind and the gracious favor of Almighty God.

In witness whereof I have hereunto set my hand and caused the seal of the United States to be affixed.

[L. S.]    Done at the CITY OF WASHINGTON this first day of January, in the year of our Lord one thousand eight hundred and sixty-three, and of the Independence of the United States of America the eighty-seventh.

By the President:

*Abraham Lincoln*

*William H Seward*    *Secretary of State.*

A true copy, with the autograph signatures of the President and the Secretary of State.

*Jno. G. Nicolay*
*Priv. Sec. to the President.*

*General Rufus Saxton, Brigadier General and Military Governor of the Department of the South, issued the following document on January 1, 1863.*

### A HAPPY NEW YEAR'S GREETING TO THE COLORED PEOPLE IN THE DEPARTMENT OF THE SOUTH.

*In accordance, as I believe, with the will of our Heavenly Father, and by direction of your great and good friend, whose name you are all familiar with, ABRAHAM LINCOLN, President of the United States, and Commander-in-Chief of the Army and Navy, on the first day of January, 1863, you will be declared "forever free."*

*When in the course of human events there comes a day which is destined to be an everlasting beacon-light, marking a joyful era in the progress of a nation and the hopes of a people, it seems to be fitting the occasion that it should not pass unnoticed by those whose hopes it comes to brighten and to bless. Such a day to you is January 1, 1863. I therefore call upon all the colored people in this Department to assemble on that day at the Headquarters of the First Regiment of South Carolina Volunteers, there to hear the President's Proclamation read, and to indulge in such other manifestations of joy as may be called forth by the occasion. It is your duty to carry this good news to your brethren who are still in slavery. Let all your voices, like merry bells, join loud and clear in the grand chorus of liberty— "We are free," "We are free," until listening you shall hear its echoes coming back from every cabin in the land,—"We are free," "We are free."*

> *R. SAXTON,*
> *Brig. Gen. and Military Governor.*

# After the Emancipation

Before the Emancipation Proclamation was issued on January 1, 1863, five colored regiments had been formed. They were the 1st South Carolina Infantry Regiment (African Descent), the 1st, 2nd, and 3rd Louisiana Native Guards and the 1st Kansas Colored Infantry.

Watch Meeting—breaking the chains of slavery.

## Ullman's Brigade, Corps d'Afrique

Shortly after the Emancipation Proclamation, on January 13, 1863, the Secretary of War authorized Brigadier General Daniel Ullman to raise a black brigade of four regiments of Louisiana Volunteer Infantry. The U.S. Volunteers recruited in that state were to serve three years, or for the length of the war. This action was initiated before the authorization was granted for the formation of the United States Colored Troops. The latter organization didn't begin, officially, until May 23, 1863, as per G.O. 143 from the War Department (O.R. S III, Vol. III, p. 14).

*Brigadier General Daniel Ullman.*

Secretary of War Stanton wanted to increase the number of men in his colored military force from Louisiana. Therefore, he sent Brigadier General Ullman an order to increase the number of black regiments to six, which would be used for scouting purposes. Ullman was directed to report to Major General N.P. Banks on March 23, 1863, and he was to complete his obligation within thirty days after his arrival in New Orleans. Ullman was ordered to establish his headquarters in Baton Rouge, or other such point as General Banks would designate. The volunteers were allowed to come from the plantations and any other source. The troops raised were to be supplied with quartermaster, commissary and ordnance stores, just as any other soldiers. General Banks was to assign these troops to duties as he deemed suitable. In the end, Ullman succeeded in raising five regiments of U.S. Volunteer Infantry (O.R. S III, Vol. III, pp. 9, 102-103).

The following men were the Regimental Commanding Officers in Ullman's Brigade:

| | |
|---|---|
| 1st Regiment Infantry | Colonel A.B. Botsford |
| 2d Regiment Infantry | Colonel Henry G. Thomas |
| 3d Regiment Infantry | Colonel Cyrus Hamlin |
| 4th Regiment Infantry | Colonel John F. Appleton |
| 5th Regiment Infantry | Colonel Ladislas L. Zulavsky |

After the Corps d'Afrique was organized under Major General Banks, Department of the Gulf, on May 1, 1863, these five regiments of Ullman's Brigade were redesignated as the 6th, 7th, 8th, 9th, and 10th Regiments of Infantry of the Corps d'Afrique as per G.O. No. 47. This was issued from the headquarters of the Department of the Gulf, 19th Army Corps, on June 6, 1863.

Eventually, these Corps d'Afrique regiments were amalgamated again into the United States Colored Troops. They became the 78th, 79th, 80th, 81st, and 82d Regiments of Infantry, U.S.C.T.

## Brigadier General Lorenzo Thomas, Adjutant General, U.S. Army

On March 25, 1863, the same day that Secretary Stanton instructed Generals Banks and Ullman to raise black troops in Louisiana, he also told Brigadier General Loranzo Thomas, Adjutant General of the Union Army to start organizing regiments of ex-slaves in the Mississippi Valley (O.R. S III, Vol. V, pp. 101-103, 118).

Secretary Stanton informed General Thomas that he should confer with Major General Ulysses S. Grant in order to explain the importance of the President's Emancipation Proclamation for the organization of their labor and military strength. Stanton informed Thomas that "no officer in the U.S. Service is regarded as in the discharge of his duties under the acts of Congress, who fails to employ to the utmost extent the aid and cooperation of the loyal colored population in performing the labor incident to military operations, and also in performing the duties of soldiers under proper organization, and that any obstacle thrown in the way of these ends is regarded by the President as a violation of the acts of Congress and the declared purposes of the Government in using every means to bring the war to an end" (O.R. S III, Vol. V, p. 100).

*General Lorenzo Thomas*

Thomas was ordered to find out what military officers were willing to take command of colored troops and if troops could be raised and organized without prejudice to the service. He was given permission to relieve officers and privates from service in white units to receive commissions as qualified in the organization of brigades, regiments and companies of African-American troops.

General Thomas took what we now would call a "Public Relations" approach to the introduction of black soldiers to the military. At Cairo, Illinois, he reviewed the troops and announced to some extent the policy of the government. He subsequently enlarged the governmental view as he came into more contact with large bodies of white troops and thousands of Negroes. He had the troops paraded and announced the purpose of his mission. He then requested the body of troops to call on such of their commanders as they might desire to make an address on the policy announced. In this way, Thomas felt the views and opinions of many generals and other officers were communicated directly to the troops. The policy was enthusiastically received by the troops (O.R. S III, Vol. V, pp. 118-119).

Grant had his assistant adjutant general, J.A. Rawlins, issue G.O. No. 25 from his headquarters of the Department of Tennessee on April 22, 1863 for compliance with Thomas' assignment to form black regiments. He told the corps, division, and post commanders to use all their facilities to help form the black regiments. The commissaries were to issue supplies, and quartermasters were to furnish stores, just as had been done for white soldiers. Grant told them, "It is expected that all commanders will especially exert themselves in carrying out the policy of the Administration, not only in organizing colored regiments and rendering them efficient, but also in removing prejudice against them" (O.R. S III, Vol. III, p. 147).

The policy was, "All officers and enlisted men were required to treat the blacks kindly and encourage their seeking the protection of the troops, to be fed and clothed as far as possible until they could be able to provide for themselves; the able-bodied men to be organized into regiments, except such laborers as were required in the several Staff Corps and department-cooks for the troops and servants for the officers" (O.R. S III, Vol. III, p. 119).

General Thomas specifically announced that "if any officer should stand in the way or oppose this policy he would not hesitate to dismiss him from the service of the United States" (O.R. S III, Vol. III, p. 119).

Thomas was authorized to appoint field and company officers and to organize such troops for military service in accordance with the rules and regulations of their service. They were to be supplied in the same manner as other soldiers.

The first regiment created by Thomas was mustered into service in May 1863, and designated the First Regiment Arkansas Volunteer Infantry (African Descent). It was then redesignated the 46th Regiment U.S.C.T. one year later on May 11, 1864 (O.R. S III, Vol. V, p. 660).

By November 1863, Thomas had organized four regiments of cavalry, six regiments of heavy artillery, four companies of light artillery, and forty regiments of infantry which totaled 56,320 men from Iowa, Arkansas, Tennessee, Mississippi, Louisiana, Alabama, Florida, and Kentucky (O.R. S III, Vol. IV, p. 921).

General Thomas had experienced great difficulty in the early part of his work in getting medical officers. But he remedied this problem by sending Surgeon B.W. Sargent of his staff through the New England states to procure as many physicians as possible from the graduates of the medical schools. He induced a number of physicians to appear for examination and receive appointments (O.R. S III, Vol. IV, p. 922; S III, Vol. V, p. 123).

As the soldiers were being organized, Lincoln wrote to the Honorable Andrew Johnson on March 26, 1863. The President knew of Johnson's idea of raising a Negro military force. Andrew Johnson was the military governor of Tennessee at this time. Lincoln felt that it was advantageous for someone in a high position, an eminent citizen of a slave state and a slave owner himself, to lend in the organization of black soldiers. Lincoln remarked that "The colored population is the great available, yet unavailed of, force for restoring the Union, the bare sight of 50,000 armed and drilled black soldiers upon the banks of the Mississippi would end the Rebellion at once. And who doubts that we can present that sight if we but take hold in earnest? If you have been thinking of it please do not dismiss the thought" (O.R. S III, Vol. V, p. 103).

*The war in the southwest—Adjutant-General Thomas addressing the Negroes in Louisiana on the duties of freedom.*

## THE NEGRO TROOPS IN THE SOUTHWEST.

*WE illustrate on this page a most interesting scene, namely, the address of Adjutant-General Thomas to the negro troops and the contrabands generally at Goodrich's Landing, Louisiana, on 4th October, 1863. Goodrich's Landing, sixty-five miles north of Vicksburg on the west bank of the river, is the head-quarters of General J.P. Hawkins, commanding the district of Northeast Louisiana and the colored troops there stationed, and of Mr. W.R. Field, President of the Board of Commissioners for the leasing of Government plantations. On Sunday, October 4, Adjutant-General Thomas requested the soldiers, officers, planters, and working hands to the Goodrich House, and addressed them on the various duties devolving upon them. The utmost attention was given by the entire audience; and it may safely be said that no so singular and impressive scene has ever been enacted during the war as the Adjutant-General of the United States Army addressing negro soldiers, civilians, and women and children, on the duties and responsibilities of freedom, and that in the most southern of all the Slave States. Our artist has drawn the scene from photographs taken on the spot.*

(*Harper's Weekly, Nov. 14, 1863.*)

Lorenzo Thomas reported to Stanton that at first the best class of officer would not volunteer due to the general prejudice in the Army. But, since the prejudice against the black soldier had been overcome by their performance in the military, a higher class of officers presented itself (O.R. S III, Vol. V, p. 120).

He stopped the recruiting effort on May 1, 1865. As a result of his efforts in the West and Southwest, 2,804 officers and 76,040 enlisted men were added to the U.S.C.T. They belonged to four regiments of cavalry, nine regiments of heavy artillery, 8 batteries of light artillery, and 57 regiments of infantry. Thomas raised 42.5% of the total number of black men to serve in the U.S. Colored Troops, and 39.4% of the officer corps (O.R. S III, Vol. V, p. 124).

## Corps d'Afrique United States Colored Volunteers

In the Department of the Gulf, Major General Nathaniel Banks, the department commander, issued G.O. No. 40 from his headquarters on May 1, 1863. This order established the Corps d'Afrique. The strength of such a regiment in the corps was initially set at 500 men, including the full compliment of noncommissioned officers and officers. At its maximum strength, the Corps contained 1 cavalry regiment, 1 heavy artillery regiment, 5 engineer regiments, and 22 regiments of infantry.

***The Banks of the Mississippi.***

*The Major General commanding the Department proposes the organization of a corps d'armee of colored troops, to be designated as the "Corps d'Afrique." It will consist ultimately of eighteen regiments, representing all arms—Infantry, Artillery, and Cavalry, organized in three Divisions of three Brigades each, with appropriate corps of Engineers and flying Hospitals for each Division. Appropriate uniforms, and the graduation of pay to correspond with value of service, will be hereafter awarded.*

*In the field, the efficiency of every corps depends upon the influence of its officers upon the troops engaged, and the practicable limits of one direct command is generally estimated at one thousand men. The most eminent military historians and commanders, among others Thiers and Chambray, express the opinion, upon a full review of the elements of military prowess of every nation may be estimated by the centuries it has devoted to military contest, or the traditional passion of its people for military glory. With a race unaccustomed to military service, much more depends on the immediate influence of officers upon individual members, than with those that have acquired more or less of warlike habits and spirit by centuries of contest. It is deemed best, therefore, in the organization of the Corps d'Afrique, to limit the regiments to the smallest number of men consistent with efficient service in the field, in order to secure the most thorough instruction and discipline, and the largest influence of the officers over the troops. At first they will be limited to five hundred men. The average of American regiments is less than that number.*

*The Commanding General desires to detail for temporary or permanent duty the best officers of the army, for the organization, instruction and discipline of this corps. With their aid, he is confident that the corps will render important service to the Government. It is not established upon any dogma of equality or other theory, but as a practical and sensible matter of business. The Government makes use of mules, horses, uneducated and educated white men, in the defense of its institutions. Why should not the negro contribute whatever is in his power for the cause in which he is as deeply interested as other men? We may properly demand from him whatever service he can render. The chief defect in organizations of this character has arisen from incorrect ideas of the officers in command. Their discipline has been lax, and in some cases the conduct of the regiments unsatisfactory and discreditable. Controversies unnecessary and injurious to the service have arisen between them and other troops. The organization proposed will reconcile and avoid many of these troubles.*

*Officers and soldiers will consider the exigencies of the service in this Department, and the absolute necessity of appropriating every element of power to the support of the Government. The prejudices or opinions of men are in no wise involved. The cooperation and active support of all officers and men, and the nomination of fit men from the ranks, and form the lists of non- commissioned and commissioned officers, are respectfully solicited from the Generals commanding the respective Divisions.*

*BY COMMAND OF MAJOR GENERAL BANKS:*

*RICHARD B. IRWIN,*
*Assistant Adjutant General.*

*OFFICIAL:*

*Aide-de-Camp.*

*General Ullman's Headquarters, 1st Division, Corps d 'Afrique, Port Hudson, La.*

From March 26, 1864, to August 28, 1864, the Corps d'Afrique, had an Invalid Battalion. This was composed of deserving soldiers who, by reason of wounds or sickness contracted in the line of duty, were unfit for further field service. They were organized, armed, uniformed, and equipped in the same manner and under the same regulations as prescribed by existing orders for the Invalid Corps of the Army.

Major Thomas L. White, 9th Infantry, Corps d'Afrique, was charged with the duty of organizing the Invalid Battalion under the direction of Colonel Frank P. Cahill. The authorization for the Invalid Battalion was revoked on August 28, 1864, and all enlisted men were to be returned to their regiments. Those not fit for active service would be sent to the hospital, and notification had to be given to their regimental commander.

Fourteen black regiments were organized at New Orleans, nine in Port Hudson, Louisiana, and the remainder were organized at Camp Parapet, Fort Pike, Fort St. Phillip, Madisonville, and New Iberia, Louisiana. (For the detailed breakdown of the Corps d'Afrique regiments, see Dyer, pp. 1718-1720.)

In 1864 the War Department decided to incorporate all black federal regiments into a single organization. These Corps d'Afrique units were redesignated the United States Colored Troops and no longer had any official ties to any state. (See Appendix III for the listing and numbers those regiments were given.)

The Louisiana regiments were all issued U.S. Regulation uniforms by 1864. Negro troops, as a rule, took more readily to dress uniforms than did whites, and it is probable that they closely followed the prescribed dress. The only suggestion of special uniforms lies in a letter from the Army Clothing and Equipage Office to the Quartermaster General. The letter was dated March 3, 1864, and it reported issuing undersized "French Zouave" clothing to the musicians and bands of black regiments (Todd, p. 414).

# 15th Regiment Corps d'Afrique Soldiers Memorial

This regiment was organized early in August 1863, and was mustered into U.S. service on the 27th of that month. The regiment was reviewed on September 8th by General Banks, Adjutant General Thomas, and Brigadier General Charles P. Stone, their respective staff members, and a large number of spectators. They received the praise of all for their extraordinary proficiency in drill during the short time they had been in the service.

The organization of the regiment was superior to that of any other in the Corps. A regimental school was established under the immediate supervision of the chaplain, in which the noncommissioned officers were first taught.

The members of the regiment received their arms on September 12 and two days later, they received orders to report to Brashear City, Louisiana, for duty. The regiment left New Orleans with full ranks which numbered 1100 men, thus equalling the number required by the General Orders from headquarters.

In the lower left hand of the memorial is a carte de visite of First Lieutenant Walter H. Hutchinson of Company C. He entered the U.S. Army on December 26, 1861, as a private of the 12th Connecticut Volunteer Infantry. He was promoted to corporal on November 20, 1863, and first lieutenant on September 3, 1863.

The photo on the lower right hand corner is First Lieutenant Joseph H. Shaw of Company K. He entered the U.S. Army on August 20, 1861, as a private in the 6th Michigan Volunteer Infantry. He was promoted to quartermaster sergeant on March 7, 1863, and reassigned to the Louisiana Artillery as first lieutenant on September 7, 1863.

The designation of the 15th Regiment, Corps d'Afrique was changed to the 5th Regiment Engineers, Corps d'Afrique on February 10, 1864 and to the 99th U.S.C.T. on April 4, 1864. It was consolidated into a battalion of five companies in December 1865 and retained in service until April 23, 1866, when it was mustered out of service. The regiment engaged in two battles, Natural Bridge and Steamer Alliance.

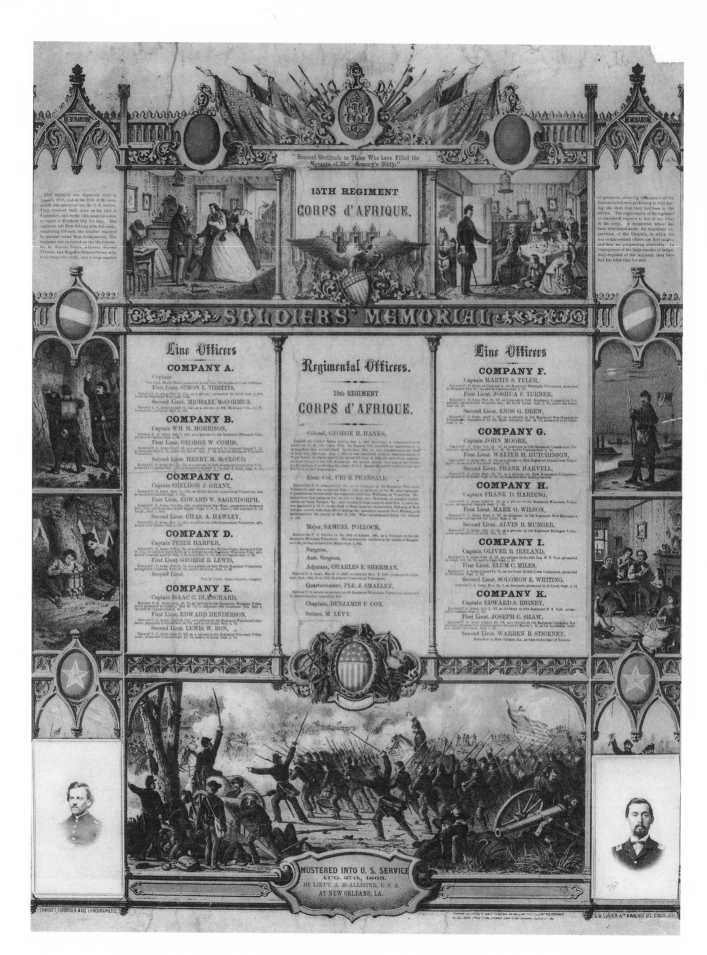

SOLDIERS' MEMORIAL

15TH REGIMENT
CORPS d'AFRIQUE.

"Honored Gratitude to Those Who have Filled the Measure of Their Country's Glory."

### Line Officers

**COMPANY A.**

Captain
Vice-Capt. Henri Milne promoted Lieut. Col. 3d Regiment Corps d'Afrique.
First Lieut. SIMON I. TIBBITS,

Second Lieut. MICHAEL McCORMICK,

**COMPANY B.**

Captain WM. H. MORRISON,

First Lieut. GEORGE W. COMBS,

Second Lieut. HENRY M. McCLOUD,

**COMPANY C.**

Captain SHELDON J. GRANT,

First Lieut. EDWARD W. SAGENDORPH,

Second Lieut. CHAS. A. HAWLEY,

**COMPANY D.**

Captain PETER HARPER,

First Lieut. GEORGE B. LEWIS,

Second Lieut.

**COMPANY E.**

Captain ISAAC C. BLANCHARD,

First Lieut. EDWARD HENDERSON,

Second Lieut. LEWIS W. BON,

### Regimental Officers.

15th REGIMENT
CORPS d'AFRIQUE.

Colonel, GEORGE H. HANKS,

Lieut. Col., URI B. PEARSALL.

Major, SAMUEL POLLOCK,

Surgeon,

Asst. Surgeon,

Adjutant, CHARLES E. SHERMAN,

Quartermaster, PLE. J. SMALLEY,

Chaplain, BENJAMIN F. COX.

Sutlers, M. LEVY.

### Line Officers

**COMPANY F.**

Captain MARTIN S. TYLER,

First Lieut. JOSHUA F. TURNER,

Second Lieut. ENOS G. DREW,

**COMPANY G.**

Captain JOHN MOORE,

First Lieut. WALTER H. HUTCHINSON,

Second Lieut. FRANK HARVELL,

**COMPANY H.**

Captain FRANK D. HARDING,

First Lieut. MARK G. WILSON,

Second Lieut. ALVIN B. MUNGER,

**COMPANY I.**

Captain OLIVER B. IRELAND,

First Lieut. ELIM C. MILES,

Second Lieut. SOLOMON E. WHITING,

**COMPANY K.**

Captain EDWARD S. RIGNEY,

First Lieut. JOSEPH C. SHAW,

Second Lieut. WARREN B. STICKNEY,
Detached in New Orleans, La., as Superintendent of Schools.

MUSTERED INTO U. S. SERVICE
AUG. 27th, 1863.
BY LIEUT. A. McALLISTER, U. S. A.
AT NEW ORLEANS, LA.

## 54th Regiment Massachusetts Volunteer Infantry

The 54th Regiment Massachusetts Volunteer Infantry is perhaps the most recognized of all the black regiments of the Civil War. Perhaps the next best known regiment is the 1st Regiment South Carolina Volunteer Infantry (African Descent). The latter was the first black regiment, while the 54th was the first black regiment from the North. However, they both had their origins as state volunteers; the 1st South Carolina was redesignated the 33d Regiment U.S.C.T., and the 54th kept its original state identification throughout the war. Even though they were colored troops, on the 33d became part of the U.S.C.T. (See Appendix IV.)

On January 26, 1863, Secretary of War Stanton authorized Governor John A. Andrew to raise a number of volunteers to fill companies of artillery for duty in the forts of Massachusetts and elsewhere, and such corps of infantry for the volunteer military service as he might find convenient. Such volunteers were to be enlisted for three years, or until sooner discharged, and could include persons of African descent, organized into a special corps. He was to make the usual needful requisition on the appropriate staff bureaus and officers for the proper transportation, organization, supplies, subsistence, arms, and equipment of these volunteers.

*Colonel Robert Gould Shaw, 54th Regiment, Massachusetts Volunteer Infantry.*

Captain Robert G. Shaw, a 25 year old student from Staten Island, New York was placed in charge of the regiment. Recruiting began in Boston on February 9, 1863. Men were also sent from Philadelphia, but the larger part of the members were obtained through the efforts of a recruiting committee appointed by Governor Andrew, largely under the direction of Major George L. Stearns. The first soldiers, a squad of 27 men, came into Camp Meigs, Reidville, Massachusetts, on February 26. Their quarters were the regulation wooden Army barracks, originally built for the 44th Massachusetts.

The men were trained, uniformed, and equipped with Enfield rifles before they left the Bay State on May 28, 1863. This regiment was looked upon as the North's showcase black regiment. Not having enough black men from Massachusetts to fill its ranks, men from other states were enlisted.

The biggest problem that the men of the 54th had was centered on the issue of pay. Although the men were promised the same pay as white soldiers in Massachusetts regiments, the government maintained its pay policy of the Act of July 17, 1862, which mandated $10.00 per month with $3.00 going towards clothing. Colonel Shaw had written to the governor about this issue because he threatened to disband his men if it was not rectified. The state of Massachusetts agreed to make up the difference in pay out of its own funds, but the men refused to take the money on moral grounds. They felt that the Federal government should recognize their stand on the same pay as the white soldiers, as was initially promised by the Governor.

This problem was eventually rectified on September 28, 1864, but it placed great hardships on the families of the volunteers. (See Quaker Oath)

Another issue that the 54th helped to break was that of being denied black officers. Six enlisted men from the ranks of this regiment and the 55th broke the color barrier of black officers.

The most memorable action of the 54th was its participation in the engagement of Fort Wagner on July 18, 1863. At Shaw's request, they were given permission to lead the attack. The colonel felt that this would be a great opportunity to show the country the capabilities of the black soldiers. They reached Morris Island at 6 P.M. on July 18, 1863, and they led the assault on Fort Wagner, planting their colors on the parapet. Colonel Shaw fell at the head of the storming column, and the rest of the regiment, under Captain Luis F. Emilio, was repulsed. All of the field officers and many of the line officers were killed or wounded. The regiment remained in an advance position after the charge until they were relieved on the morning of of the 19th. All ten companies participated in this engagement. The regiment lost 259 of its 650 officers and men. Although there were prior battles in which black soldiers performed honorably, the death of the young Colonel Shaw, the son of prominent abolitionists, changed the feeling of many of the whites who were in doubt of the fighting capabilities and contributions of the black men in Union blue.

Those men of the 54th who were captured during this engagement went to jail in Charleston. While they were there, they were tried for "insurrection." Since the black soldiers were free, they did not fit the category of the captured black soldiers who were former slaves; they were found not guilty.

The first deed for a black soldier to be a recipient of the Medal of Honor was the action of Sergeant William H. Carney. Although he was the first black soldier

*"Storming Fort Wagner" depicts Colonel Robert Gould Shaw leading his men of the 54th Massachusetts charging the ramparts on July 18, 1863. This young abolitionist reached the ramparts, turned and shouted to his men "Onward Fifth-fourth!" That was the last thing he said, for he was felled by a ball in the chest. The Rebels were so irate that colored soldiers were lead by a white officer that they stripped his body of his uniform and threw him in a common grave with his men on top of him.*

*Dr. Lincoln R. Stone (right), Camp at Readville, 54th Mass. Regt.*

to be recognized for this medal, he was the last black soldier of the Civil War to receive it; the date of reception was May 23, 1900.

The State Regimental Color lost during this battle was returned to Massachusetts in March of 1875 by General R.S. Ripley, who was in command of the defense of Charleston, South Carolina at the time of the attack on Fort Wagner.

Captain Luis F. Emilio wrote of the action in *The Assault on Fort Wagner, July 18, 1863, The Memorable Charge of the Fifty-Fourth Regiment of Massachusetts Volunteers.* Later, there was a more detailed record of the 54th entitled, *A Brave Black Regiment: History of the Fifty-Fourth Regiment of Massachusetts Volunteer Infantry, 1863-1865.*

Colonel Edward N. Hallowell, a merchant from Philadelphia, took over command of the regiment as soon as he recovered from the wounds he received at Fort Wagner. He continued as its commander until the regiment was mustered out of service on August 20, 1865, at Mount Pleasant.

Another battle that the 54th participated in was the Battle of Olustee on February 20, 1864. The 54th went into battle with the cry "Three Cheers for Massachusetts and seven dollars a month" (Headly, p. 452).

Those men captured at the battle were sent to Camp Sumter, also known as the Andersonville Prison. Four of them, Corporal James Gooding, Company C; Private Charles Rensenlear, Company C; Corporal Charles Augustus, Company I; and Private William J. Smith, Company I, died and are buried there.

On September 7, 1864, six companies of the regiment were specially detailed to guard 600 Rebel officers sent to Morris Island, and were placed under fire by the United States Government in retaliation for the same number of the regiment's prisoners in Charleston who were exposed to the fire of Union guns. The Rebel officers were confined in a large open pen to the north of Fort Wagner, and within canister range of the guns. The guard duty was severe and the utmost vigilance was necessary. None of the prisoners escaped (Headly, p. 452).

The 54th was mustered out of service on August 20, 1865 at Mount Pleasant, South Carolina. The following day they embarked for Gallop's Island, Boston Harbor. On September 1, 1865 the men received their final pay and were discharged.

The men of the 54th Regiment participated in the following engagements:

| | Killed | | Wounded | | Missing in Action | |
|---|---|---|---|---|---|---|
| | O | EM | O | EM | O | EM |
| **1863** | | | | | | |
| James Island | | 14 | | 17 | | 13 |
| Fort Wagner | 3 | 7 | 9 | 125 | | 115 |
| | | | | | | |
| **1864** | | | | | | |
| Olustee | | 5 | | 4 | | 10 |
| Honey Hill | 1 | 1 | 3 | 38 | | 5 |
| | | | | | | |
| **1865** | | | | | | |
| Boynkins Mill | 1 | 1 | 2 | 16 | | 1 |
| | | | | | | |
| Totals | 5 | 28 | 18 | 196 | | 144 |

[Official Army Register of the Volunteer Force of the United States Army, Part VIII, AGO. Washington, July 16, 1876.]

## 14th Rhode Island Regiment Heavy Artillery (Colored)

Black soldiers first fought in large numbers for Rhode Island as early as the Revolution. On August 4, 1862, the Adjutant General's Office of the State of Rhode Island issued G.O. No. 36. "The Sixth Regiment authorized by the Secretary of War, under date of October 23, 1861, will consist entirely of colored citizens. Enlistment will commence immediately." A rendezvous was opened and about one hundred men enrolled, but owing to uncertainty as to whether they were to be employed as soldiers on equal terms with other volunteers, or to be assigned to labor with pick and spade, together with other causes, the enterprise failed.

Permission was granted from the War Department on June 17, 1863, to enlist a colored company of heavy artillery. G.O. No. 24 from the Adjutant General's office of Rhode Island authorized one company of black heavy artillery to serve three years or during the war; a camp was established at Dexter Training Grounds in Providence. General Order No. 26 was issued on August 14, 1863 for a second company of heavy artillery. This camp of black troops was named "Camp Fremont," in honor of Major General John C. Fremont. Then, on September 9, 1863, authority was granted by the War Department to raise a regiment of heavy artillery composed of colored men. Lieutenant Colonel Nelson Viall commanded this regiment. The camp which had been established on the Dexter Training Grounds and known as "Camp Fremont" was changed to "Camp Smith," in recognition of the governor, James Y. Smith.

*Private John N. Sharper, a native of Providence, Rhode Island, enrolled in the 14th Regiment Rhode Island Heavy Artillery (Colored) on October 30, 1863 and was mustered into service on November 4, 1863. He was discharged on a Surgeon Certificate from the Corps d'Afrique Hospital in New Orleans on September 11, 1865.*

On August 28, 1863, the first company was mustered in. The colored ladies of Providence presented the 1st Battalion with a handsome silk flag, which bore the appropriate emblems, on December 9, 1863. Ten days later, this battalion sailed for Newport, Virginia.

The first and third battalions were stationed at Camp Parapet, New Orleans, and the second battalion was at Plaquemine, Louisiana. The regiment was divided until it was mustered out of the service. At Camp Parapet, Lieutenant Colonel Viall, with the aid of sympathetic friends, established a school for the men under his command.

The designation of the regiment was changed on April 4, 1864 to the 8th Regiment U.S.C.T. It was changed a second time to the 11th Regiment U.S. Colored Heavy Artillery on May 21, 1864. The regiment was mustered out of service on October 2, 1865 at New Orleans. On its way home, the regiment landed in New York City on October 15, 1865. It marched up Broadway preceded by a brass band and drum corps which was organized from its ranks. This scene presented one of the most imposing views that had been witnessed by the citizens of New York. Along the entire route, loud and enthusiastic exclamations of welcome and admiration went up from the crowd that had turned out to see the black soldiers. The regiment went on to Providence where a welcome reception was inspiring. A dress parade took place before Governor Smith, his staff, and an immense concourse of spectators. The men disbanded after the parade.


## 29th Regiment Connecticut Volunteer Infantry (Colored)

Wartime Governor William B. Buckingham of Connecticut called for black volunteers on November 23, 1863, to form the 29th Connecticut. They were organized at Fair Haven, a suburb of New Haven Connecticut. These men were promised the same pay and uniform as the white soldiers of the state. This promise of equal pay was given in ignorance of the law. The War Department subjected all black troops, state or federal, were subject to the same pay inadequacies.

The regiment was full by January 12, 1864, but lack of officers prevented it from mustering in until March 8, 1864. The black ladies of New Haven presented the regiment with their national colors.

With the 29th full, the governor called for black volunteers for another regiment, the 30th Connecticut, which was subject to the same conditions. By February of 1864, a battalion had been formed and addressed by Frederick Douglass.

The nucleus for Connecticut's second black regiment, the 30th Connecticut Volunteer Infantry, was consolidated with the 31st U.S.C.T. on May 18, 1864. At this time, many of the black state volunteer regiments were being redesignated into the United States Colored Troops. Black men who were drafted went only into U.S.C.T. The 31st was one of the three black regiments organized in New York City. It came to life on Hart's Island, East River, New York City. It participated in the Battle of the Crater at Petersburg and at the surrender of General Lee.

*Colonel William B. Wooster, 29th Conn. Vol. Inf. (Colored).*

*Line officers' tents, camp of the 29th Connecticut, Beaufort, S.C.*

The 29th Connecticut went to Beaufort, South Carolina, and encamped near the 1st South Carolina. After two months of drill and discipline, the men presented such a fine display of precision that their daily dress parades began to attract the general public.

At one time during a lull in the intense firing in their engagement at the Battle of Darbytown Road in Virginia on October 13, 1864, some of the men of the 29th would call out to the Rebels: "How about Fort Pillow today! Look over here Johnny, and see how niggers can shoot!" These men were so daring and aggressive that their commanding officer had to restrain them from useless exhibitions of their courage (Croffet, p. 675).

In this engagement, Sergeant Jacob F. Spencer ran far ahead of the line, captured two armed Rebels, and brought them back as prisoners. They afterward declared that they would never have surrendered to him if they had known he was a "nigger." Major General Godfrey Weitzel presented Spencer with a medal for gallantry (Croffet, p. 676).

When the 29th participated in the race for Richmond, two Companies, C and G were ordered forward as skirmishers, and the cavalry scouts had preceded them. These two companies had the distinction of being the first Union infantry to reach the burning city.

As part of the 25th Army Corps, the 29th went to Texas. It was stationed at Brownsville where it remained in camp until ordered to Connecticut to be mustered out on October 14, 1865. It sailed to New Orleans and then embarked for New York. From New York, the regiment went to Hartford, arriving on November 24, 1865. The next day, the men were paid and mustered out.

*Dress Parade, 29th Connecticut, Beaufort, S.C.*

## Army of the James

In April 1864, the Army of the James consisted of the 10th and 18th Army Corps under Major General B.F. Butler. General Butler treated his men to accolades from his headquarters before Richmond on October 11, 1864. He gave special mention to the colored soldiers of the 3d Division of the 18th and 10th Army Corps and the officers who led them. "In the charge of the enemy's works by the colored division of the 18th Corps, Newmarket, better men were never better led—better officers never led better men. With hardly an exception officers of colored troops have justified the care with which they have been selected. A few more such gallant charges and to command colored troops will be the post of honor in the American Armies. The colored soldiers by coolness, steadiness, and determined courage and dash have silenced every cavil of the doubters of their soldierly capacity, and drawn tokens of admiration from their enemies—have brought their late masters even to the consideration of the question whether they will not employ as soldiers the hitherto despised race. Be it so—the war is ended when a musket is in the hands of every able-bodied negro who wished to use one."

In the same document Butler, awarded the following battle honors:

The 2d U.S. Colored Cavalry have inscribed the word "Suffolk" on their colors, for their conduct in the battle of March 9th near that place.

The 1st, 4th, 5th, 6th, and 22d U.S. Colored Troops have the word "Petersburg" inscribed on their banners, for their gallantry in capturing the line of works and the enemy's guns on the 15th of June, 1864, at that place.

The 1st, 4th, 5th, 6th 22d, 36th, 37th, 38th U.S. Colored Troops, and the 2d U.S. Colored Cavalry have the words "New Market Heights" inscribed upon their colors, for their gallantry in carrying the enemy's works at that point on the 29th of September.

The Quartermaster is directed to furnish a new stand of colors to each of these regiments, with the inscriptions ordered.

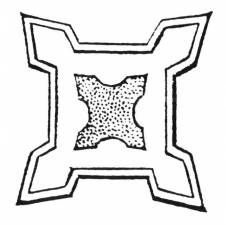

*10th Army Corps.*

*18th Army Corps.*

## 25th Army Corps

The 25th Army Corps was created by G.O. No. 297 from the War Department on December 3, 1864, by combining the black troops of the 10th and 18th Army Corps.

The 25th distinctive corps badge was in the shape of a square. The first division's version was colored red, the second division's version was white, and the third division's version was blue. The 25th Corps was the first and only all black corps in the Union Army. It was also the last federal Army Corps in the war.

Initially, the Corps had been placed in a Camp of Instruction at City Point, and from time to time, General Orders were used to express an opinion pertaining to the performance of the U.S.C.T. For example, The headquarters of the 25th Army Corps in the field at Texas issued G.O. No. 65 on October 5, 1865. An excerpt from the Order, written by General Weizel, reads: "Although none of them have as many battle-fields to be proud of, as the regiments were raised in the beginning of the war, still they have an equally brilliant record, because they have always accomplished well, everything that was required of them. Olustee, Petersburg, The Mine, Deep Bottom, Newmarket Heights, Pussell's Mills, and Nine Mile Road are among those fields where they proved their valor and settled the question as to the capacity of the colored man to make a good soldier."

The 25th Army Corps was discontinued as an organization by direction of the President on January 8, 1866 via the War Department G.O. No. 2.

After the corps was no more on January 31, 1866, General Weizel made the following comment: "Its organization was an experiment which has proven a perfect success. The conduct of its soldiers has been such as to draw praise from persons most prejudiced against color, and there is no record which should give the colored race more pride than that left by the 25th Army Corps."

*25th Army Corps.*

## Colored Soldiers C.S.A.

General Patrick R. Cleburne, Army of Tennessee, was one of the earliest Confederate Generals to push for arming the slaves for the Confederacy. Politicians started to consider arming slaves as early as the fall of 1864, and even Jefferson Davis was in favor of using blacks for the military; only with the promise of freedom, however.

Many were waiting for Robert E. Lee to express his opinion on this sensitive subject of a Negro Soldiers Bill. He said that it was not only expedient but necessary. He felt that blacks could do as well in the Confederate Army as in the Union Army, and he openly endorsed Jefferson Davis' plea of enlistment of slaves and a "racial modification" of the status of blacks in Southern society (O.R. S IV, Vol. III, pp. 797-799).

Robert E. Lee instituted a most innovative procedure. He invited soldiers in the Army of Northern Virginia to give their opinion on the plausibility of recruiting slaves and of fighting next to them. Both officer and enlisted man were in favor of this policy at this time in the war. They had faith in Lee's ability to decide what was best for the cause (Berlin, p. 281).

On March 13, 1865, the Confederate Congress passed an act to enlist slaves in the military. This was commonly called the Negro Soldiers Bill, and it became a general order for members of the military to abide. However, neither the act nor the general order promised freedom to slaves who volunteered to fight.

The Adjutant and Inspector General's Offices of the Confederate States of America issued G.O. No. 14 on March 23, 1865. This order was aimed at increasing the military force of the Confederate States in order to repel an invasion, to maintain rightful possession of the states of the Confederacy, to secure their independence, and to preserve their institutions. President Davis gave the authorization to accept slaves into the military service. Their numbers were based on what were needed, and all able-bodied Negroes would serve in the capacity that he directed.

The slaves were to be organized into companies, battalions, regiments, and brigades, according to the manner that the Secretary of War prescribed. The men would be commanded by officers who were appointed by the President.

The soldiers were to receive the same rations, clothing, and compensation as the other troops in the same branch of the service.

There were several restrictions in this general order. One stated: "Not more than 25% of the male slaves between the ages of 18-45 in any state, shall be called under the provisions of this act." And another declared: "No slave will be accepted as a recruit unless with his own consent and with the approbation of his master."

It was not the intention of the President to grant any authority for raising regiments or brigades of black soldiers. It was their intention to raise black soldiers in smaller units. All larger organizations were to be left for future action as experience may determine (O.R. S IV, Vol. III, pp. 1161-1162).

In March of 1865, two companies of black soldiers of the Confederacy paraded in Richmond. The city was invaded on April 3, 1865 lead by the black soldiers of the 5th Massachusetts Cavalry and two companies of the 29th Connecticut Infantry. With the surrender of the Army of Northern Virginia on April 9, 1865, the utilization of the black Confederate soldiers came too late.

THE BLACK CONSCIRIPTON.

"WHEN BLACK MEETS BLACK THEN COMES THE END OF WAR"—AND SLAVERY

"The Black Conscription" appeared on September 26, 1863, in Punch, a British periodical. This illustration was sold in carte de visite format.

President Jefferson Davis was an early proponent of using slaves in any way necessary to win the war. As the fighting continued through 1864, Confederate leaders began to change their opinions of using slaves in the Confederate Army. General Patrick Cleburne voiced his favor, and on January 11, 1865, General Robert E. Lee sanctioned the policy of arming slaves. The inevitable was coming—slaves would be armed. Unfortunately for them, it came too late.

To offset the balance of the supposed wickedness of using Negroes on the Northern side, artist Theodore R. Davis sent this sketch of colored Rebel pickets being used at Fredericksburg as seen through the field glasses of a Union officer and relayed to Davis. This appeared on the front page of Harper's Weekly on January 10, 1863.

Showing the Confederates using fully armed slaves on picket duty was to help those proponents of the North using soldiers of any color to help fight against the insurgents.

*A rebel captain forcing Negroes to load cannon under the fire of Berdan's Sharp-shooters.*

*..[O]ne of Mr. Mead's sketches...illustrates the way in which the cowardly rebels force their negro slaves to do dangerous work. It represents a struggle between two negroes and a rebel captain, who insisted upon their loading a cannon within range of Berdan's Sharp-shooters. The affair was witnessed by our officers through a glass. The rebel captain succeeded in forcing the negroes to expose themselves, and they were shot, one after the other.*
*(Harper's Weekly, May 10, 1862.)*

*A shell in the rebel trenches, drawn by Mr. Homer, is an event of not uncommon occurrence. The secesh chivalry generally place their negroes in the post of danger: and when our gunners get the range of their works and drop a well-aimed shell into them, the skedaddle which ensues is such as Mr. Homer has depicted.*
*(Harper's Weekly, Jan. 17, 1863.)*

# United States Colored Troops

GENERAL ORDERS,
No. 143.

WAR DEPARTMENT,
ADJUTANT GENERAL'S OFFICE
*Washington, May 22, 1863*

I. A Bureau is established in the Adjutant General's Office for the record of all matters relating to the organization of Colored Troops. An officer will be assigned to the charge of the Bureau, with such number of clerks as may be designated by the Adjutant General.

II. Three or more field officers will be detailed as Inspectors to supervise the organization of colored troops at such points as may be indicated by the War Department in the Northern and Western States.

III. Boards will be convened at such posts as may be decided upon by the War Department to examine applicants for commissions to command colored troops, who, on application to the Adjutant General, may receive authority to present themselves to the board for examination.

IV. No persons shall be allowed to recruit for colored troops except specially authorized by the War Department; and no such authority will be given to persons who have not been examined and passed by a board; nor will such authority be given any one person to raise more than one regiment.

V. The reports of Boards will specify the grade of commission for which each candidate is fit, and authority to recruit will be given in accordance. Commissions will be issued from the Adjutant General's Office when the prescribed number of men is ready for muster into service.

VI. Colored troops may be accepted by companies, to be afterwards consolidated in battalions and regiments by the Adjutant General. The regiments will be numbered *seriatim*, in the order in which they are raised, the numbers to be determined by the Adjutant General. They will be designated: "— Regiment of U. S. Colored Troops."

VII. Recruiting stations and depots will be established by the Adjutant General as circumstances shall require, and officers will be detailed to muster and inspect the troops.

VIII. The non-commissioned officers of colored troops may be selected and appointed from the best men of their number in the usual mode of appointing non-commissioned officers. Meritorious commissioned officers will be entitled to promotion to higher rank if they prove themselves equal to it.

IX. All personal applications for appointments in colored regiments, or for information concerning them, must be made to the Chief of the Bureau; all written communications should be addressed to the Chief of the Bureau, to the care of the Adjutant General.

BY ORDER OF THE SECRETARY OF WAR:

E.D. Townsend
*Assistant Adjutant General.*

**General Order No. 143 authorized the formation of the Bureau of United States Colored Troops. This order officially began the recognition of the black soldier in the U.S. Army. Men became part of the U.S. Colored Troops in three ways: redesignation of state volunteer regiments, redesignation of the Corps d'Afrique, and via the draft, enlistments, or as substitutes.**

## Major Charles W. Foster, Chief, Bureau of Colored Troops

Another of the many officers from Massachusetts involved with black soldiers was Charles Warren Foster. He first entered the military at the age of 16 when he participated in the Mexican War as a noncommissioned officer. After his discharge, he reenlisted in the U.S. Engineers for another tour of duty until 1856. After his next discharge, he was attached to the Engineer Department as the Superintendent of Harbor Improvements and Construction at Charleston, South Carolina.

When the Civil War began, he received a commission as Captain, Assistant Adjutant General, U.S. Volunteers. He then became Major Foster, Assistant Adjutant General and Chief of the Bureau of the United States Colored Troops. He served in this post until October 1867.

By October 31, 1863, Major Foster was praising for the men in the U.S.C.T. In a letter that he wrote to Secretary of War Stanton, he stated: "The colored troops have already established for themselves a commendable reputation. Their conduct in camp, on the march, in siege, and in battle attests their discipline, their endurance, and their valor" (O.R. S III, Vol. III, p. 114).

He had also been commissioned captain and assistant quartermaster, U.S. Army, on November 4, 1865. Foster had received, for faithful and meritorious services during the war, brevets of lieutenant colonel and colonel, U.S. Volunteers, on September 25, 1864, and major, lieutenant colonel, and colonel, U.S. Army, on November 4, 1864. After forty years of service, he had his name placed on the retired list on September 24, 1891.

## Major George L. Stearns

George L. Stearns of Medford, Massachusetts, began his overt efforts to free the black man by being one of John Brown's "Secret Six." This group of abolitionists backed Brown's scheme to invade the South. Another member of this select group was Thomas Wentworth Higginson, who eventually became colonel of the 1st South Carolina, the first black regiment.

Stearns began his recruiting career by joining Governor Andrew's "Black Committee." This committee to superintended the raising of black regiments in Massachusetts. Stearns appointed a number of black leaders to help raise the 54th and 55th Massachusetts Infantry, and the 5th Massachusetts Cavalry.

His work led him to be appointed major, assistant adjutant general, U.S. Volunteers. He became the recruiting commissioner for the colored troops and his first major task was to raise the black soldiers for the William Penn regiments. In order to accomplish this, he established his headquarters at the Continental Hotel in Philadelphia. He remained at his post until he was honorably discharged on March 30, 1864.

Reuben D. Mussey, Regular Army, 19th U.S. Infantry, was Stearns' assistant and was the Mustering Officer for Colored Troops in Tennessee. After Major Stearns resigned, Mussey was appointed Superintendent in his place, by Adjutant General L. Thomas. Mussey was later appointed Colonel of the 100th Regiment U.S. Colored Infantry, a regiment organized in Kentucky. For his faithful service in the recruitment and organization of colored troops, he was made brevet brigadier general on March 13, 1865. He was the only officer to be brevetted for this effort.

*Major George L. Stearns.*

*Brevet Lieutenant Colonel Alexander T. Augusta was born in Norfolk, Virginia, in March 1825. He graduated from the Trinity Medical College of the University of Toronto in 1856. During the Civil War, he was appointed surgeon of the 7th U.S. Colored Troops. His commission—the equivalent of a major—was dated October 2, 1863. Promoted to brevet lieutenant colonel on March 13, 1865, he thereby became the highest ranking black officer in the Civil War era. Augusta was on detached duty at the Camp for Colored Persons while retaining his formal affiliation with the 7th U.S. Colored Troops.*

## African-American Surgeons During the Civil War

Anderson R. Abbott
Alexander T. Augusta, 7th U.S. Colored Troops
John V. Degrasse (assistant surgeon), 35th U.S. Colored Troops (Cashiered)
William B. Ellis
William C. Powell, 127th U.S. Colored Troops
Charles B. Purvis
John Rapier
Alephus Tucker
(Abbott, Ellis, Purvis, Rapier, and Tucker probably performed their duties in hospitals as contract surgeons.)

## Black Chaplains in the Union Army

Asher, Jeremiah, Baptist, 6th U.S. Colored Troops

Bowles, John R., Baptist 55th Massachusetts Infantry

Boyd, Francis A., Christian, 109th U.S. Colored Troops (Appointment Revoked)

Harrison, Samuel, Congregational, 54th Massachusetts Infantry

Hunter, William H., African Methodist Episcopal. 4th U.S. Colored Troops

Jackson, William, Baptist, 55th Massachusetts Infantry

Leonard, Chauncey, Baptist, L'Ouverture Hospital, Alexandria Virginia

Levere, George W., Congregational, 20th U.S. Colored Troops

Randolph, Benjamin F., Presbyterian, 26th U.S. Colored Troops

Stevens, David, African Methodist Episcopal, 36th U.S. Colored Troops

Turner, Henry M., 1st U.S. Colored Troops

Underdue, James, Baptist, 39th U.S. Colored Troops

Waring, William, Baptist, 102nd U.S. Colored Troops

White, Garland H., African Methodist Episcopal, 28th U.S. Colored Troops

*Jeremiah Asher died of disease in the service on July 27, 1865.*

*John R. Bowles*

*Samuel Harrison*

*Martin R. Delaney was commissioned a major in the 104th U.S. Colored Troops on February 26, 1865. He was sent to the Department of the South to aid General Saxton in the recruitment and the organization of the 104th and 105th U.S. Colored Troops. The 104th was organized in Beaufort, South Carolina, to serve three years. The 105th failed to complete its organization. Major Delaney has been given the distinction of being the first black staff officer in the United States military, although Alexander T. Augusta, surgeon of the 7th U.S. Colored Troops held a commission dated October 2, 1863, and was made brevet lieutenant colonel on March 13, 1865.*

*First Sergeant Stephen Swails, Company F, 54th Massachusetts Infantry Regiment, was the first black soldier to break the color barrier of commissioned officers in Massachusetts regiments. Sergeant Swails was cited for his "coolness, bravery, and efficiency: during his participation in the Battle of Olustee, February 20, 1864. He was commissioned a second lieutenant in the 54th Massachusetts on March 11, 1864, by Governor John Andrew. However, the War Department would not give him a discharge to receive his commission, which he eventually received on April 28, 1865.*

*Second Lieutenant Peter Vogelsang served with the 54th Massachusetts Infantry Regiment. The 54th was the first colored regiment recruited in the North. All of the other regiments in service at the time were from the South or the border states. The 54th was organized at Camp Meigs, Readville, Massachusetts, from March 30 to May 13, 1863, to serve three years, but they were mustered out of service on August 20, 1865. The 54th Massachusetts participated in battles at James Island, Fort Wagner, Honey Hill, and Boykins Mill in South Carolina and at Olustee, Florida.*

*John F. Shorter.*                                    *William H. Dupree.*

*Governor John Andrew commissioned eight sergeants as officers in the 55th Massachusetts Infantry Regiment. Only three of these men were mustered in as officers; the others were mustered out of the regiment. Second Lieutenant John F. Shorter and Second Lieutenant William H. Dupree were commissioned at that rank. James Monroe Trotter was the third of the sergeants who were commissioned second lieutenant. These sergeants distinguished themselves in the field. Dupree was commissioned in May 1864, Shorter in March 1864, and Trotter in April 1864, but were not mustered into service as officers until some time later. Dupree received his commission on June 21, 1865, Shorter on July 1, 1865, and Trotter received his commission on June 7, 1865.*

*James Monroe Trotter was born the son of a slave in Grand Gulf, Mississippi, on November 8, 1842. He enlisted as a private on June 11, 1863, in Company K, 55th Regiment Massachusetts Volunteer Infantry (Colored). Promoted to sergeant major of the regiment, he became one of the three black soldiers later commissioned as officers in the 55th Massachusetts when he was made a second lieutenant on June 7, 1865. He became the first black music historian by writing the epochal 508-page* Music and Some Highly Musical People. *In 1888, President Grover Cleveland appointed him as recorder of deeds in Washington, D.C., which was at that time, the highest position that a black man had held in the United States—replacing Frederick Douglass.*

## Appointment of Frederick E. Camp

The war allowed some men to be active in a number of regiments. Frederick E. Camp was such an individual. He was a 30 year old citizen from Durham, Connecticut who enlisted into the 24th Connecticut Volunteer Infantry on September 2, 1862, as second lieutenant in Company F. Seven months later, he was promoted to first lieutenant.

Lieutenant Camp was wounded at the Battle of Port Hudson in June 1863, and a short time later, in September, he was mustered out of service. By November, Governor Buckingham of Connecticut, called for black volunteers to enlist in the 29th Regiment Connecticut Volunteers. Once the regiment was formed, the officers were mustered into service. Camp was appointed captain of Company D, 29th Connecticut. He remained a captain, and participated in the engagements at Petersburg, Chapin's Farm, the Siege of Darbytown Road, and Kell House, Louisiana.

The 29th Connecticut marched with Hawley's Brigade against Richmond along Darbytown Road. They were deployed on the skirmish line of its entire front, commanded by Captain Camp. The regiment made its way close to the enemy breastworks, and the men eventually ran out of ammunition. They replenished their cartridge boxes by taking what they could from the dead or wounded on the field. Captain Camp was forced to keep his men restrained because they fought with reckless and indifference to danger. They engaged the enemy for nearly 15 hours before they were relieved (Croffet, pp. 674-676).

The illustration depicts Camp's appointment in the 29th Connecticut, via the Bureau of Colored Troops, headquarters Department, Virginia and North Carolina, Army of the James. It is dated November 23, 1864. This document informed Captain Camp of his appointment to major in the 29th Connecticut from Major General Butler. Camp was to communicate his acceptance to the Bureau of Colored Troops, and he did so the following day. [At this time the 29th Connecticut, although a state regiment, was under Federal control as part of the 10th Army Corps. The commanding general had the authority to appoint staff officers. The Bureau of Colored Troops maintained the records of colored regiments.]

Camp remained at this position until January 1, 1865. On this date, he was promoted to Lieutenant Colonel of the 29th Regiment United States Colored Infantry. This regiment only engaged the enemy one time while he was in its ranks, at White Oak Road on March 31, 1865. The 29th was mustered out of service on November 6, 1865.

Lieutenant Colonel Camp continued his military career by enlisting in the 14th U.S. Infantry on February 23, 1866 as a second lieutenant. Three days later he became a first lieutenant and was transferred to the 32nd U.S. Infantry. He was promoted to captain in December 1868 and was assigned to the 2nd U.S. Infantry in January 1871. He ended his 13 year military career with his resignation on July 20, 1875, and he died on October 8, 1891.

# Bureau of Colored Troops,

### HEAD QUARTERS DEPT. VA. & N. C.,

Army of the James, *Nov. 23rd 1864.*

Sir

I am instructed by the Major General Commanding to inform you that, by virtue of the authority entrusted to him by the War Department, he has this day appointed you *Major* in the *Twenty Ninth* Regt. of *Connecticut Vols. (Colored)* subject to the approval of the President of the United States.

Immediately on receipt hereof, please to communicate to this Bureau your acceptance or non=acceptance, and report your age, birth-place, and the State of which you are a permanent resident.

You will report for duty to *the Commanding Officer 29th Conn. Vols. (Colored) in the 18th Army Corps.*

By command of *Major General Butler.*

*Edward Smith*

Asst. Adjt. Gen'l.

To *Frederick E. Camp,*
Capt. 29th Conn. Vols. (Colored)
10th Army Corps

No 19

57

## Frank M. Welch

Major Frank M. Welch, 5th Battalion (colored) Connecticut National Guard, became the highest ranking colored officer in the Connecticut National Guard. Welch began his military career as a private in Company F, 54th Regiment, Massachusetts Volunteer Infantry on May 12, 1863. This 22-year-old Philadelphia native became sergeant the next day. Welch was slightly wounded in the neck in the action at Fort Wagner, Morris Island, on July 18, 1863, and was admitted to Hospital No. 6 in Beaufort, South Carolina. He was then sent back to the company after he recovered from his wound and was appointed first sergeant on January 17, 1865 of Company F.

He was one of three enlisted men in his regiment promoted to officer rank on April 28, 1865, and mustered in on June 3, 1865. He was appointed second lieutenant on June 20, 1865, and was later appointed first lieutenant, Company F, on July 22, 1865.

Orders were received from Major General Quincy A. Gillmore directing the commanding officers of the 54th Massachusetts, who were about to be mustered out, to nominate such officers of their regiment who wanted appointments on other colored organizations. Welch wanted to continue his military career and was mustered into federal service as 2d Lieutenant, 14th U.S. Colored Heavy Artillery as of November 6, 1865. He then proceeded to Fort Macon, North Carolina, and was informed by the lieutenant colonel in command of the regiment that the regiment received orders to be mustered out of service.

He never actually reported to his unit, and Welch was mustered out on December 6, 1865. The 14th U.S. Colored Heavy Artillery was mustered out of service five days later.

Upon his return to his home in Meriden, Connecticut, Welch decided that he wanted to continue his military career. He enlisted as Captain in the Welch Guard in Bridgeport, Connecticut, Independent Battalion, Connecticut National Guard, on May 27, 1879. The state formed the 5th Battalion, Colored, Connecticut National Guard, of which Welch was appointed the commanding officer (major), on August 11, 1881. Major Welch received an honorable discharge on March 1, 1890, due to the disbanding of the 5th Battalion.

Here, he wears the standard double-breasted uniform coat of a major in the Connecticut National Guard. On his breast can be seen a five pointed star of the Grand Army of the Republic, as worn by Civil War veterans. To the right of this medal, known as the "G.A.R." medal, is a four bastioned fort shaped badge with a dark center. This was the corps badge of the 10th Army Corps. The 54th

Massachusetts was in the First Division of the 10th Army Corps. The insert of the badge appears dark in the photo because its was red. The other badge is the Long Service Medal of the Connecticut National Guard. The sword is the 1860 Field and Staff Officers sword with a gold sabre knot.

## William H. Appleton, Medal of Honor Recipient

William H. Appleton was an 18 year old machinist apprentice from Manchester, New Hampshire when he enlisted in Company I, 2d Regiment New Hampshire Volunteer Infantry. He was mustered in on June 7, 1861, just in time to participate in the first Battle of Bull Run.

His military career progressed normally; he was promoted to corporal on November 5, 1862. At the same time, he was gaining valuable military combat experience with his regiment. He remained a corporal until he was discharged at Lookout Mountain, Virginia, on July 30, 1863. There he received a commission as a second lieutenant in Company H of the 4th Regiment U.S.C.T. He joined the regiment for duty in Baltimore three days later. This regiment was then in its early stages of development, and it was the first of five U.S. Colored Troop regiments raised in Maryland. The others were the 9th, 19th, 30th, and 39th Regiments, U.S.C.T.

The twenty-one year old Appleton was promoted to first lieutenant on July 1, 1864, per Special Order No. 222 from the War Department, dated June 29, 1864.

It was during the Battle of Petersburg on June 15, 1864, that Second Lieutenant Appleton demonstrated his capabilities. His participation in this battle and the battle at Chapin's Farm on September 29, 1864, earned him his Medal of Honor. The Medal was for his behavior in two engagements. The citation reads, "The first man of the eighteenth Corps to enter the enemy's works at Petersburg, Va. 15 June 1864, Valiant service in a desperate assault at New Market Heights, Va. Inspired the Union troops by his example of steady courage."

The 4th U.S.C.T performed well in battle and participated in a total of 5 engagements. Three of its enlisted men also received the Medal of Honor in the name of Congress. They were Sergeant Major Christian Fleetwood, Color Sergeant Alfred B. Hilton, and Private Charles Veal.

[Nineteen officers of the 4th U.S.C.T. received brevet rank, and the names of which may be found in the Official Register of the Volunteer Force of the United States Army, part VIII, p. 172.]

Appleton was promoted to captain, Company E, 4th U.S.C.T., on November 26, 1864. He was mustered out of service with his regiment on May 4, 1866. G.O. No. 65, dated June 22, 1867, from the Adjutant General's Office of the War Department appointed Captain Appleton to major by brevet in the Volunteer Force, Army of the United States, for gallant and meritorious services during the war. The honor was to date from March 13, 1865. On February 18, 1891, William H. Appleton was issued the Medal of Honor.

### Free Military School for Applicants to Command Colored Troops

With the formation of the United States Colored Troops, an officer corps was required. The Government constituted a Board of Examiners, whose goal was to examine all persons, regardless of their rank, who made applications for commissions in the U.S.C.T. A major was the permanent President of the Board.

The Supervisory Committee for Recruiting Colored Regiments established the formation of the Free Military School for Applicants to command Colored Troops. On December 29, 1863, the school admitted its first 30 candidates, and it also gave directions to all its applicants for admissions to the school; it was stated that the following need not apply:

"Such as are intemperate, such as seek the service for lack of a better business; such as have been, while in the military service, frequently sick at the hospital; and such as are proved to be ill whenever their is a hard march on hand, or a battle in prospect."

The Supervisory Committee paid for the school supplies such as books and maps. These books had to be returned to the Committee, and the student paid for his own room and board.

Privates and noncommissioned officers desiring to enter the free military school at Philiadelphia were granted a 30 day furlough if their immediate commader would recommend them for commissioned appointments in the U.S.C.T. These requests for furloughs had to be approved by the next level of commander per War Department General Order No. 125, Mardh 29, 1864.

There were four class levels. The Fourth Class (the lowest level), was known as the School of the Soldier; the Third Class was the School of the Company; the Second Class was called the School of the Battalion; and the First Class was called the School of the Brigade. Six of seven days a week there were three sessions, two during the day and one during the night.

This Free Military School also taught black noncommissioned officers who were intelligent and educated men from Maryland. Arrangements had been made with the Post Commander of Camp William Penn, Lieutenant Colonel Wagner, for those students to exercise the functions of officers in assisting to drill and

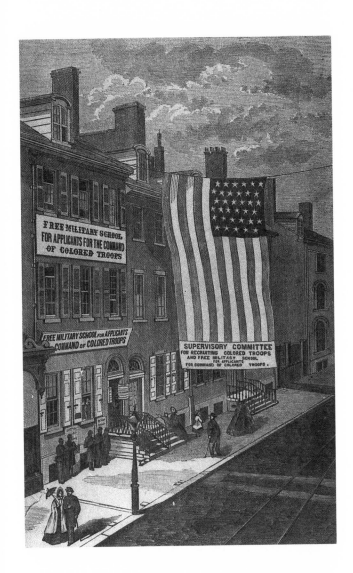

The building and banner of the Free Military School for White Applicants to Command Colored Troops, a forerunner of Officers Candidate School, is shown at 1210 Chestnut Street, Philadelphia, Pennsylvania. This was also the location of the Supervisory Committee for Recruiting Colored Troops.

This illustration expresses the opinion of those in charge of the Free Military School and the caliber of white officers that they were seeking. The quality of these white officers is self-evident—thirteen of the 7,122 officers in the United States Colored Troops were awarded the Medal of Honor.

**NO PERSON IS WANTED** as an Officer in a Colored Regiment who "feels that he is making a sacrifice in accepting a position in a Colored Regiment," or who desires the place simply for higher rank and pay. It is the aim of those having this organization in charge to make Colored Troops equal to the best of White Troops, in Drill, Discipline and Officers. It is more than possible that Colored Troops will hereafter form no inconsiderable portion of the permanent army of the United States, and it should be the aim of every officer of Colored Troops to make himself and his men fit for such an honorable position.

It can be no "sacrifice" to any man to command in a service which gives Liberty to Slaves, and Manhood to Chattels, as well as Soldiers to the Union.

Colonel John H. Taggart was the preceptor of the Free Military School, which was operational from December 26, 1863 to September 15, 1864. When it closed, Taggart opened another school, this time requiring a fee, called "The United States Military School for Officers."

This 1863 pamphlet was the first of two versions to be circulated; the second was dated 1864. The school was sponsored by the Union League of Philadelphia.

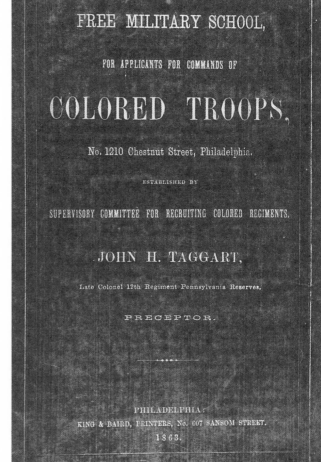

"READ THIS AND CIRCULATE IT."

FREE MILITARY SCHOOL,

FOR APPLICANTS FOR COMMANDS OF

COLORED TROOPS,

No. 1210 Chestnut Street, Philadelphia.

ESTABLISHED BY

SUPERVISORY COMMITTEE FOR RECRUITING COLORED REGIMENTS,

JOHN H. TAGGART,

Late Colonel 12th Regiment Pennsylvania Reserves,

PRECEPTOR.

PHILADELPHIA:
KING & BAIRD, PRINTERS, No. 607 SANSOM STREET.
1863.

train the regiments of the camp.

When the Supervisory Committee for Recruiting Colored Regiments of Philadelphia disbanded in the fall of 1864, the Free Military School for Applicants for the Command of Colored Troops also had to be disbanded. The school operated from December 26, 1863, until September 15, 1864. There were 484 students who passed the test given by the Examination Board.

Colonel Reuben D. Mussey, 100th U.S.C.T. opened his own school for United States Colored Troops officers. Knowledgeable officers from other branches of the service taught classes once or twice a week (Glatthaar, p. 107).

*Officers of the 101st U.S. Colored Troops*

*The 101st Infantry Regiment U.S. Colored Troops was organized from September 17, 1864 to August 5, 1865 in Tennessee to serve three years. It was composed of men unfit for service in the field but who were still able to perform ordinary fatigue and garrison duty, and also of men who were transferred from other black regiments serving in the Department of Cumberland who were incapacitated for services in the field. They participated in the Alabama battles of Scottsboro, Boyd's Station, and Madison Station. Ten of the enlisted men were killed and four were wounded. One officer was wounded and one missing.*

## Camp William Penn

An effort to raise black soldiers in Philadelphia began in March 1863. A committee was formed and a brigade was to be commanded by Colonel William Angeroth. But no further effort was put forth until the Confederate invasion of Pennsylvania in June.

By that time black men from Pennsylvania were filling the ranks of the 54th and 55th Regiments of Massachusetts Infantry and the 14th Regiment of the Rhode Island Heavy Artillery.

As a result of the refusal of Major General Couch to accept the black men answering Governor Andrew Curtin's June 15, 1863 state emergency call, Stanton gave permission to Thomas Webster of Philadelphia to raise 3 regiments of colored volunteers on June 17, 1863. Special Order No. 275 from the War Department on June 22, 1863, established Chelten Hills, near Philadelphia, as a rendezvous for the U.S.C.T. recruited in the eastern part of Pennsylvania. This camp was known as Camp William Penn. The first company of 80 black recruits was sent to Camp William Penn on June 26, 1863. This nucleus grew into the 3rd Infantry Regiment U.S.C.T. Ten other regiments were also formed at Camp William Penn.

*32nd U.S. Colored Troops, Camp William Penn.*

*Camp William Penn, Visitor's Pass.*

*General Order No. 13 was a Post General order to be complied with by the various U.S.C.T. regiments organized at Camp William Penn.*

---

## Head-Quarters Camp "William Penn,"

CHELTEN HILLS, PA.

### FEBRUARY 13TH, 1864

### GENERAL ORDER No. 13.

All Visitors to this Camp will require a Pass, to be obtained at these Head-Quarters, or at the Head-Quarters of the Supervisory Committee, No. 1210 Chestnut Street.

By order of

### LOUIS WAGNER,

Lieut.-Col. 88th Regt. P.V.

Commanding Post.

GEORGE E. HEATH,

1st Lieut. 6th Regt. U.S.C.T.

Post Adjutant.

---

### HEAD-QUARTERS CAMP "WILLIAM PENN,"

CHELTEN HILLS, PA.

_____ *1864*

The Bearer,_____

has permission to visit this Camp on _____

_____

### This Pass Not Transferable, and to be taken up when presented.

By Order of

### LOUIS WAGNER,

*Lieut.-Col.* 88*th Regt. P.V.,*

Commanding Post.

*General Agent Supervisory Committee.*

**CAMP WILLIAM PENN;**
Rendezvous for United States Colored Troops, City Line, Near North Pennsylvania Railroad, Chelten Hills, Pa.
LOUIS WAGNER, *Colonel 88th Regiment Pa. Volunteers*, Commanding Post.

Lithographed and Published by L. N. Rosenthal, 817 Walnut Street, Philadelphia.
Entered According to Act of Congress, in the year 1864, by L. N. Rosenthal, in the Clerk's office of the District Court for the Eastern District of Pennsylvania.

*Camp William Penn was located eight miles north of Philadelphia in Cheltanham Township. In its beginning stages, the soldiers lived in tents, but by December 1863, wooden barracks buildings had been erected.*

*Lieutenant Colonel Louis Wagner commanded Camp William Penn during its activation from June 1863 to May 1865.*

The men of Company A, 3rd U.S.C.T., were the same men that General Couch had refused to take to aid the first state emergency. The recruits were mustered in by companies of 80 men, and by squads, and were immediately uniformed, equipped, and sent to the camp. Each recruit was to be paid a $10.00 bounty upon the full muster of his company by the state.

Camp William Penn was located near the home of the abolitionists James and Lucretia Mott. The camp was on an elevated piece of land commanding a full view of a cultivated, rolling countryside with nearby streams. It was one-half a mile from Chelten Hills and the Department of the North Pennsylvania Railroad. The first two regiments, the 3d and 6th, lived in tents. The 8th went into regulation army wooden barracks in December 1863. The camp was set up to take two regiments at a time.

The post commander was Lieutenant Colonel Louis Wagner, who was on detached service from the 88th Regiment Pennsylvania Volunteer Infantry. Wagner had been badly wounded at Bull Run.

By December 1863, the city of Philadelphia was giving a $250.00 bounty to each colored volunteer. Black men from New York, Connecticut, New Jersey, and Delaware filled the ranks of the William Penn regiments.

The soldiers of Camp William Penn had a record in which they could take pride. The 6th, 8th, 22d, and 43d Regiments did the most fighting of the William Penn regiments, and the 6th and the 8th were listed in W.F. Fox's Regimental Losses in the American Civil War among the 300 hardest fighting regiments in the war.

Two enlisted men, Sergeant Major T. Hawkins and 1st Sergeant A. Kelly, received the Medal of Honor in the name of Congress. Two officers, Lieutenant N. Edgerton and Captain A. Wright were also recipients of the Medal of Honor.

The soldiers from Camp William Penn fought in the Battle of the Crater, at Olustee, and some of them were the first regiments to enter Richmond. One company of the 6th went into a charge at the Battle of Newmarket Heights with 32 men and returned with 3.

The 22d was chosen to be part of the funeral obsequies of President Lincoln in Washington, D.C. It was the only black regiment so honored. It was also assigned to hunt the assassins of the President. The 43rd was the first black regiment to be part of a presidential inaugural parade, marching to honor Lincoln the second time he took the executive oath.

Jeremiah Asher, Chaplain, 6th U.S.C.T. was one of the 14 black chaplains in the service of the United States, and the only one to die in service. His death resulted from malignant fever.

Camp William Penn was the largest encampment for black soldiers in the Civil War. The 3d, 6th, 8th, 22d, 24th, 25th, 32d, 41st, 43d, 45th, and 127th Regiments U.S. Volunteers and an Independent Company (100 days) were organized in the camp.

Special Order No. 227 dated May 13, 1865, began the closing of Camp William Penn. All troops were removed from the camp. Lieutenant Colonel Wagner was to assist the new camp commander, Colonel J.C. Strong of the Veterans Reserve Corps, with its closing.

It was Special Order No. 381, dated July 19, 1865, that ordered the camp to be "broken up." It was intended to be turned over to the Quartermaster Department, and it was finally closed on August 14, 1865, according to the last Post Returns.

**Infantry Soldiers**

*Unidentified first sergeant, Company G, 77th U.S. Colored Troops.*

*Sergeant Major Charles Springer, 107th U.S. Colored Troops.*

*Sergeant George Koch, 69th U.S. Colored Troops.*

*Corporal Charlie Mguda, U.S. Colored Troops.*

*Sergeant Gaither, U.S. Colored Troops.*

*"Brothers-in-arms," U.S. Colored Troops.*

# VOLUNTEER ENLISTMENT.

STATE OF *Ark.*                    COUNTY OF *Sebastian*

I, *Joseph Logan* born in *Johnson County* in the State of *Arkansas* aged *Twenty three* years, and by occupation a *Laborer* Do Hereby Acknowledge to have volunteered this *nineteenth* day of *October* 186*3*, to serve as a SOLDIER, in the **Army of the United States**, for the period of **THREE YEARS**, unless sooner discharged by proper authority: Do also agree to accept such bounty, pay, rations and clothing, as are, or may be established by law for *Colored* volunteers.

And I, *Joseph Logan* do solemnly swear that I will bear true faith and allegiance to the **United States of America**, and that I will serve them honestly and faithfully against all their enemies or opposers whomsoever; and that I will observe and obey the orders of the President of the United States, and the orders of the officers appointed over me, according to the Rules and Articles of War.

Sworn and subscribed to, at *Ft. Smith Ark.* this *19th* day of *October* 186*3*.

BEFORE *John Hayes Jr 2nd Lieut Recruiting 2nd Kas. Colored vols*

                                                                     his
                                        *Joseph  X  Logan*
                                                    mark

I CERTIFY, ON HONOR, That I have carefully examined the above named Volunteer agreeable to the General Regulations of the Army, and that in my opinion he is free from all bodily defects and mental infirmity, which would in any way disqualify him from performing the duties of a soldier.

*A. C. Turner*

EXAMINING SURGEON.

I CERTIFY, ON HONOR, That I have minutely inspected the Volunteer, previously to his enlistment, and that he was entirely sober when he enlisted; that, to the best of my judgment and belief, he is of lawful age; and that, in accepting him as duly qualified to perform the duties of an able-bodied soldier, I have strictly observed the Regulations which govern the Recruiting Service. This soldier has *black* eyes, *black* hair, *black* complexion, is *five* feet *seven* inches high.

*John Hayes Jr 2nd Lieut*

*2nd* Regiment of *Kas. Colored* Volunteers.

RECRUITING OFFICER.

*The enlistment form did not have the word "colored" as part of its text—thus the word had to be inserted, as shown in this Volunteer Enlistment for Joseph Logan, who joined the 2nd Kansas Colored Infantry. At this time, October 1863, there was no bounty for colored soldiers; the pay was less than that of white soldiers, and their three-dollar clothing allowance was deducted from their ten-dollar monthly pay. Like many laborers of the time, Logan was unable to write his name and had to make is mark, "X." The 2nd Kansas Colored Infantry was later redesignated the 83rd Regiment United States Colored Troops (new).*

*Private William Adams, Company F, 108th U.S. Colored Troops.*

*Private Jesse Keepson, Company F, 108th U.S. Colored Troops.*

*Unidentified soldiers, U.S. Colored Troops.*

*Soldier's Stencil Kit belonging to Charles E. Clark, a 19-year-old laborer from Upper Sandusky, Ohio. He enlisted in Company E of the 55th Regiment Massachusetts Volunteer Infantry (colored), on May 28, 1863 and was mustered out on August 28, 1865.*

*This "dog tag," or identification disk belonging to Henry Lindsey, Co. A, 43d PA. C.V. (43d U.S.C.T.), is a "token of remembrance" to Maria Lindsey. On the face is "Abraham Lincoln, President, U.S., War of 1861."*

# Cavalry Soldiers

This is a non-professional, hand-tinted 8x10 wet plate, albumen photograph of a cavalry private in his four-button sack coat. The crossed sabers on his kepi are tinted in gold.

This is a cased outdoor scene, quarter plate ambro-type, of a mounted cavalry soldier wearing a shell jacket, with his saber drawn. An ambro-type is a collodion positive on glass.

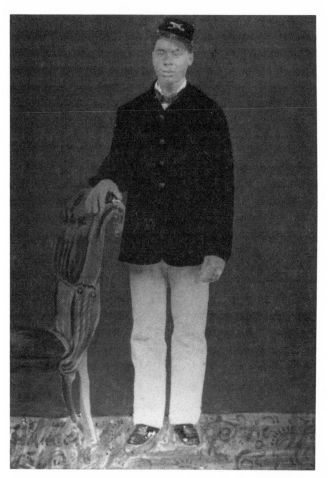

*Probably a servant, but possibly a cavalry trooper with mount.*

## The Hanging of Private Johnson, 23rd U.S. Colored Troops

On June 20, 1864, Private William Johnson, 23rd U.S.C.T., was hanged. The List of U.S. Soldiers Executed by U.S. Military Authorities during the Late War, A.G.O. 1885, does not list this execution. He was buried near Meade Station.

The facts that are known about this man is that he deserted and "attempted to commit an outrage on a white woman at Cold Harbor." Considerable importance was given to the affair, in order that the example might be made more effective. Johnson confessed his guilt and was executed within the outer breastworks about Petersburg on an elevation, and in plain view of the enemy. A white flag covered the ceremony (*Harper's Weekly*, July 9, 1864).

Noted Civil War photo historian William Frassanito found further evidence of his guilt in the personal diary of General Marsena Patrick, Provost Marshal of the Army of the Potomac. His diary recorded that "The Chaplain prayed with him; he acknowledged that he was a deserter, that he had changed his name and committed the crime charged upon him."

Frassanito provides an excellent account of the hanging and the photographing of Johnson following his execution. Two Civil War photographers took four photographs taken of the hanging and sold these images to the public.

Timothy O'Sullivan, working for Alexander Gardner took two stereo images titled "The execution of William Johnson, Jordan's Farm, Petersburg, June 20, 1864." The Brady & Co. photographer also took two images and titled them the same (Frassanito, pp. 216-222).

## Artillery Soldiers

*First Sergeant A Company, wearing frock coat with sergeant's stripes on sleeve and noncommissioned officer's brass shoulder scales.*

*An artillery private is wearing a shell jacket with red piping in this one-eighth plate tintype.*

## Soldiers Memorial for Company H, 10th Regiment U.S. Colored Heavy Artillery

The 10th Regiment U.S. Colored Heavy Artillery served longer than any other black regiment. This was because it was organized at New Orleans, Louisiana, as the 1st Regiment Louisiana Heavy Artillery (African Descent) and served a term of three years. Its designation was changed to the 1st Regiment Heavy Artillery, Corps d'Afrique, on November 19, 1863; to the 7th Regiment U.S. Colored Heavy Artillery on April 4, 1864; and to its final designation of the 10th U.S. Colored Heavy Artillery on May 21, 1864. The 77th Regiment U.S.C.T. was consolidated with it on October 1, 1865.

The regiment was in continuous service for 50 months, 24 days, and it participated in one engagement at Pass Manchas, Louisiana on March 20, 1864. It mustered out of service on February 22, 1867.

This regiment had the most brevet officers of any U.S. Colored Troops:

    1 Brevet Brigadier General
    1 Brevet Colonel
    5 Brevet Lieutenant Colonels
    11 Brevet Majors
    17 Brevet Captains
    12 Brevet Lieutenants

Brevet rank, for practical purposes, can be regarded as an honorary title, awarded for gallant or meritorious action in time of war, and having none of the authority, precedence, or pay of real or full rank.

"DEEDS, NOT WORDS---VICTORY OR DEATH!"

## 77TH REGIMENT
## U. S. Colored Infantry.

### COMPANY D.

## Regimental Officers.

Colonel CHARLES A. HARTWELL.
Lieut. Colonel HENRY STREET.
Major GEORGE WEBSTER.
Surgeon JOHN POINDEXTER.
Asst. Surgeon JOHN T. WARNER.
Chaplain WILLIAM M. MIDDLETON.
Adjutant LUCIUS CROOKER.
Regt. Q. M. ALBERT RAYBURN.

## Company Officers.

### COMMISSIONED.

Captain JESSE FETTIS.
First Lieut. WILLIAM H. BENTLEY.
Second Lieut. WILLIAM O. RICE.

### NON-COMMISSIONED.

#### SERGEANTS.

DAVID SNELL, 1st Sergt.
MAJOR CHARTER.
ROBERT LEADBETTER.
GREEN COLES.
ADOLPH ALLEN.

#### CORPORALS.

MANDERBURG STEWART.
JESSE HENDERSON.
SAMUEL ALLEN.
THEO. FIELD.

#### MUSICIANS.

THOMAS JONES.

### MUSTERED INTO U. S. SERVICE
Dec. 8, 1863.
AT FORT ST. PHILIP, LOUISIANA.

### PRIVATES.

| Names. | Remarks. |
| --- | --- |
| MITCHELL ALCON. | |
| AARON ANDERSON. | |
| ZACK BRADWELL. | |
| MITCHELL BENJAMIN. | |
| GEORGE CARTER. | |
| NIMROD DUNCAN. | |
| AUGUST DICK. | |
| PETER ELY. | |
| GEORGE FRANKLIN. | |
| WILEE FAGAN. | |
| HORACE FOSTER. | |
| JOHN GOODMAN. | |
| ZACKARIAH GROSS. | |
| ROBERT GREEN. | |
| CHARLES GIBSON. | |
| ALLEN GREEN. | |
| EWELL HUSSEN. | |
| HENRY HARDY. | |
| THOMAS HUGHES. | |
| ROBERT HILL. | |
| ROLLA HINTER. | |
| MOSES HUNTER. | |
| CHARLES HENDERSON. | |
| SIDNEY HID. | |
| SAMUEL JOHNSON. | |
| HENDERSON JOHNSON. | |
| GEORGE JOHNSON. | |
| EDWARD LEWIS. | |

### PRIVATES.

| Names. | Remarks. |
| --- | --- |
| GEORGE LEWIS. | |
| JOHN LEWIS. | |
| THOMAS MILLER. | |
| JACKSON MONTAGUE. | |
| JOSEPH NICHOLAS. | |
| IRA STEEL. | |
| URIAH SMITH. | |
| WILLIAM THOMAS. | |
| OLIVER WILLIAMS. | |
| HENRY WILLIAMS. | |
| GEORGE WASHINGTON. | |
| WOODSON WINNEGAR. | |

### DISCHARGED.

JOHN WYATT.
JORDAN WHITTAKER.

### DIED.

DICK BENNETT.
EDMUND KING.
LEWIS HENDERSON.
JACKSON JONES.
DENNIS LEE.
GEORGE OWENS.
FREDERICK REED.
DANIEL HENDRICKS.

### DESERTED.

JOHN A. BAILEY.
JOSEPH LUCERN.

### History.

The 6th Regiment of Infantry, Corps d'Afrique, was organized by its Colonel, at Fort St. Philip, La., Dec. 8th, 1863, in obedience to special orders from Headquarters, Department of the Gulf, dated Nov. 20, 1863, by the transfer from the 4th Infantry Corps d'Afrique of a portion of that regiment. May 24, 1864, its numbers were considerably augmented by the 85th U. S. Infantry Colored, consolidating within. Again, in September, it was strengthened by the addition of 135 recruits received from the Recruiting Depot U. S. Colored Troops, at New Orleans. Aside from this, the Regiment has since recruited more than 75 men. April 4, 1864, the designation of the Regiment was changed from 5th Infantry Corps d'Afrique, to 77th U. S. Infantry, Colored, in obedience to orders from the War Department, and to 77th U. S. Colored Infantry in June. From the date of its organization, until December, 1864, Fort St. Philip, La., was garrisoned by this force, which wrought in itself and the old fortifications, during that time, many changes pleasing to the eye and eminently satisfactory to the minds of soldiers free from inefficiency and ignorance to proficiency and discipline ; and the fort from filth and wretchedness to neatness and comfort. A very limited amount of picket duty on the river and Gulf coats relieved the tedium of garrison life somewhat. During the month of December, the Regiment moved from Fort St. Philip, by detachments, to the city and vicinity, and has not since been reunited as a regiment. In the latter part of December and first of January, three companies, E, H, and K, were in the field at and near Pattersonia, Miss., and although not actually under fire, proved manufactory God they are "brave of heart and strong of arm," that "the spirit is willing and the flesh not weak."

---

## Private Gordon

This is perhaps one of the most remembered photos of a black slave of the Civil War. Three different photos were taken by the Baton Rouge, Louisiana photographers, McPherson & Oliver. These photos were taken at the time of Gordon's enlistment in the Army. Illustrations of these appeared in the July 4th, 1863 issue of *Harper's Weekly* on Page 429. The article was titled "A Typical Negro." The photos made into illustrations for the *Harpers's Weekly* were captioned, "Gordon as he entered our lines," "Gordon Under Medical Inspection," and "Gordon in his uniform as a U.S. soldier." The photo shown is the "Gordon Under Medical Inspection."

The scarring on his back, called "keloids," which is an abnormal proliferation of scar tissue, had been inflicted on Christmas Day of 1862.

Gordon escaped from his master and came into Union lines in March 1863. His clothes were torn and covered with mud and dirt from his long race through the swamps and bayous while he was being chased by his master and several neighbors, along with a pack of blood-hounds.

In order to foil the scent of the dogs, he carried onions in his pockets that were taken from his former plantation. After crossing each creek or swamp, he rubbed his entire body with the onions, which threw off his scent for the dogs. Gordon had displayed unusual intelligence in his escape.

When he reached Union lines, he served as a guide. On one expedition, he was taken prisoner by the Rebels, who, infuriated beyond measure, tied him up, beat

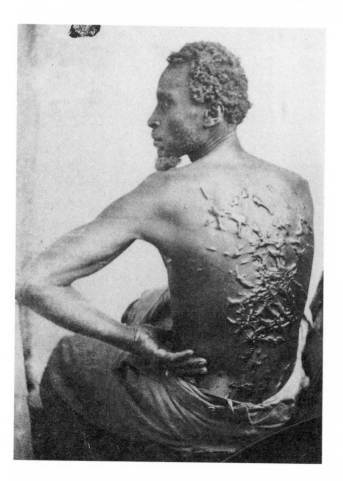 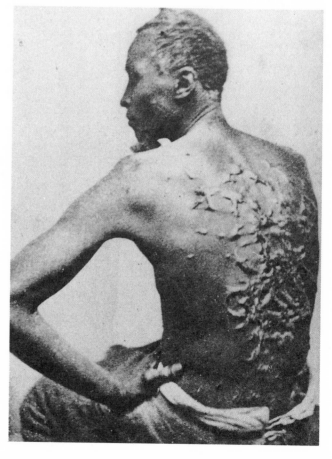

him and left him for dead. He recovered once more, however, and returned again to the Union lines.

It is not clear if Gordon was a civilian guide working for the military or a guide while a member of the Army. Most likely, he was a civilian guide. If Gordon did become a soldier, he probably joined one of the regiments in Ullman's Brigade which was being formed in that area. These regiments became part of the Corps d'Afrique and were later redesignated into the U.S.C.T.

It was customary among wet plate photographers to take more than one plate of the same subject. Seen here are the two photographs taken of Gordon's scarred back. The most obvious difference is the position of the left hand. Since it would take approximately 10 minutes between each wet plate negative, it was not uncommon for the subject to move. This is not usually noticed because we seldom have more than one photograph to view.

This photograph is also sometimes titled "The Scoured Back."

## Dutch Gap Canal

Dutch Gap Canal, sometimes called "Butler's Folly," was constructed by General Butler, who conceived of constructing a canal on the James River to permit passage of gunboats blocked at Trent Reach by Confederate Batteries and other obstructions put in the river by Butler. The formation of the canal started on August 10, 1864 and was completed by December 30, 1864. The work was performed by U.S. Colored Troops and black civilians. The canal was never used during the war because it was never totally completed until April 1865, and therefore, was of no military value.

*Dutch Gap Canal—after the canal was opened.*

*Dutch Gap Canal—bombproof shelter.*

These bombproof shelters were necessary at Dutch Gap because the Rebels were constantly throwing mortar shells into the area while the digging proceeded. When the Guard yelled "Shells!" all would hasten to the nearest shelter.

There were three Battles at Dutch Gap, Virginia. On August 24, 1864, the 22d U.S.C.T. was involved; on September 7, 1864, the 4th U.S.C.T. was involved; and on November 17, 1864, the 36th U.S.C.T. was involved.

## Men of African Descent

This term was used in most of the initial documents pertaining to the colored men in the Civil War. Authorization for permission was given to raise volunteers of African descent to comprise the 1st South Carolina Volunteers. Governor Andrews of Massachusetts was given permission to raise a special corps of men of African descent. The enlistment broadside for the men of the 54th Massachusetts called for men of African descent, while the regimental designation was that of "colored."

Major C.W. Foster, in charge of the Bureau for Colored Troops, reported to the Secretary of War on October 31, 1863, that there were 58 colored regiments at that time. All but the 1st through the 8th Regiment U.S.C.T. and the 3d, 6th, and 7th through 12th Regiments Corps d'Afrique, were to be referred to as African descent. This included the state volunteers of Rhode Island, Massachusetts, Iowa, Arkansas, Tennessee, Kansas, North Carolina, South Carolina, Alabama, Mississippi, and Louisiana (O.R. S III, Vol. III, p. 115).

The Act of July 17, 1862, The Second Confiscation Act, and the Militia Act referred to the black men as persons of "African descent." The General Orders referring to under-cooks mentioned the black men of "African descent," and the phrase "Men of Color," and "colored" came into effect sometime after the designation of "African descent."

*Unidentified man of African descent.*

81

## White Noncommissioned Officers in the United States Colored Troops

Many of the administrative duties of the noncommissioned officers required an understanding of how to comply to the military way of life. Since the black man did not have prior military experience, this type of noncommissioned officer candidate was not available in the ranks.

The ability to read and write was a prerequisite for the noncommissioned officer. This competency was lacking in many of the enlisted men; not only the black soldiers, but the white soldier as well. Although there were attempts to educate the black soldiers, those gifted and otherwise, a shortage existed in the noncommissioned officer ranks. One of the ways to fill these demands was to fill them with white soldiers. This policy also existed due to the ideas of some General Officers such as General N.P. Banks. Banks felt that black soldiers should not be permitted to become officers. By filling the ranks with noncommissioned officers to do their duties, the work load for the line officers was decreased.

Some white noncommissioned officers felt that this was the fastest road for obtaining officer status. In some cases they were correct. General Thomas found that when he authorized the first sergeants to be white that they took these positions to obtain promotion and objected if the promotions were not done as quickly as they expected. He changed the rule and urged the colonels to select intelligent blacks and instruct them. He felt that this system worked admirably because he had seen colored sergeants drill their squads as well as white sergeants (O.R. S III, Vol. V, p. 120).

Adjutant General L. Thomas generally appointed noncommissioned officers from white regiments in his endeavors to raise black regiments along the Mississippi River. As intelligent black soldiers were discovered, they were made sergeants and corporals, and ultimately, they filled all these positions (O.R. S III, Vol. IV, p. 922).

## Sergeant Major Charles M. Bucklin, 81st U.S. Colored Troops

This 18 year old farmer had enlisted in the 2nd Vermont Light Artillery, Battery B, on August 5, 1864. He remained as a Private with the Battery until his discharge to become the Sergeant Major of the 81st U.S. Colored Troops on March 9, 1865. Five months later, August 13, 1865 this white noncommissioned officer was discharged to accept his Presidential appointment as a second lieutenant in Company F, of the 81st U.S. Colored Troops.

Lieutenant Bucklin had been placed on Detached Service to search for the deserters of his regiment. Along with 5 enlisted men, he was sent to Baton Rouge, Port Hudson, and Bayou Sara Lee for the purpose of arresting these deserters.

A number of months later, he was detached from his regiment to be in charge of recruits for the 9th U.S. Cavalry, which was a black unit. Although his regiment was mustered out of service on November 30, 1866, Bucklin remained in service and was discharged on March 22, 1867.

## Under-Cooks

The Act of March 3, 1863 (the Conscription Act) authorized the enlistment of two under-cooks of African descent for each cook. They received $10.00 per month and one ration per day; three dollars of said monthly pay was for clothing.

In order for this to be effective in the military, a General Order was developed to provide this authority. War Department G.O. No. 323, dated September 28, 1863, made it official. "For a regular company, the two under-cooks will be enlisted; for a volunteer company, they will be mustered into service, as in the cases of other soldiers. In each case a remark will be made on their enlistment papers showing that they are under-cooks of African descent. Their names will be borne on the company muster-rolls, at the foot of the list of privates. They will be paid, and their accounts will be kept like other enlisted men. They will also be discharged in the same manner as other soldiers."

*The man in vest and frock coat is Gilbert Montgomery, under-cook in the 4th U.S. Colored Cavalry.*

*Servant at Camp Cameron with the 7th New York Regiment.*

*All men in uniform were not soldiers. This man lives in a make-shift home near a stable where he is a groom.*

## On Guard Duty

Some thought black soldiers could relieve white soldiers for the fighting by performing their duties of fatigue, guarding railroads, and guarding Confederate prisoners of war.

The men of the 12th, 13th, 40th, 100th, and 106th U.S.C.T. were placed on guard duty at various points of the Nashville and Northwestern Railroad in Tennessee.

Six regiments, the 19th, 27th, 30th, 31st, 39th, and 43rd U.S.C.T., guarded trains through the Wilderness during the campaign of May/June 1864.

Even more men of the sable arm guarded the Weldon Railroad. Nine regiments were assigned this duty. They were the 19th, 23rd, 27th, 28th, 29th, 30th, 31st, 39th, and 43rd Regiments of the U.S. Colored Troops.

The 40th performed guard duty its entire term on the Nashville and Louisville Railroad, the Nashville and Northwestern Railroad, and in the District of East Tennessee.

The 42nd was on guard duty in Chattanooga, Tennessee while the 103rd performed guard duty at Savannah, Georgia and various other points in Georgia and South Carolina during its entire time of duty.

After the 41st U.S.C.T. witnessed for the surrender of General Lee and his army at Appomattox, they were sent to Petersburg for a short period of time. As part of the 25th Army Corps it was sent then to Texas, and eventually arrived in Edenburg where it performed guard and provost duty until November. This regiment was mustered out at Brownsville, Texas, on November 10, 1865, and disbanded in Philadelphia, Pennsylvania, on November 14, 1865.

*Guard Mount in field.*

86

Men of color performed guard duty at Rock Island Prison Barracks, Rock Island, Illinois, near the Mississippi River. The 108th U.S.C.T. arrived there in June/July 1864. While on duty there, fifty men of the 108th died and were buried in the National Cemetery.

The 108th also performed guard duty in various points in the Department of Kentucky. However, they were not alone because this duty was also assigned to the 124th and 125th U.S. Colored Troops. There was also a contingent at Fort Monroe, as well as Elmira Prison.

There are no cases on record where a Confederate prisoner had escaped while being guarded by a U.S. Colored Troop soldier. Interestingly, however, there are several instances on record where a former slave was guarding his former master.

One of the ultimate insults to the captured Confederate soldiers was to be placed under the guard of black soldiers, especially if they were former slaves.

*Private, 67th U.S.C.T.*

*Elmira Prison—200 black soldiers were posted here.*

87

HOTEL DE MONROE

A DISTINGUISHED ARRIVAL.
Negro Soldier. — "Hi, dar! show dis
ole lady a room — one wid a closet
to put dis yar skellemtum in!"

Ent'd according to act of Congress, in the year 1865, by J. CHAPMAN in the Clerk's Office of the District Court, for the Southern District of New York.

*A Northern sarcastic form of expression of the imprisonment of Jefferson Davis in carte de visite format. Fort Monroe, a stone and brick fortress near Newport News, Virginia, was where General Ben Butler coined the phrase "Contraband of War." The fort served as headquarters for the Army of the James.*

*On May 11, 1865, Davis was captured; two days later he was placed in Fort Monroe. He was imprisoned there for two years until his friends had him released on bail. Armed sentries were posted inside and outside his cell twenty-four hours a day with orders not to converse with him.*

## A Soldier's Family

Along with the General Orders that called for the equalization of pay for all colored troops, G.O. No. 31, dated March 5, 1865, called for a bounty of one hundred dollars to be paid to the heir of the colored soldiers who were killed in battle.

Three days after the previously mentioned General Order was issued, the Secretary of War issued G.O. No. 33 to encourage enlistments and to promote the efficiency of the military forces of the United States. "The wife and children of any man mustered into the military or naval service of the U.S., shall, from and after the passage of the act, be forever free, any law, usage, or custom whatsoever to the contrary notwithstanding: and in determining who is or was the wife and who are the children of the soldier. If the parties were married or associated or cohabited as husband and wife up to the time of enlistment shall be deemed sufficient proof of marriage for the purposes of this act: and the children born of any such marriage shall be deemed all that is necessary."

Similar acts and resolutions of Congress were put into general orders, such as G.O. No. 65, dated August 11, 1865, which considered the bounties to the wife, widow, or heirs of any colored soldier, evidence that he and the woman claimed to be his wife or widow were joined in marriage by some ceremony, deemed by them obligatory, followed by their living together as husband and wife up to the time of enlistment, was all that was necessary for the purpose of securing any arrears of pay, pension, or other allowances due to any colored soldier at the time of his death; and the children born of any such marriage shall be recognized as the lawful children and heirs of the soldier.

In G.O. No. 129 on July 25, 1865, the Secretary of War ordered: "To secure equal justice and the same personal liberty to the freedmen as to other citizens and inhabitants, all orders issued by post, district, or other commanders, adopting any system of passes for them or subjecting them to any restraints or punishments not imposed on other classes, are declared void.

"Neither whites nor blacks will be restrained from seeking employment elsewhere when they cannot obtain it at a just compensation at their homes, and when not bound by voluntary agreement; nor will they be hindered from traveling from place to place on proper and legitimate business."

The President ordered in G.O. No. 138 on September 15, 1865, "to provide free transportation on Government transports and U.S. Military Railroads to such teachers of the refugees and freedmen and persons laboring voluntarily in behalf of these people. All stores and school books necessary to the subsistence, comfort, and instruction of dependent freedmen, may be transported at Government expense."

## Music of the Soldier

The music of the slave is very well documented with its disguised meanings. The rhythms often originated in Africa, but this was not true for the black soldiers during the Civil War; they sang the same songs as the white soldiers. Sometimes the words would be the same and other times different, but the music remained the same. Music such as the "Battle Cry of Freedom" and "John Brown's Body" were examples of songs sung by both blacks and whites. (See Appendix VI.)

On Emancipation Day, January 1, 1863, the 1st South Carolina Regiment had a celebration with Sunday services. They had the presentation of its colors, a large barbecue, and a number of speeches. The band of the 8th Maine played, and Colonel Higginson wrote of the event: "An incident so simple, so touching, so utterly unexpected and startling, that I can scarcely believe it on recalling. Though it gave the keynote to the whole day. The very moment the speaker had ceased, and just as I took and waved the flag, which now for the first time meant anything to these poor people. There suddenly arose close behind the platform, a strong male voice (but rather cracked and elderly), into which two women's voices instantly blended, singing, as if by an impulse that could be no more repressed than the morning note of the song of the sparrow."

> 'My country, 'tis of thee,
> sweet land of Liberty,
> of thee I sing!'

Later on the regiment sang "Marching Along" and the "John Brown Song" (Higginson, pp. 30-31).

Some regiments had distinct songs with contemporary music applied. For example:

Song: "Marching Song of the 1st Arkansas"
Words: Captain Lindley Miller
Music: "John Brown's Body"
(Published by the Supervisory Committee for Recruiting Colored Regiments, Philadelphia.)

Song: "The Second Louisiana"
Words: George H. Boker
Music: "The Charge of the Light Brigade"
(Also known as "The Black Regiment.")

Song: "Give Us A Flag"
Words: Unknown member of Company A
Music: "Hoist up the Flag" "Septimus Winner"
(54th Massachusetts Volunteer Infantry)

Song: "They Look Like Men of War"
(9th U.S.C.T. [Thomas, pp. 777-778])

Song: (Doggeral) "Captain Fiddler's Come to Town"
Words: written by a 13 year old drummer boy
Music: "Yankee Doodle"

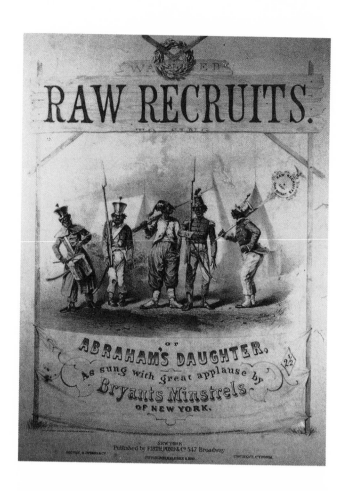

At the beginning of the Civil War, black soldiers were depicted graphically in a comical fashion. After the battles of Port Hudson, Fort Wagner, Chapin's Farm, and the Crater, the fighting capabilities of the black soldier were no longer a question. They fought well and earned the respect of their comrades-in-arms. As the war progressed, they were depicted as respected fighting men of the U.S. Army.

The political cartoonist Thomas Nast depicted this Colored Volunteer in 1863. Men of all wars trained with broomsticks and other forms of make-believe weapons.

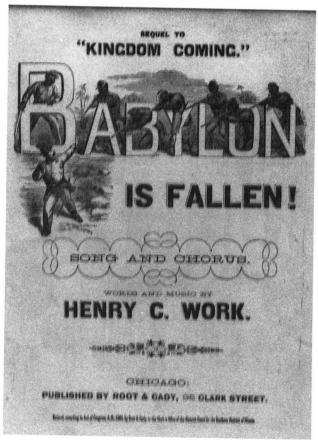

# Darkey Conscript.

AIR.—'Cars on the Track.—By CHARLIE HALL.

When I was a little moke I used to stay at home,
  Now I am a big nig to this war I'll roam ;
Although I am conscript, I feel mighty gay,
  I'll hold an office next election day.

### CHORUS.

Good-bye Susan dear I never shall come back,
  For my knapsack is strapped on my back ;—
Good-bye Susan dear, I never shall see you more
  For this poor nigger is bound for the war.

There's Horace Greely, he wants the niggers free,
  Then he promised to take them all on a spree ;
But when the time comes he says it is no fun,
  For he found out the war just begun.

  Chorus.—Good-bye Susan dear, &c.

Now then I sing to you, I hope you will be true,
  Never forsake the Red White and Blue !
But if this darkie ever comes back,
  He's bound to vote for our "little Mac."

  Chorus.— Good-bye Susan dear, &c.

Now white folks I hope you take no offence,
  This war was for the Union when it first commenced
But now it is played out like an old hack,
  All they think of is the mighty Greenback.

  Chorus.—Good-bye Susan dear

Ten illustrated Songs on Notepaper, mailed to any Address on
receipt of 50 cts. Published by Chas. Magnus, 12 Frankfort St. N.Y

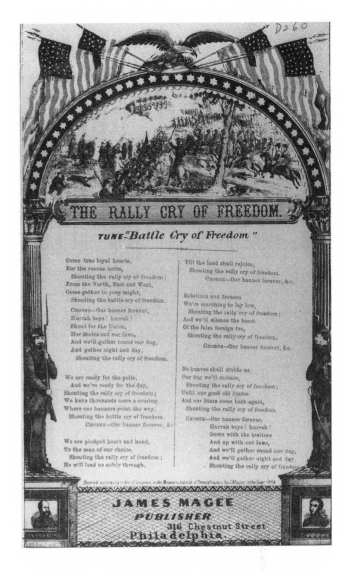

## THE RALLY CRY OF FREEDOM.

TUNE "Battle Cry of Freedom"

Come true loyal hearts,
For the rescue unite,
  Shouting the rally cry of freedom ;
From the North, East and West,
Come gather in your might,
  Shouting the battle cry of freedom.

  CHORUS—Our banner forever,
  Hurrah boys ! hurrah !
  Shout for the Union,
  Her States and our laws,
  And we'll gather round our flag,
  And gather night and day,
  Shouting the rally cry of freedom.

We are ready for the polls,
  And we're ready for the day,
Shouting the rally cry of freedom ;
We have thousands more a coming,
Where our banners point the way,
  Shouting the battle cry of freedom.
  CHORUS—Our banner forever, &c

We are pledged heart and hand,
To the man of our choice,
  Shouting the rally cry of freedom ;
He will lead us safely through,

Till the land shall rejoice,
  Shouting the rally cry of freedom.
    CHORUS—Our banner forever, &c.

Rebellion and treason
We're marching to lay low,
  Shouting the rally cry of freedom ;
And we'll silence the boast
Of the false foreign foe,
  Shouting the rally cry of freedom.
    CHORUS—Our banner forever, &c.

No knaves shall divide us,
Our flag we'll sustain,
  Shouting the rally cry of freedom ;
Until our good old States
And our Stars come back again,
  Shouting the rally cry of freedom.

CHORUS—Our banner forever,
  Hurrah boys ! hurrah !
  Down with the traitors
  And up with our laws,
  And we'll gather round our flag,
  And we'll gather night and day
  Shouting the rally cry of freedom

Entered according to Act of Congress in the Eastern District of Pennsylvania by J. Magee in the year 1864.

**JAMES MAGEE**
*PUBLISHER*
316 Chestnut Street
**Philadelphia.**

A. W. Auner, Stationer and Printer, 45 North Ninth St., Philada. Pa.

# A SOLDIER
## IN THE
# Colored Brigade.

Old Uncle Abraham wants us, and we're coming right along,
I tell you what it is, we're gwine to muster mighty strong;
Then fare you well, my honey dear, now don't you be afraid,
I's bound to be a soldier in de colored brigade.

 A soldier, a soldier, in de darkey brigade,
  I's bound to be a soldier in de colored brigade,
 A soldier, a soldier, in de darkey brigade,
  I's bound to be a soldier in de colored brigade.

O when we meet de enemy I s'pec we make 'em stare,
I tink he'll catch a tartar when he meets de woolly hair;
We'll fight while we are able, and in greenbacks we'll be paid,
And soon I'll be a colonel in de colored brigade.
 *Chor.*—A colonel, a colonel, in de darkey brigade,
  And soon I'll be a colonel in de colored brigade.

Wid musket on my shoulder and wid banjo in my hand,
For Union and de Constitution as it was I stand.
Now some folks tink de darkey for the fighting wasn't made,
We'll show dem what's de matter in de colored brigade.
 *Chor.*—De matter, de matter, in de darkey brigade,
  We'll show dem what's de matter in de colored brigade.

In days ob Gen'ral Washington we fought de British well,
Behind de bales wid "Hickory" I think we made 'em yell;
I tell you we're de chickens dat can handle gun or spade,
And Greeley he'll go wid us in de colored brigade.
 *Chor.*—Go wid us, go wid us, in de darkey brigade.
  And Greeley he'll go wid us in de colored brigade.

Some say dey lub de darkey and dey want him to be free,
I s'pec dey only fooling and dey better let him be;
For him dey'd break dis Union which de're forefadders had made,
Worth more dan twenty millions ob de colored brigade.
 *Chor.*—Dan millions, dan millions, ob de darkey brigade,
  Worth more dan twenty millions ob de colored brigade.

Den cheer up now, my honey dear, I hear de trumpets play,
And gib me just a little buss before I go away;
I'll marry you when I come back, so don't you be afraid,
We'll raise up picanninnies for de colored brigade.
 *Chor.*—Ninnies, ninnies for de darkey brigade,
  We'll raise up picanninnies for de colored brigade.

A. W. Auner, Song Publisher, 45 North Ninth Street, Philada. Pa.

# THE COLORED SOLDIER BOY!

By Samuel Nickless,
Late Corperal Company I, 24th Regiment U. S C. T.

My poor old mother and I did part, when I was very young,
Her memory still clings round my heart, like mystic morning hung;
They tell me of my mother's form, she watched me while I slept,
And with her dark and gentle hand, she wiped the tears I wept.

CHORUS.

But now my mother has gone to rest, she dreams her purest joy,
I wonder if she thinks of me, the Colored Soldier Boy.

And that same hand that held my own, when I began to walk,
The joys that sparkled in her eyes, when I began to talk;
I remember well when I was ill, she kissed my burning brow,
The tears that fell upon my cheeks, I think I feel them now.

CHORUS.—But now my mother, &c.

And then she used to kneel with me, how gloomy was that day,
She put her hands up to her breast, and taught me how to pray;
Oh, mother! mother! in this breast, thy image still shall be,
And I will strive unto the last, to always think of thee.

CHORUS.—But now my mother, &c.

## JOHNSON'S
## CARD & JOB PRINTING OFFICE,
### No. 7 North Tenth St., Phila.

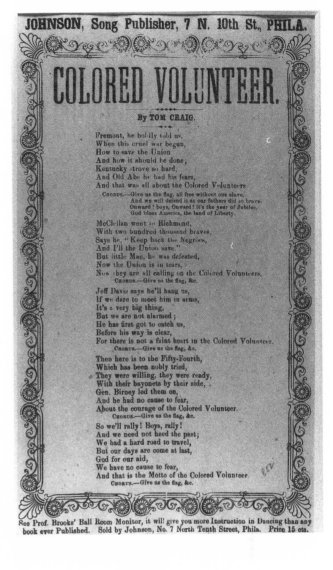

JOHNSON, Song Publisher, 7 N. 10th St., PHILA.

# COLORED VOLUNTEER.

### By TOM CRAIG.

Fremont, he boldly told us,
When this cruel war begun,
How to save the Union
And how it should be done;
Kentucky strove so hard,
And Old Abe he had his fears,
And that was all about the Colored Volunteers.
 CHORUS.—Give us the flag, all free without one slave,
  And we will defend it as our fathers did so brave.
  Onward! boys, Onward! it's the year of Jubilee.
  God bless America, the land of Liberty.

McClellan went to Richmond,
With two hundred thousand braves,
Says he, "Keep back the Negroes,
And I'll the Union save."
But little Mac, he was defeated,
Now the Union is in tears,
Now they are all calling on the Colored Volunteers.
  CHORUS.—Give us the flag, &c.

Jeff Davis says he'll hang us,
If we dare to meet him in arms,
It's a very big thing,
But we are not alarmed;
He has first got to catch us,
Before his way is clear,
For there is not a faint heart in the Colored Volunteer.
  CHORUS.—Give us the flag, &c.

Then here is to the Fifty-Fourth,
Which has been nobly tried,
They were willing, they were ready,
With their bayonets by their side,
Gen. Birney led them on,
And he had no cause to fear,
About the courage of the Colored Volunteer.
  CHORUS.—Give us the flag, &c.

So we'll rally! Boys, rally!
And we need not heed the past;
We had a hard road to travel,
But our days are come at last,
God for our aid,
We have no cause to fear,
And that is the Motto of the Colored Volunteer
  CHORUS.—Give us the flag, &c.

See Prof. Brooks' Ball Room Monitor, it will give you more Instruction in Dancing than any book ever Published. Sold by Johnson, No. 7 North Tenth Street, Phila. Price 15 cts.

The soldiers would gather around the camp fires sometimes talking and other times singing about the girls they left behind, of their loneliness of being away from home, their buddies that have died, and of the humor of being in the army. The white soldier looked back to that which was precious to him, but the black soldier had different motivation for his singing. He sang about what was ahead of him because most of these soldiers had nothing to reflect back upon. They longed for what was ahead.

Many times songs were improvised spontaneously. At Petersburg, before the Battle of the Crater, the black soldiers developed a song until they perfected it. Over and over again they would sing it, making slight changes, until they felt it was right. When the refrain struck the response of the men, at times there were as many as 500 voices upraised in song. The men sang this song until they fought in the Battle of the Crater. General Armstrong called this "The Negro Battle Hymn." They took the song into battle with them, and the chorus went as follows:

"We looks like men a-marchin' on, We looks like men er war."

After their defeat at the Crater, the song was never sung again.

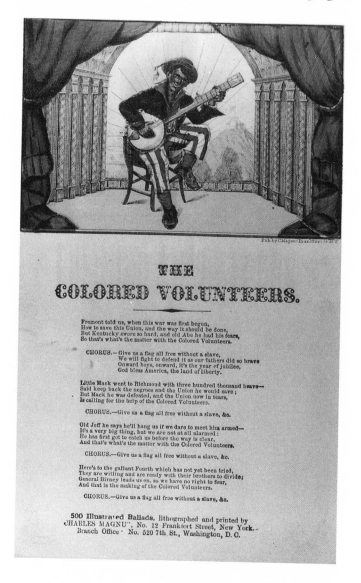

96

# The Issues

## Pay Policy

The Militia Act of July 17, 1862, established the pay policy for men of African descent employed by the government. The War Department covered this pay policy in G.O. No. 91, July 29, 1862, and the following year in G.O. No. 163, July 4, 1863, which updated the policy. The Enrollment Act of March 1863 was interpreted to have men of African descent drafted and this act did not specify lesser pay for the black soldiers.

The protest for equal pay for black soldiers spread more and more as they entered the military. This pay discrepancy gave black soldiers $10.00 per month, of which $3.00 may be in clothing, and was substantially less than the pay of white soldiers. White soldiers (privates) received $13.00 per month with a clothing allowance of $3.50. The black soldiers' pay applied to all ranks, from private to sergeant major, surgeon, chaplain, or officers of other ranks. In the case of white soldiers, the pay varied with rank.

The pay issue was the most important issue and the chief complaint of the black men in the military. This became the symbol of the larger struggle for racial justice, and in rare instances, the protests caused near mutiny, court-martials, and executions of some black soldiers.

*Paying off Negro soldiers at Hilton Head, S.C. (*Frank Leslie's Illustrated Newspaper, *Aug. 20, 1864.)*

It was the efforts of the abolitionists, regimental commanders, officers, generals, and even the Secretary of War, that led to the eventual change in the previously mentioned General Orders. This change began with the War Department's G.O. No. 215, June 22, 1864, which gave equal pay to all soldiers in the same branch of the military, regardless of their race. This order was also retroactive to January 1, 1864. There were conditions that applied to the equalization of pay, for example, only those soldiers who were "free on or before April 19, 1861," were entitled to the same pay as their white counterparts. This excluded all the slave regiments and former slaves in the other regiments. The War Department issued Circular No. 60 on August 1, 1864, to detail the procedure for those soldiers who were "free on or before April 1, 1864."

The General Order which gave equal pay to all persons of color in the military, regardless to their status of freedom was issued by the War Department on March 8, 1865. G.O. No. 31, Section 5, stated that "Any regiment of colored troops mustered in the service...the noncommissioned officers and privates should be paid the same as other troops of the same arm of the service...shall from the date of their enlistment receive the same pay and allowances to other volunteers." This order brought parity to the black soldiers.

To make things more clear, and to avoid further misunderstanding, the War Department issued another general order on August 11, 1866. G.O. No. 62, Part II, stated that the words "free on or before April 1, 1861," shall not deprive any colored soldier of the bounty to which he is entitled.

Section 2 of the Order stated that the "wife, widow or heirs of any colored soldier who were living together at the time of enlistment is sufficient proof of marriage for the purpose of securing any of the entitled benefits."

It took approximately two years for this issue to be resolved.


## Quaker Oath

The law specifically directing the enrollment of colored men was not passed until February 24, 1864. The fourth section stated "that all persons of color who were free on the nineteenth day of April, eighteen hundred and sixty-one, and who have been enlisted and mustered into the military service of the United States, shall, from the time of their enlistment, be entitled to receive the same bounty and clothing allowed to such persons by the laws existing at the time of their enlistments." This referred to the "free colored man," and not the former slave (O.R. S III, Vol. IV, p. 658).

The Secretary of War was ordered to make the necessary regulations. War Department Circular No. 60, August 1, 1864, stipulated the method of obtaining this information. All officers commanding regiments, batteries, and independent companies of colored troops were immediately to make a thorough investigation of the men who belonged to the command and were enlisted prior to January 1, 1864, with a view to ascertain who were free men on or before April 19, 1861. The fact of freedom was to be determined in each case by the statement of the soldier, under oath, taken in connection with the most reliable information that could be obtained from other sources. They were to enter the following remark next to the names of the soldiers on the muster rolls: "Free on or before April 19, 1861," and such soldier was mustered for pay accordingly. The Pay Department was ordered to pay the soldiers from the time of their entry into the service to the first day of January 1864, and pay the difference between the pay received by them as soldiers under their present enlistments and the full pay allowed by law for their white counterparts (O.R. S III, Vol. VIV, pp. 564-565).

To circumvent the above restrictions and give every one of his men full pay, Colonel N. Hallowell of the 54th Massachusetts Infantry had them take what became known as the "Quaker Oath." It stated: "You do solemnly swear that you owed no man unrequited labor on or before the 19th day of April, 1861. So help you God." Although some of the men were slaves on the fateful date, they took the oath as freedmen, for they felt that by God's higher law, they were free men, regardless of their country's law.

*Col. N. Hallowell, 54th Mass. Inf.*

The phrase "free on or before April 19, 1861" was placed on the muster rolls of these soldiers, as well as the final pay vouchers (Emilio, pp. 220-221).

The War Department issued G.O. No. 62 on August 11, 1866 which allowed the soldier to recover from any discrepancies from the past. Both the Senate and the House of Representatives resolved that the omission in the muster rolls of the designated date of freedom would not deprive any colored soldier of the bounty to which he was entitled. The presumption would stand that he was free at the time of his enlistment.

## Education

Many of the duties of the noncommissioned officers were administrative. Since there were not enough black noncommissioned officers with these capabilities, the military found it necessary to have schools that would prepare these men for their duties. The beginning of the Armed Forces Network began with the educating of the black soldier.

Chaplains, officers and their wives, as well as other educated noncommissioned officers would teach the men how to read and write. Some regiments took pride in the fact that every man contributed money for their education. "Readers" could be found in many soldiers' knapsacks, and classrooms were built on a number of posts.

Commanding generals (Banks, Grant, Weitzel, and Butler) all felt that education of the former slaves was a way to further remove the shackles of bondage. General Banks authorized an additional staff officer, with the rank and pay of captain, to be designated the "Corps Instructor" whose duty was to superintend, in garrison and as far as was consistent with military duty in the field, the education of men enrolled in the Corps d'Afrique.

*Chaplain J.M. Mickly, 43rd U.S.C.T.*

Banks then directed the commanding officer of each regiment to detail one additional staff officer, with the rank and pay of Lieutenant, to be designated the "Regimental Instructor" to teach the men of the regiment the rudiments of learning. Requisition of books and supplies were to be forwarded to the Departmental headquarters for approval (G.O. No. 72, headquarters, Department of the Gulf, New Orleans, September 28, 1863).

Chaplain Jeremiah M. Mickly, 43d U.S.C.T., wrote the regimental history and said that the "freedmen," rather than the "free men" of his regiment took to their education with greater enthusiasm, since this had been denied to them in the past.

Chaplain J.R. Reasoner of the 119th U.S.C.T. spent an average of two hours each day teaching men to read and write. The school books (McGuffey readers) were furnished by the Freedman's Aid Commission and sold at cost to the soldiers. It was thought that it was better to spend a part of their money judiciously in buying books, than to give the books to them (Berlin, p. 630).

Chaplain Reasoner also felt that "nearly all the Freedmen were eager to learn to read and write. Many of the 119th have learned to read, without any instructions."

A number of philanthropic agencies in the North sent "Yankee schoolmarms" to the South to educate the newly freed slaves. The teachers from the North were both white and black. Working adults would attend classes in the evening and whenever they had available time. They filled the classroom day and night. On "log seats or a dirt floor," many freedmen studied their "letters" in old almanacs, the Bible, or even newspapers. The African Methodist Episcopal Church, along with the Quakers, were leaders in this field.

## Substitutes

The Enrollment Act of March 1863 allowed for a man to be a substitute for a drafted man, provided that he met all the necessary requirements.

The requirements of substitute soliders were the same for both black and white soliders. The men had to be physically fit and pose no threat of desertion. However, problems did arise for both races of soliders when a black man was substituted for a white.

The Provost Marshal General's Office of the War Department issued Circular No. 54 on July 20, 1863, to clarify this matter. The document stated that "Existing laws make a distinction in the matter of pay, bounty, and other allowances between soldiers of African descent and other soldiers in the service of the United States. Men of African descent can, therefore, only be accepted as Substitutes for each other under the Enrollment Act." It was signed "James Fry, Provost Martial General" (O.R. S III, Vol. III, p. 458).

*Unidentified citizen of the South.*

## Fatigue Duty

Many military officers felt that black soldiers should be organized simply as labor battalions. U.S.C.T. regiments were assigned a disproportionate amount of labor on fortifications and labor and fatigue duties of permanent stations and camps. The fatigue duties took up so much of their time that these soldiers were not able to learn their drill or become efficient with their weapons.

The Secretary of War ordered this practice to cease. Black soldiers were only required to take their fair share of fatigue duty with the white troops. Secretary Stanton further stated that "This is necessary to prepare the black soldiers for the higher conflict with the enemy. When a commander of colored troops is required to perform an excess of labor above white troops in the same command, he is to report this to their common superior." Adjutant General L. Thomas issued this in General Order No. 21, Louisville, Kentucky, on June 14, 1864 (O.R. S III, Vol. IV, p. 431). This did not mean that the practice stopped at all locations. Many times, black soldiers were assigned to this duty and the officers complained to the command, and the problem was eventually corrected.

*Sgt. George Dean, Co. K, 67th U.S.C.T.*

## Recruiting

Recruitment of soldiers into the Regular Army in April 1861 was governed by Regulations for the Army of the United States, 1857. According to paragraph 1299, an enlistee had to be a "free white male person above the age of eighteen and under thirty-five years..." Initial calls to expand the Regular Army with the militia commenced in April 1861 under legal authority of the Militia Act of 28 February 1795, and the District of Columbia Militia Act of 3 March 1803.

A third pertinent law, not invoked in April 1861, was the Act of May 8, 1792, which established a uniform militia of the U.S. It called for enrollment of "each and every free able-bodied white male citizen of the respective states..." (USAMHI, Ethnics, Black, Early, pp. 1-2).

The phrase "able-bodied male citizen" was the crux of the interpretation. Was the free born black a citizen? Slaves freed before the war may have been accorded all the rights of federal citizenship and also of citizenship of their individual states, but citizenship for slaves freed by the war was not federally recognized until 1868. The President authorized the arming of freed slaves (Second Confiscation Act, July 17, 1862) and the War Department issued G.O. No. 1, in January 1863, which allowed freed slaves to be part of the military, and gave significance to the Enrollment Act of March 1863 which authorized the drafting of black men.

**CUTTING HIS OLD ASSOCIATES.**

MAN OF COLOR. "Ugh! Get out. I ain't one ob you no more. *I'se a Man, I is!*"

(Harper's Weekly, *Jan. 17, 1863.*)

*Negro recruits taking the cars for Murfreesboro.* (Frank Leslie's Illustrated Newspaper, *May 7, 1864.*)

*Negro recruits at Charleston.* (Harper's Weekly, *April 1, 1865.*)

The Conscription Law, also known as the Enrollment Act of March 3, 1863, authorized the conscription of "able-bodied male citizens between the ages of 20 to 45..." This implied for the the black man to be drafted into the military service of the United States as well. The Government acted accordingly and black men were drafted. This was the first time that black or white men were drafted into the military. Although the black man was drafted in the same manner as the white man, he did not receive the same pay or bounty.

The language of the War Department Order was changed in February 1864 when Congress revised the Enrollment Act. This was clarified in G.O. No. 75, February 25, 1864. Section 24 specifically referred to "all able-bodied male colored persons between ages 20-45 years, resident of the United States, shall be enrolled according to provisions of this Act." It is interesting to note that "able-bodied colored persons" was written and not "men of African descent."

The general order also referred to drafting slaves of loyal masters, making the slave free and giving the bounty of $100.00 to the master. A slave master in each of the slave states represented in Congress was to receive up to $300.00 compensation for each black volunteer. The volunteer was then made free.

This general order no longer allowed men to be drafted, enlisted, or volunteer into state units. They were mustered into regiments or companies as United States Colored Troops.

This practice of involuntary conscription caused Major General W.T. Sherman to issued Special Field Orders No. 16 from his headquarters of the Military Division in Mississippi on June 14, 1864. He ordered the following: "1. Recruiting officers will not enlist as soldiers any negroes who are profitably employed by any of the army departments, and any staff officer having a negro employed in useful labor on account of the Government will refuse to release him from his employment by virtue of a supposed enlistment as a soldier. 2. Commanding officers of the military posts will arrest, and, if need be, imprison any recruiting officer who, to make up companies of negro soldiers, interferes with the necessary gangs of hired negroes in the employment of the quartermaster's or commissary or other department of the Government without full consent of the officers having them in charge" (O.R. S III, Vol. V, p. 434).

Not all states were given credit for furnishing black soldiers. Some black recruits were furnished under the direct authority of the Federal government. A total of 99,337 of the men were mustered in under federal authority, while 79,638 were mustered in by state authority. This provided the grand total of 178,975 men in federal service.

It is interesting to note that Attorney General Edward Bates observed in 1864 that Congress had never "prohibited the enlistment of free colored men into either branch of the national military service." The insertion of the restrictive adjective "white" into the pre-Civil War Army Regulations (1821-1857) was a striking instance of legislation by an executive department, according to Colonel William Winthrop, military law expert.

To determine whether or not individual states permitted the enlistment of blacks in April 1861, one must examine state, not federal, militia law (USAMHI, Ethinics, Black, Early, p. 2).

In Philadelphia, the Supervisory Committee for Recruiting Colored Regiments was given permission by Secretary of War, Edwin M. Stanton to raise three regiments of colored troops at Camp William Penn in Cheltanham Township. These became the 3rd, 6th, and 8th U.S. Colored Troops. This Supervisory Committee was founded by the Union League of Philadelphia.

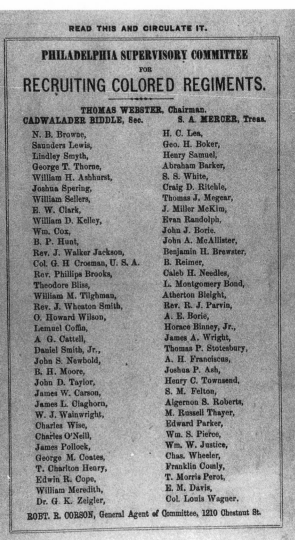

READ THIS AND CIRCULATE IT.

**PHILADELPHIA SUPERVISORY COMMITTEE**
FOR
**RECRUITING COLORED REGIMENTS.**

THOMAS WEBSTER, Chairman.
CADWALADER BIDDLE, Sec.      S. A. MERCER, Treas.

| | |
|---|---|
| N. B. Browne, | H. C. Lea, |
| Saunders Lewis, | Geo. H. Boker, |
| Lindley Smyth, | Henry Samuel, |
| George T. Thorne, | Abraham Barker, |
| William H. Ashhurst, | S. S. White, |
| Joshua Spering, | Craig D. Ritchie, |
| William Sellers, | Thomas J. Megear, |
| E. W. Clark, | J. Miller McKim, |
| William D. Kelley, | Evan Randolph, |
| Wm. Cox, | John J. Borie. |
| B. P. Hunt, | John A. McAllister, |
| Rev. J. Walker Jackson, | Benjamin H. Brewster, |
| Col. G. H Croeman, U. S. A. | B. Reimer, |
| Rev. Phillips Brooks, | Caleb H. Needles, |
| Theodore Bliss, | L. Montgomery Bond, |
| William M. Tilghman, | Atherton Bleight, |
| Rev. J. Wheaton Smith, | Rev. R. J. Parvin, |
| O. Howard Wilson, | A. E. Borie, |
| Lemuel Coffin, | Horace Binney, Jr., |
| A G. Cattell, | James A. Wright, |
| Daniel Smith, Jr., | Thomas P. Stotesbury, |
| John S. Newbold, | A. H. Franciscus, |
| B. H. Moore, | Joshua P. Ash, |
| John D. Taylor, | Henry C. Townsend, |
| James W. Carson, | S. M. Felton, |
| James L. Claghorn, | Algernon S. Roberts, |
| W. J. Wainwright, | M. Russell Thayer, |
| Charles Wise, | Edward Parker, |
| Charles O'Neill, | Wm. S. Pierce, |
| James Pollock, | Wm. W. Justice, |
| George M. Coates, | Chas. Wheeler, |
| T. Charlton Henry, | Franklin Comly, |
| Edwin R. Cope, | T. Morris Perot, |
| William Meredith, | E. M. Davis, |
| Dr. G. K. Zeigler, | Col. Louis Wagner. |

ROBT. R. CORSON, General Agent of Committee, 1210 Chestnut St.

Price Five Cents.

THE

UNITED STATES

CONSCRIPTION

LAW

OF

1863.

OFFICIAL AND COMPLETE

NEW YORK:
JAMES W. FORTUNE, PUBLISHER,
No. 102 Centre Street.

*The greatest single force in the progress of the colored soldier was the adoption of national conscription in March 1863. This act had no racial restrictions.*

*Teaching the Negro recruits the use of the Minie rifle.*

*...So much ignorant prejudice is still entertained in many parts of the North to the employment of colored troops that it is due to the country that the capacity of the negro to drill and fight can not be too strongly insisted upon.*

*...The drill masters in the Department of the South report that the negroes in the South Carolina regiments evince great aptitude at learning the manual of arms. They are more docile than white recruits, and when once they have mastered a movement they retain the knowledge perfectly. Similar testimony is borne by officers in the West. One of them predicts that with proper drill and training the negroes will be the steadiest rank and file in the world.*

*(Harper's Weekly, March 14, 1863.)*

## June 1863 Confederate Invasion of Pennsylvania

Confederate General Robert E. Lee invaded the state of Pennsylvania in June 1863. President Lincoln issued a proclamation on June 15, 1863 calling for 100,000 men, 50,000 of which would be from Pennsylvania, for six months of service unless released sooner (O.R. S I, Vol. XXVII, pp. 136-137). Governor Curtin then issued a proclamation of a state emergency which called for all able-bodied men, making no distinction of color, to be uniformed and armed, and to report to General Couch in Harrisburg.

A committee of 46 leading black citizens, businessmen, scholars, and clergy was formed to aid in the recruiting of "Men of Color." The emergency call was for "every man who can shoulder a musket or handle a pick to share with others the burden and duties of entrenching an defending the city."

The broadside illustrated was made for the attention of the black population of Philadelphia.

The Bethel Church was one of the leading gathering places for responsible black citizens in Philadelphia. On July 17, 1863, a meeting was held with regard to "Men of Color" to enlist for the state defense. A committee had been formed, and they proposed that the black men tender to the government their services for six months or the length of the emergency. There was no definite understanding as to the terms on which black men would be received into the state service.

At this meeting, the committee also pledged to the displaced slave the protection of their homes and firesides, a part of their personal property and a share of their daily bread, even to a portion of the last crumb.

Frederick Douglass urged immediate action. He stated that "Those present could enroll their names: if their services were not accepted, the responsibility would rest with the authorities."

Black men from many cities and towns of the state answered this call. A company of 90 black men, raised by Captain Babe, of the City Police Department, appeared at the City Arsenal in Philadelphia. They received uniforms and guns without any hesitation. They were sent to Harrisburg and arrived there within 12 hours. General Couch refused to accept these men due to the fact that since they were black, their term of service was for three years and not the state of emergency of six months or sooner (O.R. S I, Vol. XXVII, Part III, p. 203). When Secretary of War Stanton heard of Couch's rejection, he telegraphed Couch "to receive into service any volunteer troops without regard to color." General Couch still refused to accept the black volunteers.

Although the black men that arrived in Harrisburg were refused participation in the state emergency, they did engage the enemy in the Battle of Columbia Bridge. (See "The Battle of Columbia Bridge.")

# MEN OF COLOR
## OF PHILADELPHIA!

The Country Demands your Services. The Enemy is Approaching. You know his object. It is to Subjugate the North and Enslave us. Already many of our Class in this State have been Captured and Carried South to Slavery, Stripes and Mutilation. For our own sake and for the sake of our Common Country we are called upon now to

# COME FORWARD!

Let us seize this great opportunity of vindicating our manhood and patriotism through all time. The General Commanding at this post is arranging for the

# DEFENCE OF THE CITY!

He will need the aid of every Man who can shoulder a musket or handle a pick. We have assured him of the readiness of our people to do their whole duty in the emergency. We need not ask you to justify us in having made this assurance. The undersigned have been designated a Committee to have this matter in charge. Members of this Committee will sit every day at

## BETHEL CHURCH, cor. of 6th & Lombard Streets
### AND AT
## UNION CHURCH, Coates Street below York Avenue

Their business will be to receive the Names of all Able Bodied Men of Color who are willing to share with others the burdens and duties of Entrenching and Defending the City. Men of Color! you who are able and willing to fight or labor in the work now to be done, call immediately and report yourselves at one or the other of the above named places.

| | | | | |
|---|---|---|---|---|
| E. D. Bassett, | Wm. D. Forten, | Fred. Douglass, | John P. Burr, | Jas. R. Gordon. |
| Wm. Whipper, | Rev. S. Smith, | Rev. J. Asher, | Robt. Jones, | Samuel Stewart, |
| D. D. Turner, | N. W. Depee, | Rev. J. C. Gibbs, | O. V. Catto, | David B. Bowser, |
| Jas. McCrummell, | Dr J. H. Wilson, | Daniel George, | Thos. J. Dorsey, | Henry Minton, |
| A. S. Cassey, | J. W. Cassey, | Robert M. Adger, | I. D. Cliff, | Daniel Colley, |
| A. M. Green, | P. J. Armstrong, | Henry M. Cropper, | Jacob C. White, | J. C. White, Jr., |
| J. W. Page, | J. W. Simpson, | Rev. J. B. Reeve, | Morris Hall, | Rev. J. P. Campbell, |
| L. R. Seymour, | Rev. J. B. Trusty, | Rev. J. A. Williams, | James Needham, | Rev. W. J. Alston |
| Rev. J. Underdue. | | Rev. A. L. Stanford, | | J. P. Johnson, |
| John W. Price | | Thomas J. Bowers, | | Franklin Turner. |

*The Confederate Invasion in the State of Pennsylvania in June 1863 called for all able-bodied men to help defend the state. This was the first of a number of Men of Color Broadsides.*

# MEN OF COLOR

## To Arms!  To Arms!

# NOW OR NEVER

This is our golden moment!  The Government of the United States calls for every Able-bodied Colored Man to enter the Army for the

## THREE YEARS' SERVICE!

### AND JOIN IN FIGHTING THE

## BATTLES OF LIBERTY AND THE UNION

A new era is open to us.  For generations we have suffered under the horrors of slavery, outrage and wrong; our manhood has been denied, our citizenship blotted out, our souls seared and burned, our spirits cowed and crushed, and the hopes of the future of our race involved in doubt and darkness.    But now our relations to the white race are changed.  Now, therefore, is our most precious moment.  Let us rush to arms!

## FAIL NOW, & OUR RACE IS DOOMED

On this the soil of our birth.  We must now awake, arise, or be forever fallen.  If we value liberty, if we wish to be free in this land, if we love our country, if we love our families, our children, our home, we must strike now while the country calls; we must rise up in the dignity of our manhood, and show by our own right arms that we are worthy to be freemen.  Our enemies have made the country believe that we are craven cowards, without soul, without manhood, without the spirit of soldiers.  Shall we die with this stigma resting upon our graves?  Shall we leave this inheritance of Shame to our Children!  No! a thousand times NO!  We WILL Rise!  The alternative is upon us.  Let us rather die freemen than live to be slaves.  What is life without liberty!  We say that we have manhood: now is the time to prove it.  A union or a people that cannot fight may be pitied, but cannot be respected.  If we would be regarded men, if we would forever

## SILENCE THE TONGUE OF CALUMNY

Of Prejudice and Hate, let us Rise Now and Fly to Arms!  We have seen what

## VALOR AND HEROISM

### OUR BROTHERS DISPLAYED AT

## PORT HUDSON AND MILLIKEN'S BEND.

Though they are just from the galling, poisoning grasp of Slavery, they have startled the World by the most exalted heroism.  If they have proved themselves heroes, cannot WE PROVE OURSELVES MEN!

## ARE FREEMEN LESS BRAVE THAN SLAVES

More than a Million White Men have left Comfortable Homes and joined the Armies of the Union to save their Country.  Cannot we leave ours, and swell the Hosts of the Union, to save our liberties, vindicate our manhood, and deserve well of our Country.  MEN OF COLOR! the Englishman, the Irishman, the Frenchman, the German, the American, have been called to assert their claim to freedom and a manly character, by an appeal to the sword.  The day that has seen an enslaved race in arms has, in all history, seen their last trial.  We now are that

## OUR LAST OPPORTUNITY HAS COME

If we are not lower in the scale of humanity than Englishmen, Irishmen, White Americans, and other Races, we can show it now.

## MEN OF COLOR, BROTHERS AND FATHERS!

# WE APPEAL TO YOU!

By all your concern for yourselves and your liberties, by all your regard for God and humanity, by all your desire for Citizenship and Equality before the law, by all your love for the Country, to stop at no subterfuge, listen to nothing that shall deter you from rallying for the Army.  Come Forward, and at once Enroll your Names for the Three Years' Service.

## STRIKE NOW!

### And you are henceforth and forever FREEMEN!

E. D. Bassett,
Wm. Whipper,
D. D. Turner,
Jas. McCrummell,
A. S. Cassey,
A. M. Green,
J. W. Page,
L. R. Seymour,

Rev. J. Underdue,
John W. Price,
Augustus Dorsey,
William D. Forten,
Rev. Stephen Smith,
N. W. Depee,
Dr. J. B. Wilson,
J. W. Cassey,

Frederick Douglass,
P. J. Armstrong,
J. W. Simpson,
Rev. J. B. Trusty,
S. Morgan Smith,
William E. Gipson,
Rev. J. Boulden,
Rev. J. Asher,

Rev. J. C. Gibbs,
Daniel George,
Robert M. Adger,
Henry M. Cropper,
Rev. J. B. Reeve,
Rev. J. A. Williams,
Rev. A. L. Stanford,
Thomas J. Bowers,

Elijah J. Davis,
John P. Burr,
Robert Jones,
O. V. Catto,
Thos. J. Dorsey,
I. D. Cliff,
Jacob C. White,
Morris Hall,

James Needham,
Rev. Elisha Weaver,
Ebenezer Black,
Rev. William T. Catto,
James R. Gordon,
Samuel Stewart,
David B. Bowser,
Henry Minton,

Daniel Colley,
J. C. White, Jr,
Rev. J. P. Campbell,
Rev. W. J. Alston,
J. P. Johnson,
Franklin Turner,
Jesse E. Glasgow.

U. S. Steam-Power Book and Job Printing Establishment, Ledger Buildings, Third and Chestnut Streets, Philadelphia.

This is a copy from the 6 ft. High original published in 1863

## Recruiting, Camp William Penn

This broadside is perhaps one of the best known that depicts the recruiting of the black soldier during the Civil War. This was for the black men to enlist in the 3rd Regiment of Infantry, U.S.C.T., Camp William Penn, Chelton Hills, near Philadelphia. Permission was given to Mr. Thomas Webster, Chairman of the Supervisory Committee for recruiting colored troops. The committee was part of the Union League of Philadelphia. On the bottom of this 8 foot broadside is a listing of the leading black citizens of Philadelphia. Among the names is that of Reverand J. Asher. He became the chaplain of the second regiment to be formed at this camp, the 6th Regiment U.S.C.T. Asher was one of 14 black chaplains, and the only one that died during his service.

Most of us only see the words in bold, but the small print is equally important. It was here that Frederick Douglass and the other leading citizens implored the black men to participate in the war.

After permission was received on June 22, 1863, to raise three regiments of infantry composed of colored men in Philadelphia or the eastern portion of Pennsylvania, a group of men immediately took interest in the action. A mass meeting was called at National Hall on July 6, 1863. A committee was formed with Reverand Stephen Smith as president. Twenty-seven men were made vice-presidents, and Eben D. Bassett, Jacob C. White, Jr., and Octavius V. Catto were the secretaries of the group. The three regiments raised became the 3d, 6th, and 8th U.S. Colored Infantry.

## Independent Company A

It had been approximately one year since the Pennsylvania state emergency was called due to the Confederate Invasion which led to the Battle at Gettysburg. At this point, another state emergency was called due to the raid of two of Jubal Early's Cavalry Brigades.

Nearly 2,000 horsemen, commanded by Brigadier General John McCausland had orders from Early to demand $100,000 in gold or $500,000 in greenbacks from the citizens of Chambersburg. This was to be compensation for the three Virginia houses that were burned by Major General David Hunter's men. If payment was not to be made, the town was to be burned. The citizens did not pay, and on July 31, 1864, the town of Chambersburg was burned.

# RALLY! RALLY! RALLY!

## TO MEN OF COLOR!

### AUTHORITY HAS BEEN RECEIVED TO RAISE

# A REGIMENT

of

# MEN OF COLOR

# FOR 100 DAYS

## Rally, Men of Color, at Once for Your Country

Arm for the Defence of your Homes! Enroll yourselves for the Emergency. A Regiment ought to be Raised within TWO DAYS. Chester and Delaware Counties will send Three Companies—Bucks and Montgomery will do as well. What will Philadelphia do?

# COL. TAGGART

Late Colonel 12th Regiment Pennsylvania Reserves, will command, and the Officers will be the Graduates of the Military Board at Washington.

# $50 CITY BOUNTY

Will be Paid each Man. Come, then, to Head-quarters,

# No. 1210 CHESTNUT STREET

AND ENROLL YOUR NAMES.

U. S. Steam-Power Book and Job Printing Establishment, Ledger Buildings, Third and Chestnut Streets, Philadelphia.

The President called for 12,000 militia or volunteer infantry to serve at Washington and its vicinity for 100 days, unless sooner discharged. They were to be organized according to the general regulations of the service to be armed, clothed, paid, transported, subsisted, and supplied as other troops in the United States Service (O.R. S I, Vol. XXXVII, Part II, pp. 74-76). Governor Curtain issued his state emergency call to the citizens of Philadelphia on July 10, 1864.

Once again, men of Pennsylvania stepped forward to protect their homes. This call was also for all able-bodied men and did not make any distinction of color. By June of 1864, black men from Pennsylvania were already filling the ranks of the Camp William Penn Regiments. Black soldiers had marched through the streets of Philadelphia. They had also helped fill the ranks of the 54th and 55th Massachusetts Regiments. Their participation as a vital military force was well established.

This new state emergency call did not refuse the black volunteer as it did the previous year. The same "Men of Color" was the rallying cry. These volunteers were to report to the same address as the Free Military School and the recruiting office of the William Penn soldiers. Colonel Taggart, in charge of the Free Military School, was to command. The officers were to be the graduates of the Military Board of Washington.

These volunteers were to receive a $50.00 bounty from the city of Philadelphia, and they would also receive the same pay as the white soldiers. It was thought that only two days would be necessary to answer the governor's call, and Chester, Bucks, and Montgomery counties sent six companies.

Although a regiment was authorized to be formed under the command of Captain Converse Southard, only a company took the field.

This company was organized at Camp William Penn on July 20, 1864. This was in accordance to G.O. No. 143 which stated that "Colored Troops may be accepted as companies to be afterward consolidated into battalions and regiments by the Adjutant General." But authorities were also willing to accept company-sized units due to the urgency of the situation. Company A was composed of a captain, first lieutenant, second lieutenant, first sergeant, 7 sergeants, 10 corporals, 2 musicians, and 60 privates. They remained at Camp William Penn for 100 days.

After the emergency passed, Captain Southard was discharged and received an appointment as captain in the 119th U.S.C.T. Second Lieutenant George W. Keyes, of Independent Company A, was transferred to the 41st Regiment U.S.C.T which was being formed at Camp William Penn; he became the adjutant of the regiment. Forty-three enlisted men of Company A enlisted in the 41st U.S.C.T.

## Drafted Slaves

By May of 1864, a question arose concerning whether slaves could be drafted under the terms of the Enrollment Act. The Government expressed its rulings on drafted slaves via William Whiting, Solicitor of the War Department. The February 1864 enrollment was for "all able-bodied men between the ages of 20-45."

A slave of a loyal master in any of the loyal states, having been drafted in the U.S. armed forces, was to be made free prior to entering the service, and his master received $100.00 in bounty. When the slave volunteered, as opposed to being drafted, he was entitled to his freedom and his master was compensated up to $300.00 (O.R. S III, Vol. V, pp. 396-397).

No one could lawfully prevent a drafted slave from entering the military service of the United States by procuring a substitute or paying commutation to him without his authority or against his consent.

If the drafted slave preferred to avoid the military and to remain in slavery, it was his personal privilege to secure a qualified exemption from that draft by payment of $300.00 or procurement of an acceptable substitute (O.R. S III, Vol. V, p. 397).

*This claim for compensation for George Holman, a slave, was submitted by William R., Mary C., Martha A., and Sarah C. Holman. By signing the Oath of Allegiance on this form, the claimants would be entitled to the bounty for having their slave enlisted in the U.S. Colored Troops. Note that the slave was given the family name of his owners.*

# CLAIM FOR COMPENSATION FOR ENLISTED SLAVE.

No.

We *William R Holman  mary C Holman  Martha A Holman  Sarah C Holman* a loyal citizens and residents of *Lebanon*, County of *Wilson*, State of *Tennessee*, hereby claim compensation, under the provisions of Section 24, Act approved February 24, 1864, and Sec. 2, Act approved July 28, 1866, for my slave *George Holman* enlisted *September 29*, 1863. at *Gallatin, Tenn.* by *James N Holmes  Agent* in the *14 Inf.* Regiment U. S. Colored Troops, Co. *"A"*, certificate of which enlistment, and a descriptive list, as required, accompanying this application.

In proof of my loyalty to the Constitution and Government of the United States, I present the accompanying oath, which I have taken, signed and acknowledged; to be filed with this application, in accordance with requirement of General Order, No. 329, 1863, War Department, Adjutant General's Office.

*February* 186*7*.

## OATH OF ALLEGIANCE.

We the undersigned the owners and claimants do solemnly swear that the foregoing claim is a just and true claim, due to us as masters and owners of the said slave, and that the facts alleged in said claim in respect to the enlistment of said slave into the military service of the United States, are true. And we do further swear that we have never joined, *or been concerned in any insurrection* or rebellion; *that we have never borne arms* against the United States: *that we have never given any aid, countenance, council or encouragement* to any person or persons engaged, or whom we had reason to believe were about to engage, in insurrection, rebellion, or armed hostility *against the United States;* that we have neither sought, nor accepted, nor attempted to exercise the functions of any office, civil or military, nor to perform any service whatever under any authority, or pretended authority, in hostility to the United States; that we have not yielded a voluntary support to any insurrection, rebellion, or pretended government, authority, power or constitution within the United States, hostile thereto. And we do further swear that, to the best of our knowledge and ability, we have supported and defended, and will continue to support and defend, the United States *against all enemies, foreign and domestic, and that we have supported, defended and obeyed, and will continue to support, defend and obey the Constitution and laws of the United States;* that we will bear true faith and allegiance to the same; and that we take this oath freely, without any mental reservation or evasion. So help us God.

Sworn to and subscribed before me, at *Lebanon Tenn*, this day of *February*, 186*7*.

FIVE CENT REVENUE STAMP.

*Clerk County Court*

(Affidavits of disinterested loyal parties will be required to prove the active loyalty of claimant during the war.)

# PROOF OF OWNERSHIP.

**State of Maryland,**
*St. Mary's* **County,** } SCT.

On this *1st* day of *April* A. D. 186*5*, before me, a Justice of the Peace, in and for the County aforesaid, personally appeared *George Forbes* a resident of *St Mary's County Maryland* a person whom I certify to be respectable and entitled to credit, and who, being by me, duly sworn according to law, says that he was the owner of *Alfred Hall* (a man of African descent) at the time of his enlistment; that he enlisted from the *County of St Mary's* State of Maryland, on the *23d* day of *October* 186*3*, in the *7th* Regiment United States Colored Troops, Co. *I*, as set forth in the annexed Certificate of the Board of Claims: at the same time, before me, personally appeared *W. O. Robson* and *Wm B Goddard* residents of said County, and persons whom I certify to be respectable and entitled to credit, and who, being by me, duly sworn according to law, say that they are personally well acquainted with the above named *George Forbes* and that they are cognizant of the fact that he was the owner of the said *Alfred Hall* at the time of his enlistment into the United States service, as aforesaid, and that they have no interest, direct or indirect, in the prosecution of the claim of said *George Forbes* against the State of Maryland

*Geo Forbes*
Signature of Claimant.

*W. O. Robson*
*Wm B Goddard*
Signature of Witnesses.

Sworn to and subscribed before me, on the day and year first above written, the said affidavits having been by me first read to and fully understood by the affiants, and I hereby certify that I have no interest, direct or indirect, in the prosecution of said claim.

*C. Camalier J.P.*
Signature of Officer.

**State of** *Maryland*
*Saint Marys County* } SS.

I hereby certify that *C. Camalier* Esq., before whom the foregoing affidavits were made and subscribed, and who has thereunto subscribed his name, was, at the time so doing, a Justice of the Peace of the State of Maryland, in and for *Saint Marys* County aforesaid, duly commissioned and sworn, and that his signature thereto is genuine.

In Testimony Whereof, I have hereunto set my hand, and affixed the seal of the Circuit Court for *Saint Marys County* and State aforesaid, this *first* day of *April A. D.* 186*5*

*Jno. A. Camalier* Clerk.

116

## Prisoners of War

Along with war comes its prisoners. Union and Confederate officials signed a cartel on July 22, 1862, to define the system of exchange of its prisoners. A general for a general, a captain for a captain, a sergeant for a sergeant, and so on. The main problem with this exchange agreement was that the Confederates would not and could not recognize captured black soldiers as equal to captured white Confederate soldiers. Within the numbers of captured black soldiers, some were free born and some were former slaves, and this posed yet another problem of distinction.

The Confederate States denied prisoner of war status to captured black soldiers or their white officers. Confederate commanders were ordered to turn captured black soldiers over to various state governments to be dealt with according to the appropriate state statutes (O.R. S I, Vol. IV, p. 599).

All these states had laws that prescribed death to black insurrectionists, which was well known by 1863. General Grant ordered that all prisoner exchanges cease. The Confederate Congress issued a joint resolution in May 1863 which restated the Confederate policy: "Officers of black regiments would be treated as criminals and soldiers who had been slaves would be turned over to state authorities." One of the problems was in what to do with the free black soldiers that were captured. Since they had not been former slaves, this Confederate policy did not apply to them. As captured soldiers, they should be treated as other captured soldiers, but as free black men, they could not be treated equal. By 1864 these free black men were treated like white prisoners of war, except when it came to exchanging them for a Confederate prisoner of war. The Rebels could not consider them equal (Berlin, p. 568).

*Union prisoners of war at Camp Sumter, Andersonville, Ga. Northeastern view taken from the stockade.*

At this time, Lieutenant Colonel William H. Ludlow was the Union Agent for the Exchange of Prisoners. On June 14, 1863, he asked the Honorable Robert Ould, Confederate Agent for the Exchange of Prisoners, for a copy of the Joint Resolution of May 1863 of the Confederate Congress as to officially know of Rebel intentions toward men and officers captured in arms who had been duly mustered into the service of the United States. Ludlow was interested in how Confederates would treat captured black soldiers. He gave Ould formal notice that the United States Government would throw its protection around all its officers and men, without regard to color, and would promptly retaliate for all cases violating the cartel or the laws and usages of war (O.R. S II, Vol. VI, pp. 17-18).

President Lincoln had also issued his policy which was converted in to General Order No. 252, dated July 30, 1863, for the military to abide. This order was from the Executive Mansion, and it stated that:

> It is the duty of every Government to give protection to its citizens, of whatever class, color, or condition, and especially to those who are duly organized as soldiers in the public service. The law of nations, and the usages and customs of war, as carried on by civilized powers, permit no distinction as to color in the treatment of prisoners of war as public enemies: To sell or enslave any captured person on account of his color, and for no offence against the laws of war, is a relapse into barbarism, and a crime against the civilization of the age.
>
> The Government of the United States will give the same protection to all its soldiers: and if the enemy shall sell or enslave any one because of his color, the offence shall be punished by retaliation upon the enemy's prisoners in our possession.
>
> It is therefore ordered, that for every soldier of the United States killed in violation of the laws of war, a Rebel soldier will be executed; and for every one enslaved by the enemy or sold into slavery, a Rebel soldier shall be placed at hard labor on the public works, and continued at such labor until the other shall be released and receive the treatment due to a prisoner of war.
>
> Abraham Lincoln

General Grant informed Major General Butler of his orders with respect to exchange of colored prisoners from his headquarters on April 17, 1864. He told Butler that there was be no distinction whatever made between white and colored prisoners; the only question being, whether they were in the service of the United States military at the time of their capture. If they were, the same terms for the treatment of white prisoners and conditions of release and exchange was to be exacted in the case of both white and black soldiers.

The non-acquiescence by the Confederate authorities was to be regarded as a refusal on their part to agree to the further exchange of prisoners, and would be so treated by the Union (O.R. S II, Vol. VII, pp. 62-63).

The Union ended all prisoner exchanges when the South excluded captured black soldiers from the exchange. Prisoner of war exchanges began again in February of 1865.

There were 284 known deaths of black soldiers who were Confederate prisoners of war.

According to the Reports of Committees of the House of Representative made during the Third Session of the Fortieth Congress in 1869, two hundred and thirty-six black Prisoners of War were exchanged, and seventy-seven escaped.

## Major Bogle, Prisoner of War

The Confederates did not treat white officers who commanded black soldiers in battle too kindly. One of the few accounts of such treatment is that of Major Archibald Bogle, 35th Regiment, U.S.C.T.

Bogle, like many other officers in the United States Colored Troops had prior military experience. It is safe to say that the officer corps of the Colored Troops contained many men who, not only had prior military experience, but had engaged the enemy in combat. This Scottish born officer had been mustered into the 17th Massachusetts Volunteer Infantry as a 2d Lieutenant. He had received a promotion to captain, by brevet, for gallant conduct in the field.

Twenty-two year-old Bogle was wounded twice during the Battle of Olustee, Florida, on February 20, 1864. He had been left on the field for dead, but Bogle was captured there on the same day.

The Confederates showed their distaste of a white officer leading black soldiers in battle by sending him to an enlisted man's prison, Camp Sumter (Andersonville Prison). He arrived there on about March 14, 1864.

First Lieutenant George W. French, Company H, 8th U.S.C.T. was another officer of a U.S.C.T. regiment who was sent there. He was taken prisoner during the same engagement. French never left Camp Sumter, and he was buried there. Grave number 2888 marks his burial place among the other 62 prisoners who died of "fever remittent."

Bogle was feeling very faint when he arrived at the stockade. He was on crutches, and he had been severely wounded in the bowels and the lower part of the right leg, where two bones were fractured.

He shared a tent with the black soldiers in the Southwest corner of the stockade, and since he had the highest rank, he was in charge of the men. Some of the black soldiers received extra rations for the extra heavy labor that they performed for the Rebels, and in that sense, they were better off than most of the prisoners.

Bogle had heard that there was some sort of hospital in the Camp. After he was helped there by some of his men, he was refused both admittance and treatment. He went there a second time in a very weakened state, suffering from exposure, starvation and diarrhea, and his wounds had turned gangrenous. Before he was captured he weighed 170 pounds, at this time, he weighed a mere 70 to 80 pounds.

One of the Union soldiers, Corporal Burns, an acting hospital steward, bandaged up the wounds on Bogle's leg. While he was in the process, a Confederate officer in charge of the prison hospital, Surgeon White, entered the picture and demanded that Burns stop what he was doing. He wanted Bogle back out with his "niggers." Burns finished dressing his leg, and Bogle's own men took care of him after that incident.

The next month, April, Bogle tried the hospital once again. This time, Confederate Hospital Steward Robinson, who was Dr. White's right hand man, came in an asked if he was the Major of a Negro regiment. Bogle's answer was that he was an officer in the United States military. When Bogle answered the next question of identifying his regiment, Robinson asked him to leave. Sometime later, Corporal Burns told Bogle that if he didn't leave he would be "ball and chained." Afterwards, Bogle learned what Burns was really told: "If Bogle didn't leave the hospital, Bogle would be shot, and Burns would be ball and chained." Needless to say, Bogle left the hospital.

While Bogle was imprisoned at Camp Sumter, he was engaged in a tunneling operation in which he plotted to release all the prisoners of the stockade. The plan failed because one of the prisoners informed a guard about it.

After a series of harsh treatments, and because he was a white officer of a black regiment, he was finally released. He was held prisoner for 13 months, and was paroled on March 1, 1865.

Bogle wrote a letter to Brigadier General Lorenzo Thomas after his return to his regiment from "The Citadel" in Charleston, South Carolina. His aim was to bring Surgeon White, Captain Wirz, Hospital Steward Robinson, from Camp Sumter, and Captain Vowels, Commandant of prisons at Millen, Georgia to justice. In his letter, Bogle related all his misfortunes of being a captured white officer of a black regiment in the hands of the Rebels. At a later time, Bogle was summoned to appear at the Captain Wirz trial in October 1865.

One month before he was discharged, Major Bogle wrote to Lieutenant General U.S. Grant from the headquarters of the 35th U.S.C.T. at Summerville, South Carolina. He wanted to apply for a commission in the Regular Army with the understanding that his rank would be determined by a "Board of Examination." It was a common practice with the reorganization of the Army and the over abundance of capable officers to be reduced in rank to remain in service.

Major Bogle was mustered out of service on May 21, 1866. He was appointed brevet lieutenant colonel and brevet colonel in the Volunteer Force for gallant and meritorious services during the war, to date from March 13, 1865.

He continued his military service by becoming a first lieutenant in the 39th Infantry on May 27, 1867. This regiment was one of the four infantry regiments composed of black men. This regiment was later consolidated with the 40th Infantry to be designated the 25th Regiment by the Act of Congress of March 3, 1869. Bogle became a first lieutenant in the 25th Regiment on April 20, 1869. He remained in the service until he was dismissed on December 20, 1871, as listed in War Department G.O. No. 18 of April 18, 1872.

# Slaves and Slavery

### Recruitment of Plantation Negroes

Union officials felt that the South was a great source of manpower. By using this manpower source under their jurisdiction, the labor force, both male and female, received employment and had food and shelter as well. It also prevented them from crowding the roads with mass movements of displaced people.

The issue of using former slaves working on plantations controlled by Union Plantation Superintendents (usually white men from the North) going into the Army and Navy presented a problem. Plantation agents wanted the blacks to grow cotton but blacks wanted to grow food for themselves. This presented a conflict that was never really solved. Some men went into the army (before the Plantation Superintendent could prevent it), and others were refused permission to enter the army.

*The Sanctuary—A Negro family has just come in sight of the fortified lines of the Union army. The old mother has thrown herself on her knees, praising the Lord, while the rest of the family are grouped behind, conetmplating the scene in silent wonder. [Lithograph Plate No. 40 by Edwin Forbes, copyrighted 1876.]*

Special Order No. 11 dated May 28, 1863, was for the recruitment of men for the 1st Regiment U.S. Volunteers, Ullman's Brigade. The Order stated that "You are hereby authorized to enlist negroes on any plantations this side of the Mississippi River. Should any person or persons interfere with your business you will report such person or persons immediately at these Headquarters."

The 1st Regiment U.S. Volunteers, Ullman's Brigade was redesignated as the 6th Regiment Corps d'Afrique which was later redesignated into the 79th (old) U.S Colored Troops in June 1863.

# Peculiar Institution

*"Peculiar Institution" is a euphemistic Southern phrase for slavery which originated after John C. Calhoun had defended the "Peculiar Labor" of the South in 1828, and the "Peculiar Domestic Institution." In 1830 the phrase came into general use.*

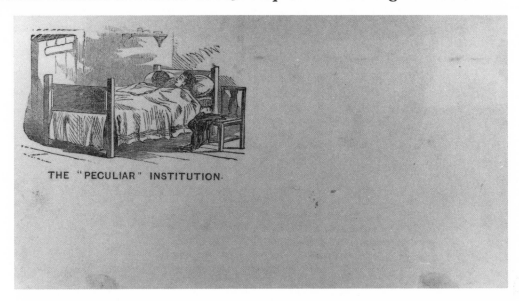

*This is one of a number of political Civl War Patriotic Envelopes.*

*Planting sweet potatoes on a slave plantation, May 1862.*

# Branded Slaves

*Wilson Chin was about 60 years old at the time of this photo. He was raised by Isaac Howard of Woodford County, Kentucky. When he was 21 years old, he was taken down the river and sold to Volsey B. Marmillion, a sugar grower. This man traditionally branded his slaves, and Wilson Chin illustrates this brand of "VBM" on his forehead. Of the 210 slaves that lived on this plantation, 105 left at one time and came into the Union camp. Thirty of them had been branded like cattle with a hot iron, four of them on their forehead, and the others on the breast or arm.*

*The other photo is an unidentified slave who has been branded on the forehead also.*

**WILSON CHINN, a Branded Slave from Louisiana.**
Also exhibiting Instruments of Torture
used to punish Slaves.

Photographed by KIMBALL, 477 Broadway, N.Y

Entered according to Act of Congress, in the year 1863, by
GEO. H. HANKS, in the Clerk's Office of the United States for
the Southern District of New-York.

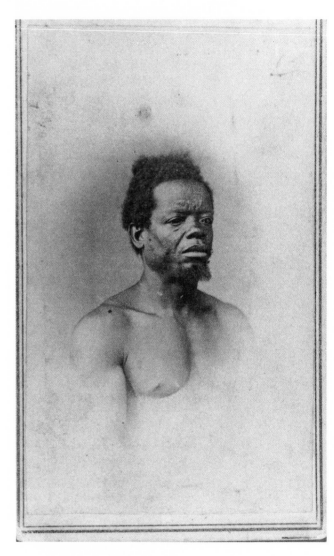

## Slave Children from New Orleans

Many slave children from New Orleans were set free by General Butler. The children attended the first school in Louisiana for emancipated slaves, which was established by Major General Nathanial Banks.

A series of carte de visites of five slave children and three adults from New Orleans was sold during 1863 and 1864. They were photographed by at least five different photographers in more than 20 different poses.

This was probably the earliest photograph that was used to raise money to educate a group of people. The statement on the back of the photos in the series reads, "The nett proceeds from the sale of these photographs will be devoted to the education of colored people in the department of the Gulf, now under the command of Maj. Gen. Banks."

The names of the subjects are as follows:

| | | |
|---|---|---|
| Rosina Downs (Rosa) | age | 6 years |
| Charles Taylor | | 8 years |
| Augusta Broujey | | 9 years |
| Rebecca Huger | | 11 years |
| Isaac White | | 8 years |
| Wilson Chin | | 60 years |
| Robert Whitehead | | a regularly ordained preacher |
| Mary Johnson | | a cook |

The carte de visites were for sale by the National Freedman's Relief Association, No. 1 Mercer Street, New York City, New York. They were sold for 25 cents each.

LEARNING IS WEALTH.
WILSON, CHARLEY, REBECCA & ROSA.
Slaves from New Orleans

OUR PROTECTION.
ROSA, CHARLEY, REBECCA.
Slave Children from New Orleans.

## Slave Children in Philadelphia

These slave children from New Orleans were turned out of their hotel, the St. Lawrence Hotel in Philadelphia, because they were black. They were on a tour of northern cities when they reached Philadelphia in January of 1864. The hotel management did not recognize these fair skinned children as being black, and they were registered into the hotel. When the landlord found out that these children were not "white," they were asked to leave. They went to the neighboring Continental Hotel where they were accepted. This is the same hotel that Major Stearns used as his headquarters for recruiting colored soldiers.

A local photographer, McClees, was so irate over the incident at the St. Lawrence Hotel, that he created a carte de visite of the three well-dressed children with the caption "THESE CHILDREN were turned out of the St. Lawrence Hotel, Chestnut ST., Philadelphia, on account of color." He used the money he raised to further the education of the slave children of New Orleans. The cartes were sold for 25 cents each.

These children, Rebecca, Charley, and Augusta, are shown in another carte de visite with the children identified, and the caption "Slave Children of New Orleans."

An article in the January 30, 1864 issue of *Harper's Weekly* described the incident. The editors ended their blasting commentary with, "And so, by God's blessing, the humanity and wisdom of the American People is at this moment touching Slavery to its destruction. Little Children like these in the picture this country no longer turns away into untold horrors and despair; but its heart whispers to them, gently, 'Suffer little children to come unto me!'."

THESE CHILDREN
Were turned out of the St. Lawrence Hotel, Chestnut St., Philadelphia, on account of Color.

126

## A Redeemed Slave Child

This child was photographed in at least 26 different poses, mainly in the carte de visite format, by at least 5 different photographers.

The following is entered on the bottom of the carte de visite shown here: "Fannie Virginia Casseopia Lawrence, A Redeemed SLAVE CHILD, 5 years of age. Redeemed in Virginia by Catherine S. Lawrence; Baptized in Brooklyn, at Plymouth Church, by Henry Ward Beecher, May 1863.

"Entered according to an Act of Congress, in the year 1863, by C. Lawrence, in the Clerk's Office of the District Court of the United States, for the Southern District of New York."

In order to understand who Fannie V.C. Lawrence was, one must understand the relationship between Fannie and Miss Lawrence. Catherine S. Lawrence, teacher, missionary, and temperance lecturer of Scholarie Village, Scholarie County, New York, enlisted as an Army nurse in 1861. She entered the City Hospital in New York to receive her military instructions. Next she reported to Dorothea C. Dix, Superintendent of Union Women War Nurses in Washington, D.C. Nurse Lawrence served at many hospitals, such as Fortress Monroe Hospital and the National Hotel Hospital, in Washington, D.C. She was Directress of Kolerarama Hospital, also in Washington, and she also served in the hospital at

FANNIE VIRGINIA CASSEOPIA LAWRENCE.
A Redeemed SLAVE CHILD, 5 years of age. Redeemed in Virginia by Catharine S. Lawrence; Baptized in Brooklyn, at Plymouth Church, by Henry Ward Beecher, May, 1863.
Entered according to Act of Congress, in the year 1863, by C. S. Lawrence, in the Clerk's Office of the District Court of the United States, for the Southern District of New York.

Redeemed in Virginia

By Catharine S. Lawrence. Baptized in Brooklyn, at Plymouth Church, by Henry Ward Beecher, May, 1863. Fannie Virginia Casseopia Lawrence, a Redeemed SLAVE CHILD, 5 years of age.
Entered according to Act of Congress, in the year 1863, by C. S. Lawrence, in the Clerk's Office of the district Court of the United States, for the Southern District of New York.
Photograph by Renowden, 65 Fulton Av. Brooklyn.

Armory Square in Falls Church, Virginia, as well as the Old Convalescent Camp in Alexandria Heights, Virginia.

Detailed information on the life of Nurse Lawrence can be found in her autobiography, *Sketch of Life and Labors of Miss Catherine S. Lawrence* "who in early life distinguished herself as a bitter opponent of Slavery and Intemperance, and late in life as a nurse in the late war: and for other patriotic and philanthropic services." The proceeds of the sale of the book were to supplement her $12.00 a month pension from the government for being an army nurse.

When Miss Lawrence first became aware of Fannie, the child's surname was Ayres. Fannie had two sisters, Vianna and Sarah, and her father was a lawyer who had migrated to Fairfax, Virginia with his wife, mother, and family. Although he was not averse to owning a large number of slaves, he considered himself a Union man. At or just before the outbreak of the war, Mr. Ayres was taken ill and died. Before his death, he made an act of justice by giving all his slaves their freedom. His wife died within a short period of time, and the freed slaves remained with the aged grandmother.

The Confederates knew that Ayres was a Union sympathizer, and after his death they proceeded to confiscate everything they could find. The grandmother was also dying, and she called upon her faithful blacks to leave with the three orphan girls. She told them to take whatever clothing and supplies that they could carry, and to try to reach the Union lines. Soon thereafter, the grandmother died, and the blacks left and joined a party of refugees and headed for the Union lines. They eventually made their way to the Union lines at Fairfax, Virginia, which was a hundred miles away.

Fannie's eldest sister, Vianna went to Miss Lawrence and asked her if she would take the child. She told her that they had no place to stay, and that she could not take care of her youngest sister. Miss Lawrence was in doubt regarding Fannie's birthright, and whether it was black or white. Miss Lawrence took the child with the intention of educating and baptizing her. Fannie was baptized when she was three years old.

After the war, Miss Lawrence traveled a great deal for a woman during that period. She made various trips to New England with Fannie, and introduced her to many public figures such as Governor Andrew of Massachusetts, the Honorable Edward Everett, Wendell Phillips, William Lloyd Garrison, John Whittier, and many others.

Miss Lawrence did not abandon Fannie's two sisters; she felt that the girls should not be separated, so she adopted all three of them. She also had them baptized, and Sarah, called Sally, stayed with Miss Lawrence's brother. The elder sister, Vianna, was baptized in the United Church in Seneca Falls, New York. Eventually, both of the elder girls were placed in what Lawrence felt were appropriate homes.

## Captain Riley's Slave Children

At the time that this photo was taken, Captain Girrard Riley was serving in Company K, 6th U.S.C.T. He had prior military service through his enlistment as a private in Captain Clark's Company of the 50th Regiment, Ohio Infantry at the age of 41 in August of 1862. He eventually became a chaplain in this regiment, but resigned his post to become captain in the 6th U.S.C.T.

Captain Riley was sent to Mathews County, Virginia, to rescue some Union families and about thirty slaves. These two children, Levi Douglas White, age 7, and his sister Jane White, age 9, were rescued by Captain Riley and sent to the Association for the care of Colored Orphans instituted in Philadelphia. Once separated from their family, they were given a proper education and never returned to Virginia.

**AS WE FOUND THEM.**

These children were owned by Thomas White, of Mathews Co., Va., until Feb. 20th. when Capt. Riley, 6th U. S. C. I , took them and gave them to the Society of Friends to educate at the Orphan's Shelter, Philadelphia.

Profits from sale, for the benefit of the children.

## Sojourner Truth

Born to a slave in 1797, Isabella Baumfree has become known to the world as Sojourner Truth. She was an advocate of temperance, an evangelist, and an early public speaker against slavery. She was born in Hurley, Ulster County, New York, where slavery was abolished in 1827.

Isabella ran away one year before she was to be given her freedom, but it was eventually granted to her. She went to work in New York as a domestic, and in the 1840s she was told by God to take the name "Sojourner," and to walk the land to speak the truth about slavery.

Sojourner Truth settled in Battle Creek, Michigan, in the early 1850s. This area provided the setting for many of her photos.

A book on her life, *Narrative of Sojourner Truth*, written in 1853 by Olive Gilbert, supported her for many years in her preachings against slavery. In 1863, she decided, after being ill for a number of months, that she would sell photographs of herself. The caption read, "I'll sell the Shadow to Support the Substance." The shadow referred to the photograph, and the subtance referred to her body. In other words, she would sell the photograph to support her physical being.

During the war, she helped the black soldiers from Michigan, and she was received by President Lincoln in October 1864 at the White House.

Following the war, Sojourner Truth continued to travel and preach the truth of slavery. She supported herself by selling her pictures and her book.

*I Sell the Shadow to Support the Substance.*
SOJOURNER TRUTH.

## To Aid the Prisoner of War

Colonel Samuel A. Duncan, 4th U.S.C.T., commanded three regiments of colored soldiers, the 4th, 5th, and 6th U.S.C.T., and they reported to Brigadier General Isaac J. Wistar. Wistar, along with another brigade of three white regiments and a cavalry regiment, was to perform a surprise raid to capture Richmond and release the Union prisoners. This plan was proposed by General Butler, and activity began on February 6, 1864. Each infantry soldier carried six days rations and 40 rounds in his knapsack, along with 30 rounds of cartridges in his box.

Unfortunately, the Richmond expedition was not successful. The enemy was waiting for them, and when the flag-of-truce boat arrived from Richmond which brought in the morning *Examiner*, the other side of the story became known. A Yankee deserter, who was under the sentence of death for the murder of a lieutenant, was allowed to escape by a private in the 139th New York Volunteers. The culprit was Private William Boyle of the New York Mounted Rifles. He would have been hanged were it not for President Lincoln's order to suspend the execution of capital sentences until further orders.

When Boyle reached Richmond he was placed in Castle Thunder. It was there that he told the Confederates of the plans of the Wistar raid. They believed him and sent three regiments of infantry, one of cavalry, and four batteries of artillery to oppose the raiding force.

*Castle Thunder, Richmond, Va.*

The information of the raid was also printed in the *Richmond Sentinel* the day after the attack. Wistar and Butler felt that if the raid did anything, they succeeded in forcing the Confederates to keep some troops in Richmond to defend any other potential raids. General Wistar reported that "The Infantry marched in four days 33, 28, 18, and 25 miles, respectively, with alacrity and cheerfulness, and almost without stragglers, the colored troops being in his respect, as usual, remarkable" (O.R. S I, Vol. XXIII, pp. 143-146). This was before the well known Kilpatrick-Dahlgren Raid.

An aspect of the contribution of the black man during the Civil War can be seen in his service to the Union prisoners in Confederate confinement or on the run. It was expressed rather elegantly after the war the Report of Committees, House of Representatives, Third Session, Fortieth Congress, 1869.

> ...[I]t is in kindness and humanity to the prisoner that the conduct and example of these loyal and faithful friends of the Union shine with the greatest brilliancy. In the gloom of the walled prison they brought him food from their slender stores, and, notwithstanding the terrible punishment which followed their detection, persevered in affording aid to the suffering. They smuggled vegetables and other luxuries into the stockade for the use of the prisoners, outwitting the vigilance of the guard in their attempts at relief. But to the escaped and wandering prisoner, beset by men and hounds following sharply on his train, the presence was most welcome and their aid never withheld.

There has never been a recorded case of an escaped Union prisoner being turned over to the Confederate authorities by a black man. He was remembered as the friend of the Union prisoner.

Lest we forget, those who do not carry weapons also serve.

*The new citizen of the South.*

# Contraband

## General Butler and the Contraband of War

It was the policy of the Army when the war began to return runaway slaves to their masters, as stated in the Fugitive Slave Law. In May of 1861, three runaway slaves, who had been working on a Confederate battery, reached Fortress Monroe, Virginia. They were the property of Confederate Colonel Mallory. Major Carey, representing Colonel Mallory, requested, under a flag of truce, that these three runaways be returned. General Butler described the incident in his book, entitled *Butler's Book.* He made the following reply to Carey:

> You say you have seceded, so you cannot consistently claim them. I shall hold these negroes as contraband of war, since they are engaged in the construction of your battery and are claimed as your property. The question is simply whether they shall be used for or against the Government of the United States. Yet though I greatly need the labor which has providentially come to my hands, if Colonel Mallory will come into the fort and take the Oath of Allegiance to the United States, he shall have his negroes, and I will endeavor to hire them from him.

The reply of the Major was that "Colonel Mallory is absent," but General Butler knew that Colonel Mallory could not take the Oath of Allegiance to the United States. No man could take this oath and continue fighting against the country. This incident inspired the Union soldiery's nickname for runaway slaves—"contrabands."

On May 30, 1861, Secretary of War Simon Cameron wrote to Major General Butler approving of the action that he took with the contrabands. He further stated that Butler should employ the black men and keep a record of their labor, its value, and maintain their expenses (O.R. S III, Vol. I, p. 243).

The first legislation by Congress that affected black people was an act of March 13, 1862. This act prohibited military personnel from returning runaway slaves to their masters. Any officer found guilty by a court martial would be discharged from the military service.

To feed adult refugees and adult runaways, the War Department issued G.O. No. 30 on January 25, 1864. Through this order, the government provided for those people not employed by the government, and who had no means of providing for themselves, and gave them rations; for children under fourteen years of age, half rations were issued. These rations were issued by the Subsistence Department.

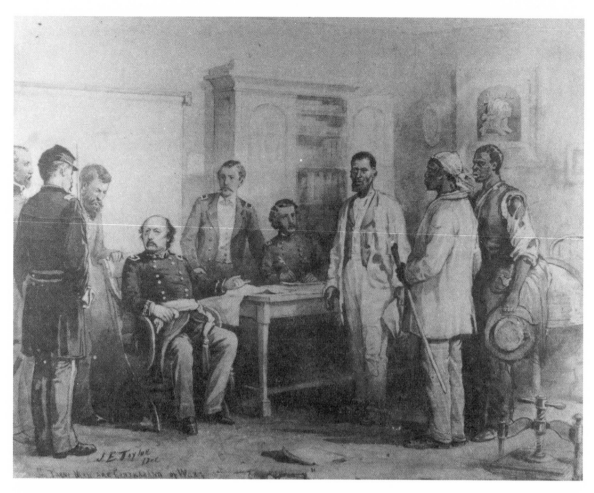

*General Butler proclaiming, "These men are contraband of War," by J.E. Taylor.*

*Patriotic envelope: White master—"Come back here you black rascal." Slave—"Can't come back nohow, massa; dis chile's CONTRABAN'."*

## Contraband Camp—Contraband Labor

These camps were for the displaced black men and their families. They were on the outskirts of large Southern cities, and were usually made from the discards of the military. The canvas, boxes, and barrels taxed the ingenuity of the former slaves.

For many of the black people, this was their first taste of freedom, and their first home. To have your own residence was the goal of everyone, white or black, native or immigrant.

The camp was also an invaluable manpower source that soon found employment within the various departments of the military. Men, women, and children were now able, for the first time, to earn money and support themselves.

Over a period of time, the black man found employment working for the military in a sundry of jobs. He began to become an asset to himself and his family, and was also a valuable source of manpower for the military recruiter. It was not taken lightly when the recruiter for the army would intimidate, cajole, and entice these men to leave their jobs to do their duty and satisfy their moral obligation by enlisting as soldiers. This became a problem for Major General W.T. Sherman because it was depleting his civilian work force.

Sherman issued General Field Order No. 16 on June 3, 1864, which stated that "Recruiting officers will not enlist as soldiers any negroes who are profitably employed by any of the army departments, and any staff officer having a negro employed in useful labor on account of the Government will refuse to release him from his employment by virtue of a supposed enlistment as a soldier." Sherman continued by stating that "Commanding officers of the military posts will arrest, and, if need be, imprison any recruiting officer who, to make up companies of negro soldiers, interferes with the necessary gangs of hired negroes in the employment of the quartermaster's or commissary or other department of the Government without full consent of the officers having them in charge" (O.R. S III, Vol. V, p. 434).

This order presented a problem for Adjutant General L. Thomas in the recruiting of men as directed. Thomas felt that this order would stop the enlistment of the black man. He also considered the threat of imprisonment to recruiting officers especially harsh.

Since the black men were no longer being taken up into the military as soldiers, he was readily sought after for civilian work forces. In subsequent wars, men were made exempt from military service if their jobs were felt to be more valuable than their service as soldiers. This was probably the first time that free black men were considered so valuable a commodity.

*Contraband Camp, Harpers Ferry.*

## Teamsters

This illustration from the March 7, 1863, issue of *Harper's Weekly* depicts an army of teamsters being paid off in March 1862. The artist was Alfred Waud, and he wrote: "In the Army of the Potomac there are probably 8,000-10,000 negroes employed as teamsters. This is a business they are well fitted for, and, of course, it relieves an equal number of white men for other duties. A teamster's life is a very hard one particularly at this season of the year. It does not matter how much it storms, or how deep the mud, subsistence must be hauled to the camps, day and night, taking along with tired horses and mules. The creaking wagons are kept busy carrying to and from commissary, quartermaster and ordnance stores, in addition to keeping the camps supplied with fire-wood."

The government was in favor of finding work for this available source of manpower, and on August 16, 1862, the War Department issued G.O. No. 109 that referred to the presidential order of July 22, 1862, "...that military and naval commanders shall employ laborers, with and from said states, so many persons of African descent as can be advantageously used for military and naval purposes, giving them reasonable wages for their labor."

In view of the fact that the government was also supplying several hundred women and children of the same class who were unable to support themselves, the Secretary of War ordered that $5.00 per month be deducted from the pay of the teamsters and laborers in the Quartermaster's Department, to be paid over to a commissioner. The commissioner would then expend the fund and thus accrue for the benefit of the women and children, and as a hospital fund for the sick among the men from whom it was derived.

# WANTED IMMEDIATELY!

# 100

# Colored Teamsters!

## For the Army of the Potomac.

### WAGES,

# $20 PER MONTH

## AND RATIONS.

# FRANK PFEIFFER,

## Master Mechanic.

*The TEAMSTERS' DUEL, from a sketch by Mr. Waud, is one of the humorous scenes in which our camps abound. When a quarrel arises between two colored teamsters a challenge passes, and the combatants lash each other with their long whips until one of them confesses that he can endure no more, and "throws up the sponge." The other is pronounced the victor, and very frequently admonishes his vanquished foe of the necessity of better behavior in future, amidst the roars and laughter of the white spectators.*
(Harper's Weekly, *Jan. 17, 1863.*)

*Colored Army Teamsters, Cobb Hill, Va.*

## Negro Passports

This Negro Passport is the kind of Civil War artifact that is not usually found because it was originally in the hands of the slave, and was perishable. When it was no longer needed, it was usually discarded.

Issued by the War Department, Confederate States of America, Richmond, June 4th, 1863, this Negro Passport was used to "Pass Billey Smith to Petersburg by the South Side R.R." This transportation was "Subject to the discretion of the Military authorities," and it was signed by the Provost Marshall, James Turner. Billey Smith was described as be 33 years of age, 6 feet tall, and possessed a "light color."

*Harper's Weekly* artist, F.B. Schell, illustrated the examination of passes on the road leading to the levee of the Mississippi River in the vicinity of Vicksburg, as it was surrounded by the Union Army. The plantation police or home guard was given this task because it became a matter of vital interest to the owners of the plantations that their slaves should be kept at home and not permitted to get within the Federal lines. This emergency called for the formation of a home guard and for a system of passes to prevent an exodus of the slaves.

## Servants and Officers

Robert A. Potter was mustered in the 2d Regiment, Connecticut Volunteer Heavy Artillery, as second lieutenant of Company D on September 11, 1862. He was promoted to first lieutenant almost a year later, August 24, 1863, and was promoted a third time, to captain of Company E, on August 25, 1864. He was mustered out of service on August 18, 1865.

Captain Potter is seen here with his servant, Robert Morton. It was not uncommon to see a servant of black men working around the camp wearing a military uniform. They were provided with rations and clothing because most of them did not have any of their own.

Captain Potter received money to provide for his servant. Nothing is known of servant Robert Morton, but he was fortunate because he had a job, earned money, and was given shelter. It was not only those who were issued weapons who served in the War of the Rebellion. Black women served on and off in various military posts, where they found work doing laundry, as nurses, spies, cooks, and even the "oldest profession known to man." Young black men also worked in and around the camps doing various jobs. Some worked as servants, while the older men found jobs as teamsters, stevedores, cooks, foragers, servants, spies, scouts, blacksmiths, and any other task that they could perform. They also worked on the fortifications and as a field hand to bring in a food crop for the army population.

Approximately 225,000 black civilians worked for the Government. If the black man would have performed as many services for the South as he did for the North, the result of the war may have been very different. By the end of the war, the South realized this fact, and knew that this source of manpower could have been used to aid their cause instead of being utilized by the North.

*Captain Robert Potter, 2nd Connecticut Heavy Artillery.*

*Young Robert Morton, servant to Captain Potter.*

No. 3.

# The United States,

To Col. A.M. Blackman

| ON WHAT ACCOUNT. | COMMENCEMENT AND EXPIRATION. | | TERM OF SERVICE CHARGED. | | PAY PER MONTH. | | AMOUNT. | |
|---|---|---|---|---|---|---|---|---|
| | FROM— | TO— | MONTHS. | DAYS. | DOLLARS. | CENTS. | DOLLARS. | CENTS. |
| PAY. For myself . . . . . | the of 18 | the of 18 | 1 | | 95 | | 75 | |
| For 2 private servants not soldiers . | the of 18 | the of 18 | 1 | | 11 | | 22 | |
| CLOTHING. For 2 private servants not soldiers . | the of 18 | the of 18 | 1 | 1 | 2 | 50 | 5 | |
| FORAGE. For horses . . . . . | the of 18 | the of 18 | | | | | | |

|  | No. of days. | No. of Rations per day. | Total No. of Rations. | Post or place where due. | Price of Rations. CENTS. | | |
|---|---|---|---|---|---|---|---|
| SUBSISTENCE. For myself for year service . . | 30 | 8 | 240 | | 30 | 72 | |
| For 2 private servant [not soldiers . | | 2 | | | | 194 00 | |
| | | | | | | 7 20 | |
| | | | | | | 186 80 | |

Commencement: October 31 1864 — December 30 1864

REMARKS.

I hereby certify, on honor, that I am on detached service by authority of Special Order No. X. dated Jan. 24 1861 Headquarters of 3d Div. 25. Ar. At Fischer at Point—N.C.

A.M. Blackman
Col. 43d U.S.C.T.

I hereby certify that I have been and noted this payment on the above-mentioned Order.

J. Holliday
Paymaster U.S.A.

I HEREBY CERTIFY, That the foregoing account is accurate and just; that I have not been absent WITH OR WITHOUT ... during any part of the time charged for; that I have not received pay, nor drawn rations, forage, or clothing, in kind, or received money in lieu of any part thereof, for any part of the time therein charged; that I actually owed, and kept in service the horses, and employed the private servants for which I charge, for the whole of the time charged, and that I did not, during the term so charged, or any part thereof, keep or employ a soldier as a waiter or servant; that the amount is an accurate description of my servant; that for the whole period charged for my staff appointment, I actually and legally held the appointment, and did duty in the department; that I was the actual and only commanding officer at the double-ration post charged for; and that no officer, within my knowledge, has a right to claim, or does claim, for said services for any part of the period charged; that for the whole time brevet pay is claimed, I had the command stated; that I was actually in the command of a company for the whole time additional pay is charged; that I have not been in the performance of any staff duty for which I claim or have received extra compensation during the time an additional ration is charged for; that I have been in the United States Army as a commissioned officer for the number of years stated in the charge for extra rations; that I am not in arrears with the United States on any account whatsoever, and that the last payment I received was from Paymaster Wm. J. Clarkson, and to the 31 day of October, 1864.

I at the same time acknowledge that I have RECEIVED of J.F. Holliday, Paymaster U.S. Army, this 1 day of February, 1865, the sum of One hundred eighty five dollars and eighty cents, being the amount and in full of said account. Also I certify that I am not indebted to the U.S. for hospital attendance.

A.M. Blackman
Col. 43d U.S.C.T.

(SIGNED IN DUPLICATE.)

| DESCRIPTION OF SERVANTS. | | HEIGHT. | | COMPLEXION. | EYES. | HAIR. |
|---|---|---|---|---|---|---|
| NAMES. | | Feet. | Inches. | | | |
| Ben. White | | 5 | 6 | | | |
| Harriel Jackson | | 5 | 3 | | | |

| RECAPITULATION. | |
|---|---|
| Pay . . . . . . . | |
| Subsistence . . . . | |
| Forage . . . . . | |
| Clothing . . . . | |
| AMOUNT . . . $ | |

Carall @ 8% $144

*This subsistence voucher for Col. A.M. Blackman indicated that he had two "contraband" servants.*

## Cooks, Nurses, and the Medical Department

Besides establishing the General Orders for the Military, the War Department also established the policies for employment of civilians who worked for various departments in the military. For example, G.O. No. 390, dated December 8, 1863, stipulated that the "Officers of the Medical Department in charge of Hospitals for blacks are authorized to employ as cooks or nurses, either males or females, who will be paid by the Medical Purveyor or storekeeper at the rate of $10.00 per month. In cases where white females are employed, they will receive 40 cents per day. All such persons will also receive one ration per day." This 40 cents per day equaled $12.00 per month for white nurses and cooks, while the black women still only received $10.00.

A short time later, this General Order was superseded by another one that allowed black men and women to work in all U.S. General Hospitals. War Department G.O. No. 23, January 16, 1864 states that "The employment of persons of African descent, male or female, as cooks or nurses, will be permitted in all U.S. General Hospitals.

When so employed they will receive ten dollars per month and one ration. They will be paid by the nearest Medical Disbursing Officer, on rolls similar to those used in the payment of men of the Hospital Corps."

By using the available black manpower, the military solved its labor shortage. This employment gave the black men wages, in nearly every case, for the first time. On the other hand, many blacks were cheated by wicked money grabbers because the farmer did not know how to read numbers.

*The colored man among the group of soldiers in front of the winter hut at Brady Station is probably a cook for the group. Contrabands found employment around camp, and they knew where to acquire supplies and knew the people and the area. This provided a great asset to an organization in the field.*

# Medals, Flags, and Battles

*Sixteen Men of Color were awarded the Medal of Honor for their service in the U.S. Army. Seven of these recipients were recognized for protecting the colors. Five enlisted men earned the Medal for taking command of their company and leading their men in battle after all the officers had been killed or wounded. Four others earned the award for various deeds of gallantry.*

| Enlisted Men | Rank | Regiment | Date of Issue |
|---|---|---|---|
| 1. Barnes, William H. | Private | 38th | April 6, 1865 |
| 2. Beaty, Powhatan | Private | 5th | April 6, 1865 |
| 3. Bronson, James H. | 1st Sgt. | 5th | April 6, 1865 |
| 4. Carney, William H. | Sergeant | 54th Mass. | May 23, 1900 |
| 5. Dorsey, Decautur | Sergeant | 39th | Nov. 8, 1865 |
| 6. Fleetwood, Christian | Sgt. Major | 4th | April 6, 1865 |
| 7. Gardiner, James | Private | 36th | April 6, 1865 |
| 8. Harris, James H. | Sergeant | 38th | Feb. 18, 1874 |
| 9. Hawkins, Thomas | Sgt. Major | 6th | Feb. 8, 1870 |
| 10. Hilton, Alfred B. | Sergeant | 4th | April 6, 1865 |
| 11. Holland, Milton M. | Sgt. Major | 5th | April 6, 1865 |
| 12. James, Miles | Corporal | 36th | April 6, 1865 |
| 13. Kelley, Alexander | 1st Sgt. | 6th | April 6, 1865 |
| 14. Pinn, Robert | 1st Sgt. | 5th | April 6, 1865 |
| 15. Ratcliff, Edward | 1st Sgt. | 38th | April 6, 1865 |
| 16. Veal, Charles | Private | 4th | April 6, 1865 |

*Medal of Honor composite photograph collected for the Colored Conference in the Paris 1900 Exposition. Identified as follows, top to bottom, left to right:*
*Row 1: Robert A. Pinn, Milton N. Holland, John W. Lawson*
*Row 2: John Denny, Isaiah Mays, Powhatan Beaty, Brent Woods*
*Row 3: William H. Carney, Thomas R. Hawkins, Dennis Bell, James H. Harris*
*Row 4: Thomas Shaw, Alexander Kelly, James Gardiner, Christian A. Fleetwood*
*[From the Christian A. Fleetwood files, Library of Congress, Box #2.]*

*Sergeant William H. Carney, Company C, 54th Massachusetts, received the Medal of Honor on May 23, 1900 for his participation in the Battle of Fort Wagner. He was the first colored soldier to be recognized (July 18, 1863); ironically, he was the last one to actually recieve his award.*

Richard Walzl,     Baltimore.

*Christian Fleetwood, 4th U.S. Colored Troops. On his chest are an Army of the James Medal and a Medal of Honor. Fleetwood received the Medal of Honor for his participation in the Battle of Chapin's Farm on September 29 and 30, 1864.*

147

# U.S. Navy Medal of Honor

| | Enlisted Men | Rank | Date of Issue |
|---|---|---|---|
| 1. | Anderson, Aaron | Landsman | June 22, 1865 |
| 2. | Blake, Robert | Landsman | April 16, 1864 |
| 3. | Brown, William H. | Landsman | August 5, 1864 |
| 4. | Brown, Wilson | Landsman | December 31, 1864 |
| 5. | Dees, Clement | Seaman | |
| 6. | Lawson, John | Landsman | December 31, 1864 |
| 7. | Mifflin, James | Engineer's Cook | August 5, 1864 |
| 8. | Pease, Joachim | Seaman | December 31, 1864 |

*Cased Navy Medal of Honor.*

*The U.S. Navy was authorized to enlist "contrabands" for naval services as of September 25, 1861, under the same forms and regulations that applied to other enlistments. They were allowed no higher rating than boys, at a compensation of $10 per month and one ration a day.*

(Copy of Naval Discharge.)

# Discharge.

**This is to Certify,** That No. 5219 *Samuel Woodland* a *Landsman* has this day been ~~DISCHARGED~~ from the U.S. *Reg Ship Princeton at Philada Late of the U.S. Houghton*

and from the Naval Service.

Dated this 22 Augst 186

APPROVED:

*J. M. Colbourn*
Captain.

*Geo D Murray*
Paymaster.

| NAME. | ENLISTED—WHEN. | | | WHERE BORN, AND PERSONAL DESCRIPTION. | | | | | | | |
|---|---|---|---|---|---|---|---|---|---|---|---|
| | When. | Term. | Rating. | City, Town or County. | Date. | Age. | Occupation. | Eyes. | Hair. | Complexion. | Height. feet inch. |
| Samuel Woodland | Meh 11 1864 | | Lds | Md | | 41 | | | | Negro | 5 9 |
| | | | | | | | | | Frank Watson | | |

The Gillmore Medal was authorized on October 28, 1863. It was considered a Medal of Honor for Gallant and Meritorious conduct during the operations before Charleston, South Carolina. Only three percent of the men that saw action or duty in the batteries or trenches could be awarded this medal. General Quincy A. Gillmore had 400 bronze medals struck. A number of soldiers in the U.S. Colored Troops were recipients of this prestigious award. Although a detailed list of the recipients is unavailable, William H. Carney is wearing the medal in the previous photograph.

The Army of the James Medal, commonly called the Butler Medal, is the only medal ever struck for colored troops. General Benjamin Butler designed and paid for these medals after the Battle of Chapin's Farm; only 197 silver medals were produced. Inscribed in Latin, the translation of the front reads: "Liberty came to them by the sword U.S. Colored Troops." On the back it reads: "Distinguished for Courage, Campaign before Richmond" The medal had a red, white, and blue ribbon with a wreath embossed with "Army of the James."

The Civil War Campaign Medal was authorized by the War Department in 1907 for military service from April 15, 1861 to April 9, 1865 or for service in Texas through August 20, 1866. This included men of the U.S. Colored Troops. The original ribbon had a narrow white stripe in the center, flanked on either side by equal stripes of red, white, and blue. This was changed in 1913 to half blue on the left, and half gray on the right.

## Headquarters Flags

General Order No. 169 issued from the headquarters of the Department of the Gulf, New Orleans, on November 30th, 1864, read in part: "The flags to designate the different headquarters of the organizations in the U.S. Colored Troops, Department of the Gulf, and the positions of Commanders on the march, and in the field shall be as follows:

1st. Headquarters U.S. Colored Troops, Department of the Gulf. Flag four feet square, with a blue border nine inches wide, around a white centre two feet six inches square, in the centre of which, a red shield eighteen inches wide, and eighteen inches long, with the letters, U.S.C.T. in white thereon.

2d. Headquarters of Divisions; same pattern and size as above, with the following exception: the border will be red instead of blue; the shield blue, instead of red, with the number of the Division in a white figure, one foot long, in the centre thereof.

3d. Headquarters of Brigades. Flag four feet square, with a blue border nine inches wide, around a white centre, two feet six inches square. The number of the brigade, a black figure ten inches long, in the upper corner of the white square nearest the staff; the figure three inches from the nearest edges of the square. The number of the Division in red; same size figure similarly placed in the lower corner of the white square, farthest from the staff.

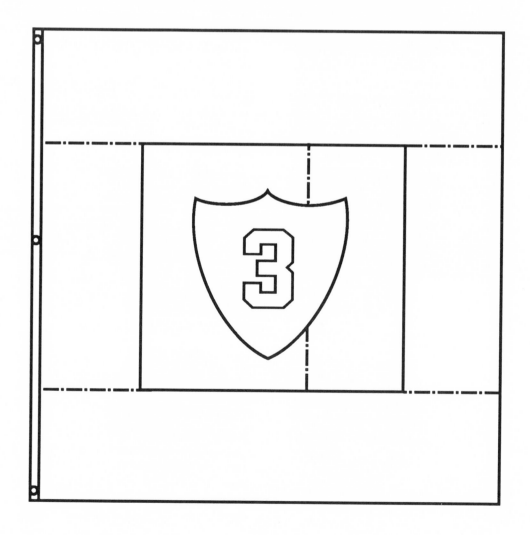

# Regimental Flags

*Color sergeant of the 108th Regiment U.S. Colored Troops, with regimental flag. Each infantry regiment had a blue silk flag similar to the one shown. This is a regulation flag.*

*A non-regulation regimental flag of the 24th U.S. Colored Troops attributed to David Bustill Bowser. Its motto, "Let Soldiers in War be Citizens in Peace" is most significant in the spirit of Frederick Douglass. The flag was presented by the citizens of Philadelphia.*

## David Bustill Bowser

It was not uncommon for men who participated in the Civil War to have fathers or grandfathers who participated in the Revolutionary War. David B. Bowser's grandfather was a baker in the Continental Army and later became one of the first black teachers in Pennsylvania. Bowser, 41-years-of-age at the time that the Civil War began, was an established artist and painter of signs in Philadelphia.

One of his contributions in the Civil War was the distinct non-regimental flags of the colored regiments. He was hired by the Supervisory Committee for Recruiting Colored Regiments of Philadelphia to paint the regimental flags of the Camp William Penn Regiments. These flags were of regimental size and often contained the national arms on the reverse and an allegorical painting depicting various scenes of the black man in uniform. The flag would also be inscribed with a "motto" and the name of the organization that presented the flag. He also painted similar flags for other colored regiments, and he sold albumen photos of both sides of the flags in carte de visite format. Some of them have a Bowser imprint on the reverse, and none of the flags are known to have existed.

Bowser took pride in having painted live portraits of Abraham Lincoln and John Brown. The John Brown painting was on one side of the flag of the 32nd U.S.C.T, a William Penn Regiment.

Bowser's name appears on the bottom of the two "Men of Color" Philadelphia Broadsides for the recruitment of the black man to serve his country.

[Further information on the flags of David Bustill Bowser can be found in Richard Sauer's *Advance The Colors*, Capitol Preservation Committee, Common-wealth of Pennsylvania, 1987.]

*Obverse (left) and reverse (right) of the regimental color of the 6th U.S. Colored Troops. The artwork on this flag is also attributed to David Bustill Bowser of Philadelphia and has the motto "Freedom for All" on the obverse. This flag was rescued by Sergeant Major Thomas R. Hawkins during the assault at New Market Heights, Virginia, on September 29, 1864. Five years after the end of the war, Hawkins received the Medal of Honor for his valor.*

## Flag Raising Ceremonies 3d Regiment U.S.C.T.

Traditionally in white regiments, the presentation of the colors was an occasion to be shared by the group presenting the colors, local citizens, and the regiment; there was no difference in the flag presentation ceremonies of black regiments. Leading public officials would give patriotic speeches, and the regiment would have an open house. The soldiers would perform the regimental drill and parade before the guests. If they didn't have their own band, a local regiment would lend their talents to the occasion. The flags served as a link between the home and community and their obligation to perform with honor and the men in the field.

The flag raising ceremony of the 3rd Regiment U.S.C.T. at Camp William Penn was the first for the eleven regiments of black troops at the Camp. Guests of the 3rd arrived by train via the North Pennsylvania Railroad and walked to the tented encampment. The soldiers went through the regimental drill, and at the close of the drill the American flag was raised. Two bands immediately struck up "The Star Spangled Banner," and the crowd gave its cheering approval.

The keynote speaker, Mr. George H. Earle, spoke of God and the country. He thrilled the audience when he stated: "Our country now calls upon the colored man to defend the flag you have just raised. That flag which is at this time especially the flag of freedom. You are organizing that you may say to foreign states, who would interfere in our affairs, 'Stand Back!' and to the Rebel hordes, 'Disperse!' Your enemies around you and your enemies in the South have opposed arming you—first, because a musket in your hands was the embodiment of power that might prove hurtful to them and second, because the arming of you was calculated to advance your social status. Never was a colored man more respected than now. Your enemies have said you would not fight. You have already shown how base was that charge. Could you not fight for freedom? Could you not feel for your own children? Do you not realize that when you struggle for the Union, there would be a feeling of gratitude for you hereafter? If you have not fought heretofore, it was not from want of courage, nor from want of loyalty, nor honesty of purpose" (Liberator, August 13, 1863).

The regimental color was presented by a committee of ladies sponsored by the Supervisory Committee for Recruiting Colored Troops of Philadelphia on the evening of November 17, 1863. This color was regulation size but illustrated a non-regulation painting by David Bustill Bowser for a supposed cost of $150.00.

There are countless stories of gallantry by both white and black soldiers who protected their flag. One such story is that of the 35th Regiment U.S.C.T. Colonel James Beecher of the 35th U.S.C.T. was in the North when the 35th engaged the enemy in their first battle at Olustee, Florida, on February 20, 1864. One of the officers wrote to Colonel Beecher describing the incident: "Our men were brave beyond description, and as their comrades fell around them, they stood up nobly without once shrinking. When the right arm of our color sergeant was broken, he knelt down and held up the dear old flag with his left until he was relieved" (Smith, p. 313).

# MEN OF COLOR

## IN CONSEQUENCE OF

## INDISPOSITION,

### OF

# FRED'K DOUGLASS

## The Meeting for Promoting Recruiting for

## 3d REGIMENT

# U.S. COLORED TROOPS

## IS POSTPONED UNTIL

# FRIDAY, JULY 24, 1863.

*The 3d Regiment U.S. Colored Troops was the first of 11 regiments and an independent company (100 days), organized at Camp William Penn.*

## Mottos of Colored Troops

Regiments were presented with the National Standard (American flag), a regimental flag, sometimes a state flag, and also sometimes a non-regulation regimental flag.

The National Standard of each regiment was inscribed with the regimental designation and the battle honors each acquired. Many of the regiments also used mottos for their soldiers; they were inscribed on non-regulation regimental flags. The following list provides the inscriptions of various flags of regiments and the type of flag that it was inscribed upon.

| Regiment | Flag Type | Inscription |
| --- | --- | --- |
| 2d U.S. Colored Cavalry | National Standard | SUFFOLK<br>NEW MARKET HEIGHTS |
| 5th U.S. Colored Heavy | Regimental | Presented by the<br>Artillery Colored Citizens<br>of Natchez, Miss.<br>To the 5th Regt.<br>U.S. Heavy Artillery "C" |
| 10th U.S. Colored Heavy Artillery | Soldiers Memorial | WE FIGHT FOR OUR<br>RIGHTS, LIBERTY,<br>JUSTICE, AND UNION |
| 11th U.S. Colored Heavy Artillery | Soldiers Memorial | FREEDOM TO ALL,<br>DEATH TO COPPERHEADS<br>AND TRAITORS |
| 1st Regt. U.S.C.T. | National Standard | PETERSBURG<br>NEW MARKET HEIGHTS |
| 3d U.S. Colored Infantry | Non-Regulation Regimental | RATHER DIE FREEMEN<br>THAN LIVE TO BE A SLAVE |
| 4th U.S. Colored Infantry | National Standard | PETERSBURG<br>NEW MARKET HEIGHTS |
| 4th U.S. Colored Infantry | Regimental | FOURTH REGIMENT,<br>U.S. COLORED INFANTRY |
| 5th U.S. Colored Infantry | National Standard | PETERSBURG<br>NEW MARKET HEIGHTS |
| 6th U.S. Colored Infantry | National Standard | PETERSBURG<br>NEW MARKET HEIGHTS |
| 6th U.S. Colored Infantry | Non-Regulation Regimental | FREEDOM FOR ALL<br>Presented by the Colored Ladies<br>of Philadelphia Aug. 31st, 1863 |

| | | |
|---|---|---|
| 12th U.S. Colored Infantry | Non-Regulation Regimental | LIBERTY OR DEATH |
| 13th U.S. Colored Infantry | Regimental | 13 REGIMENT U.S. COLORED INFANTRY |
| 22nd U.S. Colored Infantry | National Standard | PETERSBURG NEW MARKET HEIGHTS |
| 22nd U.S. Colored Infantry | Non-Regulation Regimental | SIC SEMPER TYRANNIS (May it be ever thus to tyrants) |
| 24th U.S. Colored Infantry | Non-Regulation Regimental | LET SOLDIERS IN WAR BE CITIZENS IN PEACE Presented by the citizens of Philad April 14, 1865 |
| 25th U.S. Colored Infantry | Non-Regulation Regimental | STRIKE FOR GOD AND LIBERTY |
| 26th U.S. Colored Infantry | Regimental | GOD AND LIBERTY |
| 34th U.S. Colored Infantry | National Standard | MORRIS ISLAND CHARLESTOWN |
| 36th U.S. Colored Infantry | National Standard | NEW MARKET HEIGHTS 36th REGT. 2d BRIG. 3d DIV. 24 AC |
| 37th U.S. Colored Infantry | National Standard | NEW MARKET HEIGHTS 37th REGT. 1 BRIG. 3d DIV. 24 AC |
| 38th U.S. Colored Infantry | National Standard | NEW MARKET HEIGHTS |
| 45th U.S. Colored Infantry | Non-Regulation Regimental | ONE CAUSE ONE COUNTRY |
| 51st U.S. Colored Infantry | National Standard | MILLIKENS BEND FORT BLAKELY |
| 55th U.S. Colored Infantry | National Standard | GUN TOWN |
| 73rd U.S. Colored Infantry | National Standard | PORT HUDSON FORT BLAKELY |
| 75th U.S. Colored Infantry | National Standard | PORT HUDSON |
| 77th U.S.C.T. Company D Infantry | Soldiers Memorial | DEEDS NOT WORDS — VICTORY OR DEATH |
| 81st U.S. Colored Infantry | National Standard | PORT HUDSON |

| | | |
|---|---|---|
| 82nd U.S. Colored Infantry | National Standard | PORT HUDSON<br>PINE BARREN CREEK<br>MARIANNA FORT BLAKELY<br>BLAKELY |
| 84th U.S. Colored Infantry | National Standard | 84th REGT U.S. Colored Infantry<br>Port Hudson, La.<br>July 1863 Mansura, La.<br>May 1863 Bayou De Glaise, La.<br>May 1864<br>White Ranch, Texas<br>May 1865 Pleasant Hill |
| 92nd U.S. Colored Infantry | National Standard | PLEASANT HILL<br>MANSURA YELLOW BAYOU |
| 96th U.S. Colored Infantry | National Standard | FORT GAINES<br>PORT HUDSON<br>FORT MORGAN<br>FORT BLAKELY |
| 127th U.S.C.T. | Non-Regulation<br>Regimental | WE WILL PROVE<br>OURSELVES MEN |
| 12th Regt. Infantry | Soldiers Memorial | Honored Gratitude<br>to Corps d'Afrique those<br>who have filled the measure<br>of the country's Glory. |
| 54th Mass. Vol. Infantry | Non-Regulation<br>Regimental | IN HOC SIGNO VINCES<br>(In this sig conquer) |
| 1st Regt. North Carolina | National Standard | 1 Regiment N.C.C Volunteers<br>Presented to the 1 Regiment<br>N.C.C. Volunteers by<br>Colored Women of Newberne, N.C. |
| 1st South Carolina | National Standard | God Gives Liberty Vol. (A.D.) |
| 1st South Carolina | National Standard | Presented to the<br>First South Volunteers<br>by the mothers, wives, sisters,<br>and children, January 1863 |
| 1st South Carolina | National Standard | 1st Regt. S.C.V. Vol. (A.D.) |

*This is the flag of the 5th Regiment U.S. Colored Heavy Artillery. The scroll above and below the crossed cannons is inscribed with the words: "Presented by the colored citizens of Natchez, Miss. to the 5th Regt U.S. Heavy Artillery 'C'."*

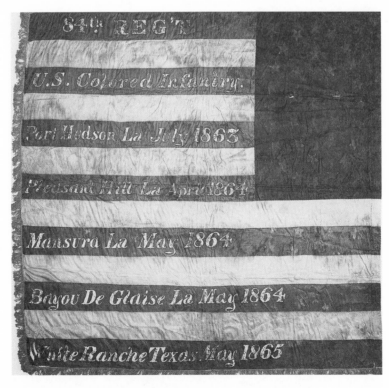

*The original regimental flag of the 84th Regiment of the U.S. Colored Infanry contained the following inscription: "84th REG'T, U.S. Colored Infantry. Port Hudson La. July 1863, Pleasant Hill La. April 1864, Mansura La. May 1864, Bayou De Glaise La. May 1864, White Ranch Texas May 1865."*

*This is the national color of the 37th Regiment, U.S. Colored Troops, 1st Brigade, 3rd Division, 18th Army Corps*

*The 37th Regiment was organized at Norfolk, Virginia, from January 30 to September 19, 1864, as the 3rd Regiment North Carolina Volunteer Infantry (African Descent), to serve three years. Its designation was changed to the 37th Regiment U.S.C.T. on February 8, 1864. It was mustered out of service on February 11, 1867.*

*General Butler had ordered the 37th U.S. Colored Troops to have the words "New Market Heights" inscribed upon their colors for their gallantry in carrying the enemy's works at that point of September 29, 1864. The quartermaster was directed to furnish a new standard of colors to this regiment with the inscription ordered. The flag was supplied, but contained an error—they were part of the 18th Army Corps and not the 24th as the flag indicated. The flag was probably never issued.*

## Battle of Port Hudson

This political cartoon depicts two subjects: "A mule and forty acres," and the battle of Port Hudson. The quote "Here is your mule if you want the forty acres you will have to go to Port Hudson and fight" represents the legislation that promised black men forty acres and a mule.

The Freedman's Bureau Act of 3 March 1865 stated that "The confiscated and abandoned lands would be divided into forty acre pieces and leased to a male head of family for a period of three years...During this time the farmer has the right to purchase the land." General Howard, Head of the Bureau of Refugees, Freedmen & abandoned Lands signed Circular No. 13 on July 28, 1865 to put this Act into effect. The mules were to be provided from the sale of other abandoned lands. Nothing of this Act ever materialized, and the Act was rescinded by Circular No. 15.

Port Hudson was the first major engagement of black soldiers in combat. The First Louisiana Native Guards participated in this battle. As Colonel Stafford turned over the regimental colors to the color guard, he made a brief statement to the soldier: "Color Guard: Protect, defend, die for, but do not surrender these colors." The gallant flag-sergeant, Plancianos, received these words and replied, "Colonel, I will bring back these colors to you in honor, or report to God with the reasons why."

Six times, with desperate valor, they charged over ground where success was hopeless. A deep bayou between them and the enemy at the point of attack rendered it impossible to reach them, yet six times they were ordered forward and six times they went to useless death, until they were swept back by blazing shot and shell. The colors returned, stained with the blood of the gallant soldiers, including that of Plancianos, who reported to God in the battle (Fleetwood, p. 12).

*In some cases, part of the Port Hudson Experiment, black people were promised 40 acres and a mule. This promise was seldom kept.*

## Action at Columbia Bridge

Most students of the Civil War do not associate the black man with the Battle of Gettysburg, but they were involved in the Gettysburg Campaign. One of the early engagements, before the battle at Gettysburg, was the Battle at Columbia Bridge in York County, Pennsylvania.

The War Department had obtained information that a large Rebel force, composed of cavalry, artillery, and infantry, was expected to make a raid in Pennsylvania. Governor Curtin was directed by the President to make plans accordingly to repel the enemy. He declared a state emergency and issued a call for the militia on June 12, 1863.

One of the Confederate objectives was to gain control of the state capitol in Harrisburg. An approach to Harrisburg was to cross the west side of the Susquehanna River at Wrightsville; on the other side of the river was Columbia. The Susquehanna River provided the line of defense for the protection of the capitol.

On June 18, 1863, several hundred black men, many of them contrabands, began digging entrenchments on the western outskirts of Wrightsville. Colonel Jacob Frick had been placed in command of all the bridges and fords on the line of the Susquehanna, and he was ordered to make such disposition as would effectively secure the crossings. This order originated from Major General D.N. Couch, on June 24, 1863. Frick commanded the 27th Pennsylvania Militia (O.R. S I, Vol. XXVII, Part 3, pp. 297, 298).

Along with the men that Colonel Frick had sent to Wrightsville, four companies of minutemen from Columbia, three white and one black, were also in the area to aid in securing the defensive positions west of Wrightsville. The white militia companies refused the tiresome labor assigned to this group, and the all the work of digging rifle pits was performed by black men. These black men were not mustered into the service, as were the other units (O.R. S I, Vol. XXVI, p. 215; S I, Vol. XXVII, p. 277).

When it became apparent that the enemy was going to begin action, the black volunteer was armed and in the trenches with the 26th and 27th Pa. Militia.

During this battle, enemy artillery fired some 40 rounds into the Union forces. Reports state that one black man was decapitated (*Daily Evening Press*, Lancaster, Pa. June 30, 1863). The command had to evacuate across the other side of the Susquehanna to Columbia, and subsequently burn the bridge.

In Colonel Frick's report of July 1863, he spoke of the black men who served with him:

> Before closing this report, justice compels me to make mention of the excellent conduct of the company of negroes from Columbia. After working industriously in the rifle pits all day, when the fight commenced they took their guns and stood up to their work bravely. They fell back only when ordered to do so (O.R. S I, Vol. XXVII, p. 279).

## The Battle of the Crater

This photograph was taken after the Battle of the Crater (July 30, 1864). The soldier on guard duty could be from any of the nine infantry regiments of colored troops that were in the Army of the Potomac. They were in the 4th Division of the 9th Army Corps, and the division had two brigades.

The first brigade, under Colonel Henry G. Thomas, was composed of the 19th and 23d, a battalion, and six companies of the 28th, 29th, and 31st U.S.C.T. On the day of the action, the division numbered 4,300, of which 2,000 were in the second brigade.

Brigadier General Ferrero specially trained the black soldiers to spearhead the assault on the crater, but Generals Grant and Meade changed the order the day before the battle. It was felt that public opinion would be against them if the attack was a failure, and the black troops leading the attack could be considered as having been used as cannon fodder. The attack was a failure, for other reasons, and the outraged Confederates shot many of the colored troops from the rim of the crater after they had surrendered.

*General Edward Ferrero.*

*The charge to the Crater. (Battles and Leaders.)*

First Lieutenant Freeman S. Bawley, 30th U.S.C.T., wrote of his account at the Battle of the Crater (July 30, 1864), in a Washington, D.C. newspaper on November 6, 1864. The following is an excerpt of what happened to the colored soldiers who were taken prisoner by the victorious Confederates. "The colored soldiers that were taken prisoners by the Rebels were part of the grand spectacle for the benefit of the Petersburg citizens. First came General Bartlett (his cork leg had been broken) mounted on a very sorry looking nag without any saddle; then four wounded negro soldiers stripped of everything but their shirt and drawers; then four officers and four more wounded blacks, the four officers, and so on, alternating the white and blacks as far as they went. The unwounded colored soldiers had been sent off to work on the fortifications. They marched through all the streets of Petersburg, taunted by the women, stoned by the boys and cursed by the men."

Losses for the 30th U.S.C.T. at the Battle of the Crater, also known as the Battle of Petersburg, were as follows: 14 enlisted men killed; 6 officers, 138 enlisted men wounded; 5 officers, 64 enlisted men missing.

## The Battle of Olustee

Three colored regiments participated in the Battle of Olustee, Florida, on February 20, 1864. They were the 8th and 35th U.S. Colored Troops and the 54th Massachusetts Infantry Regiment. Those colored soldiers captured by the Confederates were sent to Andersonville.

## The Fort Pillow Massacre

The Fort Pillow massacre of colored soldiers on April 12, 1864 devastated Battery F, 2nd Light Artillery, and the 11th U.S. Colored Troops (new). An investigation by the U.S. Congress' Committee on the Conduct of the War followed. After this massacre, colored troops had "Remember Fort Pillow" as their battle cry. The Confederate forces were part of Major General Nathan Bedford Forrest's command.

## The Battle of Nashville

The two-day Battle of Nashville, Tennessee, on December 15 an d16, 1864, involved Battery A, 2nd Light Artillery and the 12th, 13th, 14th, 17th, 18th, and 100th Infantry Regiments of the U.S. Colored Troops. This was part of the Franklin and Nashville Campaign. Six officers and 80 enlisted men were killed; fourteen officers and 309 enlisted men were wounded. The 18th Regiment had the heaviest losses.

*A Negro regiment in action. (Harper's Weekly, March 14, 1863.)*

*On February 21, 1865, the 55th Massachusetts paraded through Charleston. This illustration shows the men of the 55th marching with their rifles at right-shoulder-arms and their kepis flopping on the tips of the bayonets.*

## A Manual of Camp and Garrison Duty

Colonel Samuel M . Quincy, 73d U.S. Colored Infantry, wrote *A Manual of Camp and Garrison Duty* in July 1865. The colonel felt that a text book had been long needed to supply more detailed instructions than those found in the regulations. He felt that this manual would help train and form the mind of the disciplined solder. The manual included information on funeral escorts, uniform and dress, and the Manual of the Saber. In the conclusion of the text, Quincy wrote, with respect to the officers, "Their task will be to raise their men in their own estimation; to create and foster among them a feeling of soldierly pride and self respect, causing them to realize that the service required of them is no longer the cowering submission of the slave to his master, but the manly and respectful obedience of the soldier to his officer. The soldier of the Union, white or black, henceforth standing erect and invincible upon the soil of the greatest of free nations, THE UNITED STATES OF AMERICA" (Quincy, p. 43).

This manual had the approval of Brigadier General George L. Andrews, Chief of Staff, Department of Louisiana and Texas. He recommended it for the use of the Volunteer Army (Quincy, p. 3).

When the 73d U.S.C.T consolidated with the 96th, Colonel Quincy became colonel of the newly formed unit. He was discharged from this command and later became colonel of the 81st U.S.C.T. He was breveted brigadier general, and he was also president of the Examining Board for the U.S.C.T., Department of the Gulf, and acting assistant inspector general. He served on the staff at Port Hudson and as military mayor of New Orleans.

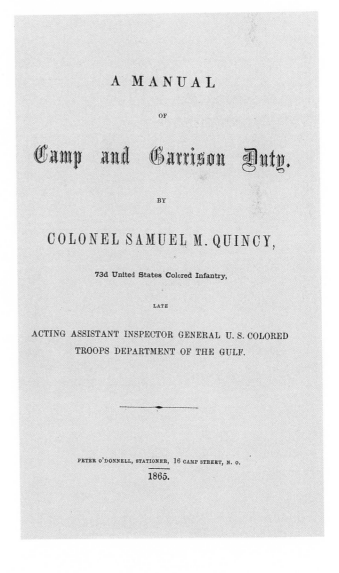

A MANUAL

OF

Camp and Garrison Duty.

BY

COLONEL SAMUEL M. QUINCY,

73d United States Colored Infantry,

LATE

ACTING ASSISTANT INSPECTOR GENERAL U. S. COLORED
TROOPS DEPARTMENT OF THE GULF.

PETER O'DONNELL, STATIONER, 16 CAMP STREET, N. O.

1865.

## Relief Fund

This is an illustration of a Relief Fund Allocation. This one was offered to the parents of Private John Wynhos, 20th U.S.C.T., Marbletown, Ulster County, New York, on December 14, 1863, while the regiment was still being formed. The 20th was not mustered in until February 9, 1864. This document has a New York state seal in the left hand corner, but the regiment was federal not state.

The 20th U.S.C.T. was one of the three regiments formed in New York state, particularly, New York City. They marched down Broadway to the cheers of New Yorkers, eight months after the Race Riots, when black people were killed on the streets, men hanged from lampposts, and a children's orphan asylum was burned.

The regiment was organized under the auspices of the Union League of New York city. The wives, sisters, and mothers of the Union League presented the regiment with its Tiffany-made flags.

The 20th and 26th Regiments were organized on Rikers Island, East River, and the 31st was organized on Harts Island, East River, and completed in the field in Virginia, each to serve three years. The 30th Connecticut Colored Volunteers was consolidated with the 31st U.S.C.T. on May 18, 1864.

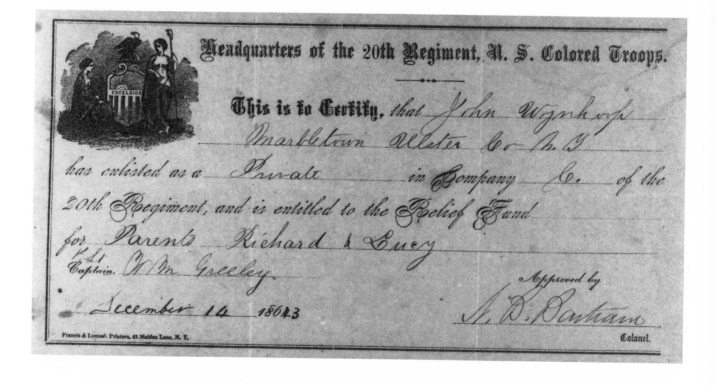

# When the Fighting Stopped

### The Surrender of the Confederate Armies

Black soldiers were at the surrenders of the two largest Confederate armies. On April 9, 1965, General Robert E. Lee surrendered the Army of Northern Virginia to General U.S. Grant in the McLean House at Appomattox Court House, Virginia. There were several black infantry regiments of the 25th Army Corps present at the time: 7th, 8th, 29th, 31st, 41st, 45th, 109th, 116th, and 117th United States Colored Troops.

On April 26, 1865, General Joseph E. Johnston surrendered his army to General William T. Sherman at Bennett's House near Durham Station, North Carolina. The 4th, 6th, 27th, 30th, 39th, and 107th Regiments United States Colored Troops were among those who witnessed this event.

*McLean House, Appomattox Court House, Virginia.*

SURRENDER OF GEN. JOHNSON, APRIL 26TH, 1865.

*In the haste to depict the surrender of Johnston, note that "Johnston" is spelled incorrectly.*

### At War's End

On June 1, 1865, the War Department via the Provost Marshal General's Bureau, directed by Major General R. Saxton, Superintendent of Recruiting for Colored Troops, issued that all enlistments of black troops be immediately discontinued throughout the United States. This directive was also sent to General Palmer in Louisville, Kentucky; General Gilmore in Hilton Head, South Carolina; General Wilson in Macon, Georgia; Colonel Sidell, in Louisville; and Captain Smith in Hilton Head.

At the war's end, soldiers with an honorable discharge from the service were authorized to retain their arms and accoutrements after paying for them in accord with G.O. No. 101 from the War Department Attorney General's Office, issued May 30, 1865. A few weeks later, June 15, 1865, these same honorably discharged soldiers were permitted to retain, without charge, their knapsacks, haversacks, and canteens, as per G.O. No. 114.

The government issued orders relative to the mustering-out of certain volunteers, specifically, organizations of Colored Troops enlisted in Northern States. The Secretary of War directed, via the War Department, Circular No. 44 on September 9, 1865, which stated that all organizations of Colored Troops which were enlisted in the Northern States must be mustered out of service immediately. (See Appendix IX).

General Grant ordered War Department G.O. No. 144 on October 14, 1865. Section IV stated that all sea coast forts, south of Fort Monroe, Virginia, except Forts Taylor and Jefferson, Florida, would be garrisoned by black troops.

Major General E.R.S. Canby, commanding the Military Division of the Gulf, issued General Orders No. 62 from his headquarters, Department of Louisiana, New Orleans, on October 28, 1865. Canby said, "Colored Troops mustered out of service and finally discharged in this Department, will not be permitted for the present, and until further orders, to purchase their arms, under General Orders No. 101, current series, War Department."

## The Last Battle

The last battle with the Confederates was Palmetto Ranch, Brazos Island, Texas, on May 12 and 13, 1865. The 1st Regiment Missouri Volunteer Infantry (colored) was organized at Benton Barracks, Missouri and redesignated into a battalion of the 62d U.S. Colored Infantry. It had the distinction of being the last black unit to engage the enemy in the last battle of the Civil War. They sustained one enlisted man wounded in the action. The battle was a Confederate victory.

The 62d U.S. Colored Infantry was mustered out of service on March 1, 1866.

*Lt. Col. David Branson commanded the 62nd U.S.C.T.*

*Capt. Henry R. Parsons, 62nd U.S.C.T., with his wife Sarah.*

**"MUSTERED OUT" COLORED VOLUNTEERS.**

*"Standing before the office of Colonel PAGE, Quarter-master," says our artist..."the scene which I have sketched was very interesting, occasioned by the meeting of 'mustered out' colored troops with their wives and friends at Little Rock, Arkansas. Just in from Duvall's Bluff, where they had been stationed, their landing created a furor among the resident colored families, many of whom, I am afraid, were disappointed in not meeting those whom they expected. Others rushed into the arms of their husbands with an outburst of uncontrollable affection. Ceremonious introductions between comrades and wives displayed a degree of politeness quite commendatory to all the parties concerned. Children ran about with bundles of blankets or knapsacks for their papas, or begged the privilege of carrying a gun for some sable warrior, and all were in high good humor, with the exception of those who missed the faces of their husbands or brothers."*

(Harper's Weekly, *May 9, 1865.*)

## To all whom it may Concern.

**Know ye,** That _Henry Jones_
a _Private_ of Captain _F. K. Fletcher_
Company, (_F_) _19_ Regiment of _U.S. Colored Troops_
VOLUNTEERS, who was enrolled on the _Sixth_ day of _January_
one thousand eight hundred and _Sixty four_ to serve _three_ years or
during the war, is hereby **Discharged** from the service of the United States
this _fifteenth_ day of _January_ ; 1867 , at _Brownsville_
_Texas_ by reason of _Special Field Orders No 1 Hd Qrs Dist of Tx AGO 24 66_
(No objection to his being re-enlisted is known to exist.*)

Said _Henry Jones_ was born in _Talbot Co_
in the State of _Maryland_ , is _25_ years of age,
_5_ feet _5 3/4_ inches high, _Griff_ complexion _Black_ eyes,
_Black_ hair, and by occupation, when enrolled, a _Farmer_

Given at _Brownsville_ this _fifteenth_ day of
_January_ 1867 .

_☞ *This sentence will be erased should there be anything_
_in the conduct or physical condition of the soldier_
_rendering him unfit for the Army._

[A. G. O., No. 99.]

J E Lockwood
Capt 11 U S C I
_Commanding the Reg't._

A C Musters
D rty Texas

Fred K Fletcher
Capt 19th U S C I
and Bvt Maj Vols Comdg F Co

**Discharge of Henry Jones, Company F, 19th U.S.C.T.**

179

## Veterans

The most important veteran organization for Civil War soldiers of the North was The Grand Army of the Republic, commonly called "GAR." This was a social political organization that acted as a voice for the veterans. The first post was formed on April 1, 1866, in Springfield, Massachusetts.

It was the policy, but not always the practice, of the GAR to not discriminate against the black soldier. Some of the posts were integrated, and some cities that had a large population of black veterans had all black posts. Philadelphia alone had three all black posts.

There was a Blue-Gray Reunion in Gettysburg in 1938. This marked the 75th anniversary of the battle, and there were some black veterans in attendance, although none had actually participated in the engagement at Gettysburg.

The last black man who participated in the Civil War was Sylvester Mack Magee; he served both sides. Magee, born a slave, listed his duties as a body servant, messenger, and in the Vicksburg Burial Details. He died on October 15, 1971 at the age of 130 years, 4 months, and 17 days.

The last black soldier in the Civil War was Joseph Clovese of Company G, 63d U.S.C.T. He attended the Gettysburg Reunion, as well as the last GAR meeting in 1949, as one of the final seven members. Clovese was born a slave, and he fled captivity when the Union Army was approaching their lines. He joined the army and served as a drummer. His final days were spent in Dearborn, Michigan in the Veterans Home, and he died on July 15, 1951.

*Reunion badge of a member of Company G, 5th U.S. Colored Troops, redesignated from the 127th Ohio Regiment Volunteer Infantry (colored).*

*All black soldiers from the State Volunteers, Corps d'Afrique, or the U.S. Colored Troops were entitled to the Grand Army of the Republic Medal, if they were members.*

*This Grand Army of the Republic veteran from Massachusetts still sits on a horse in military fashion. He may have been in the 5th Massachusetts Cavalry. He has a GAR wreath on his hat. Notice, also, the two reunion ribbons on his coat.*

*25th Army Corps veteran's badge of Private Alfred Willis, Company D, 45th U.S.C.T. Willis was mustered into service on July 1, 1864 and mustered out with his company on November 4, 1865.*

181

## The Buffalo Soldiers

By the end of July 1866 Congress passed Public Act No. 181 to increase and fix the miltary peace establishment, the Army of the United States. This act initiated through War Department General Orders No. 56, August 1, 1866, and stated that all cavalry regiments would include two regiments of black soldiers, and all infantry regiments would include four regiments of black soldiers. The term of enlistment for the cavalry became 5 years, and 3 years for the infantry. The order further stipulated that officers who served with the U.S.C.T. were also eligible as officers of Volunteers.

General Orders No. 92, dated November 23, 1866, identified the two black cavalry regiments as the 9th and 10th, and the four black infantry regiments as the 38th, 39th, 40th, and 41st. General Orders No. 16, dated March 11, 1869, further modified this situation by merging the 38th and 41st regiments to form the 24th U.S. Infantry, and the 39th and 40th to form the 25th U.S. Infantry.

These six regiments were instrumental in the further development of the West. They were commonly known as "Buffalo Soldiers"; the name was given to them by the Indians out of respect. The Army identified the period of settlement in the West as the "Indian Campaigns," which consisted of the years between the Civil War and the Spanish-American War, 1866-1898.

During this period, black soldiers earned a total of 18 Medals of Honor, and seven black sailors were graced with the same honor.

The soldiers of the U.S. Army who earned these medals are as follows:

Boyne, Thomas, Sergeant 9th U.S. Cav. New Mexico
Brown, Benjamin, Sergeant 24th U.S. Inf. Arizona
Denny, John, Sergeant 9th U.S. Cav. Las Animos Canyon, NM
Factor, Pompey, Private Indian Scouts Pecos River, TX
Greaves, Clinton, Sergeant 9th U.S. Cav. Florida Mtns., NM
Johnson, Henry, Sergeant 9th U.S. Cav. Milk River, CO
Jordan, George, Sergeant 9th U.S. Cav. Ft. Tularosa, NM
Mays, Isaiah, Corporal 24th U.S. Inf. Arizona
McBryar, William, Sergeant 10th U.S. Cav. Arizona
Paine, Adam, Private Indian Scouts Canyon Blanco, TX
Payne, Isaac, Trumpeter Indian Scouts Pecos River, TX
Shaw, Thomas, Sergeant 9th U.S. Cav. Carrizo Canyon, NM
Stance, Emanuel, Sergeant 9th U.S. Cav. Kickapoo Springs, TX
Walley, Augustus, Private 9th U.S. Cav. Cuchillo Negro Mtns., NM
Ward, John, Sergeant 24th U.S. Inf. Sioux Campaign
Williams, Moses, 1st Sergeant 9th U.S. Cav. New Mexico
Wilson, William O., Corporal 9th U.S. Cav.
Woods, Brent, Sergeant 9th U.S. Cav.

The next list shows the seven black sailors who received the award during the interim period, 1866 to 1870.

Atkins, Daniel, Ship's Cook Gallant Conduct
Davis, John, Ordinary Seaman Rescue
Johnson, John, Seaman Heroism
Johnson, William, Cooper Rescue
Noil, Joseph B., Seaman Rescue
Smith, John, Seaman Rescue
Sweeney, Robert A., Ordinary Seaman Rescue

*Three unidentified "Buffalo Soldiers." The two men below were members of the 25th U.S. Infantry. The photo at bottom, left, was identified as having been taken at Fort Custer, Montana.*

FRANCHISE.
AND NOT THIS MAN?"

(Harper's Weekly, *Aug. 5, 1865.*)

## Appendix I

## Medal of Honor Recipients

### Army

| Name | Regiment | Place of Birth |
|------|----------|----------------|
| Barnes, William H. | 38 USCT | St. Mary's County, MD |
| Beaty, Powhatan | 5 USCT | Richmond, VA |
| Bronson, James | 5 USCT | Delaware County, OH |
| Carney, William H. | 54 MASS | Norfold, VA |
| Dorsey, Decautur | 39 USCT | Howard County, MD |
| Fleetwood, Christian | 4 USCT | Baltimore, MD |
| Gardiner, James | 36 USCT | Glouster, VA |
| Harris, James | 38 USCT | St. Mary's County, MD |
| Hawkins, Thomas R. | 6 USCT | Cincinnati, OH |
| Hilton, Alfred | 4 USCT | Harford County, MD |
| Holland, Milton | 5 USCT | Austin, TX |
| James, Miles | 36 USCT | Princess Anne County, MD |
| Kelly, Alexander | 6 USCT | Pennsylvania |
| Pinn, Robert | 5 USCT | Stark County, OH |
| Ratcliff, Edward | 38 USCT | James County, MD |
| Veal, Charles | 4 USCT | Portsmouth, VA |

### Navy

| Name | Ship | Place of Birth |
|------|------|----------------|
| Anderson, Aaron | USS *Marblehead* | Virginia |
| Blake, Robert | USS *Marblehead* | Virginia |
| Brown, William | USS *Brooklyn* | Baltimore, Maryland |
| Brown, Wilson | USS *Hartford* | Natchez, Mississippi |
| Dees, Clement (Forfeited by Desertion) | USS *Pontoosic* | Cape Verde Island |
| Lawson, John | USS *Hartford* | Pennsylvania |
| Mifflin, James | USS *Brooklyn* | Richmond, Virginia |
| Pease, Joachim | USS *Kearsarge* | Long Island, New York |

## Descriptions of Recipients

### Army

Barnes, William H. Private, 38th Regiment U.S.C.T.
> Place and Date: Chapins Farm, VA. 29 September 1864
> Entered Service:_____ Birth: St. Mary's County, MD
> Date of Issue: 6 April 1865
> Citation: Among the first to enter the enemy works although wounded.

Beaty, Powhatan. First Sergeant, Company G, 5th U.S.C.T.
   Place and Date: Chapins Farm, VA 29 September 1864
   Entered Service: Delaware County, OH Birth: Richmond, VA
   Date of Issue: 6 April 1865
   Citation:  Took command of his company, all the officers having been
      killed or wounded, and gallantly led it.

Bronson, James J. 1st Sergeant, 5th U.S.C.T.
   Place and Date: Chapins Farm, VA 29 September 1864
   Entered Service: Delaware County, OH Birth: Indiana County, PA
   Date of Issue: 6 April 1865
   Citation:  Took command of his company, all the officers having been
killed or wounded, and gallantly led it.

Carney, William H. Sergeant, 54th Massachusetts Volunteer Infantry
   Place and Date: Fort Wagner, SC 18 July 1863
   Entered Service: New Bedford, MA Birth: Norfolk, VA
   Date of Issue: 23 May 1900
   Citation:  When the color sergeant was shot down, this soldier grasped the
      flag, led the way to the parapet, and planted the colors thereon.
      When the troops fell back he brought off the flag, under a fierce
      fire in which he was twice severely wounded.

Dorsey, Decautur. Sergeant, 39th U.S.C.T.
   Place and Date: Petersburg, VA 30 July 1864
   Entered Service: Baltimore County, MD Birth: Howard County, MD
   Date of Issue: 8 November 1865
   Citation:  Planted his colors on the Confederate works in advance of his
      regiment, and when the regiment was driven back to the Union
      works he carried the colors there and bravely rallied the men.

Fleetwood, Christian A. Sergeant Major, 4th U.S.C.T.
   Place and Date: Chapins Farm, VA 29 September 1864
   Entered Service: _____ Birth: Baltimore, MD
   Date of Issue: 6 April 1865
   Citation:  Siezed the colors, after two color bearers had been shot down,
      and bore them nobly through the fight.

Gardiner, James. Private, 36th U.S.C.T.
   Place and Date: Chapins Farm, VA 29 September 1864
   Entered Service: ____ Birth: Gloucester, VA
   Date of Issue: 6 April 1865
   Citation:  Rushed in advance of his brigade, shot a Rebel officer who was
      on the parapet rallying his men, and then ran him through with
      his bayonet.
[Also spelled Gardner]

Harris, James H. Sergeant, Company B, 38th U.S.C.T.
   Place and Date: New Market Heights, VA 29 September 1864
   Entered Service: _____ Birth: St. Mary's County, MD
   Date of Issue: 18 February 1874
   Citation: Gallantry in the assault.

Hawkins, Thomas R. Sergeant Major, 6th U.S.C.T.
   Place and Date: Chapin's Farm, VA 29 September 1864
   Entered Service: Philadelphia, PA Birth: Cincinnati, OH
   Date of Issue: 8 February 1870
   Citation: Rescue of regimental colors.

Hilton, Alfred B. Sergeant, Company H, 4th U.S.C.T.
   Place and Date: Chapin's Farm, VA 29 September 1864
   Entered Service: _____ Birth: Harford County, MD
   Date of Issue: 6 April 1865
   Citation: When the regimental color bearer fell, this soldier siezed the color and carried it forward, together with the national standard, until disabled at the enemy's inner line.

Holland, Milton M. Sergeant Major, 5th U.S.C.T.
   Place and Date: Chapin's Farm 29 September 1864
   Entered Service: Athens, OH Birth: Austin, TX, 1844
   Date of Issue: 6 April 1865
   Citation:  Took command of Company C, after all the officers had been killed or wounded, and gallantly led it.

James, Miles. Corporal, Company B, 36th U.S.C.T.
   Place and Date: Chapin's Farm, VA 29 September 1864
   Entered Service: Norfolk, VA Birth: Princess Anne County, VA
   Date of Issue: 6 April 1865
   Citation:  Having had his arm mutilated, making immediate amputation necessary, he loaded and discharged his piece with one hand and urged his men forward: this within 30 yards of the enemy's works.

Kelly, Alexander. First Sergeant, Company F, 6th U.S.C.T.
   Place and Date: Chapin's Farm, VA 29 September 1864
   Entered Service: _____ Birth: Pennsylvania
   Date of Issue: 6 April 1865
   Citation:  Gallantly siezed the colors, which had fallen near the enemy's lines of abatis, raised them and rallied the men at a time of confusion and in a place of the greatest danger.

Pinn, Robert. First Sergeant, Company I, 5th U.S.C.T.
Place and Date: Chapin's Farm, VA 29 September 1864
Entered Service: Massillon, OH Birth: Stark County, OH
Date of Issue: 6 April 1865

Citation: Took command of his company after all the officers had been killed or wounded and gallantly led it in battle.

Ratcliff, Edward. First Sergeant, Company C, 38th U.S.C.T.
Place and Date: Chapin's Farm, VA 29 September 1864
Entered Service: ____ Birth: James County, VA
Date of Issue: 6 April 1865
Citation: Commanded and gallantly led his company after the commanding officer had been killed; was the first enlisted man to enter the enemy's works.

Veal, Charles. Private, Company D, 4th U.S.C.T.
Place and Date: Chapin's Farm, VA 29 September 1864
Entered Service: Portsmouth, VA Birth: Portsmouth, VA
Date of Issue: 6 April 1865
Citation: Seized the national colors, after 2 color bearers had been shot down close to the enemy's works, and bore them through the remainder of the battle.


## Navy

Anderson, Aaron. Rank and Organization: Landsman, U.S. Navy
Entered Service: Philadelphia, PA
Birth: North Carolina
Citation: Served on board the USS *Wyandank* during a boat expedition up Mattox Creek, 17 March 1865. Participating with a boat crew in the clearing of Mattox Creek. Landsman Anderson carried out his dutiescourageously in the face of a devastating fire which cut away half the oars, pierced the launch in many places and cut the barrel off a musket being fired at the enemy.

Blake, Robert. Rank and Organization: Contraband, U.S. Navy
Entered Service: Virginia
Accredited to: Virginia
Citation: On board the U.S. Steam Gunboat *Marblehead* off Legareville, Stono River, 25 December 1863, in an engagement with the enemy on John's Island. Serving the rifle gun, Blake, an escaped slave, carried out his duties bravely throughout the engagement which resulted in the enemy's abandonment of positions, leaving a caisson and one gun behind.

Brown, William H. Rank and Organization: U.S. Navy
Accredited to: Maryland
Birth: Baltimore, MD
Citation: On board the USS *Brooklyn* during successful attacks against Fort Morgan Rebel gunboats and the ram Tennessee in Mobile Bay on 5 August 1864. Stationed in the immediate vicinity of the shell

whips which were twice cleared of men by bursting shells, Brown remained steadfast at his post and performed his duties in the powder division throughout the furious action which resulted in the surrender of the prize Rebel ram Tennessee and in the damaging and destuction of batteries at Fort Morgan.

Brown, Wilson. Rank and Organization: Landsman, U.S. Navy
    Accredited to: Mississippi
    Birth: Natchez, MS
    Citation: On board the flagship USS *Hartford* during the successful attacks against Fort Morgan, Rebel gunboats and the ram Tennessee in Mobile Bay 5 August 1864. Knocked unconscious into the hold of the ship when an enemy shellburst fatally wounded a man on the ladder above him, Brown, upon regaining consciousness, promptly returned to the shell whip on the berth deck and zealously continued to perform his duties although 4 of the 6 men at this station had been either killed or wounded by the enemy's terrific fire.

Dees, Clement. Rank and Organization: Seaman, U.S. Navy
    [Medal was forfeited by his desertion]
    Birth: Cape Verde Islands
    Citation: Served as Seaman aboard the USS *Pontoosic* during the capture of Fort Fisher and Wilmington, 4 December 1864 to February 1865, carrying out his duties faithfully throughout this period. Dees was recommended for gallantry and skill and for his cool courage while under the fire of the enemy throughout these actions.

Lawson, John. Rank and Organization: Landsman, U.S. Navy
    Accredited to: Pennsylvania
    Birth: Pennsylvania
    Citation: On board the flagship USS *Hartford* during successful attacks against Fort Morgan, Rebel gunboats and the ram Tennessee in Mobile Bay on 5 August 1864. Wounded in the leg and thrown violently against the side of the ship when an enemy shell killed or wounded the 6-man crew as the shell whipped the berth deck, Lawson, upon regaining his composure, proptly returned to his station and, although urged to go below for treatment, steadfastly continued his duties throughout the remainder of the action.

Mifflin, James. Rank and Organization: Engineer's Cook, U.S. Navy
    Accredited to: Virginia
    Birth: Richmond, Virginia
    Citation: On board the USS *Brooklyn* during the successful attacks against Fort Morgan, Rebel gunboats and the ram Tennessee in Mobile Bay on 5 August 1864. Stationed in the immediate vicinity of the shell whips which were twice cleared of men by bursting shells, Mifflin remained steadfast at his post and performed his duties in

the powder division throughout the furious action which resulted in the surrender to the prize Rebel ram Tennessee and in the damaging and destruction of batteries at Fort Morgan.

Pease, Joachim. Rank and Organization: Seaman, U.S. Navy
    Accredited to: New York
    Birth: Long Island, New York
    Citation: Served as seaman on board the USS *Kearsarge* when she destroyed the Alabama off Cherbourg, France, 19 June 1864. Acting as loader on the No. 2 gun during this bitter engagement, Pease exhibited marked coolness and good conduct and was highly recommended by the divisional officers for gallantry under fire.

[As listed in "Medal of Honor Recipients 1863-1978," Prepared by the Committee on Veteran's Affairs, United States Senate, February 14, 1979, Government Printing Office 1979, 96th Congress, 1st Session, Senate Committee Print No. 3.]

### *White Officers in the United States Colored Troops Who Were Recipients of the Medal of Honor*

Appleton, William H. Rank and Organization: First Lieutenant, Company H, 4th U.S.C.T.
    Place and Date: Petersburg, VA 15 June 1864
    New Market Heights, VA 29 September 1864
    Entered Service: Portsmouth, NH
    Birth: Chichester, NH
    Date of Issue: 18 February 1891
    Citation: The first man of the Eighteenth Corps to enter the enemy's works at Petersburg, Virginia 15 June 1864, Valiant service in a desperate assault at New Market Heights, Virginia, inspiring the Union troops by his example of steady courage.

Barrell, Charles L. Rank and Organization: First Lieutenant, Company C, 102d U.S.C.T.
    Place and Date: near Camden, SC April 1865
    Entered Service: Leighton, Allegan County, Michigan
    Date of Issue: 14 May 1891
    Citation: Hazardous service in marching through the enemy's country to bring relief to his command.

Bates, Delavan. Rank and Organization: Colonel, 30th U.S.C.T.
    Place and Date: Cemetery Hill, VA 30 July 1864
    Entered Service: Oswego County, NY
    Birth: Schorarie County, NY
    Date of Issue: 22 June 1891

Citation: Gallantry in action where he fell, shot through the face, at the head of his regiment.

Bennett, Orson W. Rank and Organization: First Lieutenant, Company A, 102d U.S.C.T.
  Place and Date: Honey Hill, SC 30 November 1864
  Entered Service: Michigan
  Birth: Union City, Branch County, Michigan
  Date of Issue: 9 March 1887
  Citation: After several unsuccessful efforts to recover 3 pieces of abandoned artillery, this officer gallantly led a small force fully 100 yards in advance of the Union lines and brought in the guns, preventing their capture.

Brush, George W. Rank and Organization: Lieutenant, Company B, 34th U.S.C.T.
  Place and Date: Ashepoo River, SC 24 May 1864
  Entered Service: New York
  Birth: West Kill, NY
  Date of Issue: 21 January 1897
  Citation: Voluntarily commanded a boat crew, which went to the rescue of a large number of Union soldiers on board the stranded steamer Boston, and with great gallantry succeeded in conveying them to shore, being exposed during the entire time to heavy fire from a Confederate battery.

Davidson, Andrew. Rank and Organization: First Lieutenant, Company H, 30th U.S.C.T.
  Place and Date: At the mine, Petersburg, VA 30 July 1864
  Entered Service: Otsego County, NY
  Birth: Scotland
  Date of Issue: 17 October 1892
  Citation: One of the first to enter the enemy's works, where, after his colonel, major, and one-third of the company officers had fallen, he gallantly assisted in rallying and saving the remnant of the command.

Edgerton, Nathan H. Rank and Organization: Lieutenant and Adjutant, 6th U.S.C.T.
  Place and Date: Chapin's Farm, VA 29 September 1864
  Entered Service: Philadelphia, PA
  Date of Issue: 30 March 1898
  Citation: Took up the flag after 3 color bearers had been shot down and bore it forward, though himself wounded.

Ellsworth, Thomas F. Rank and Organization: Captain, Company B, 55th Massachusetts Infantry
  Place and Date: Honey Hill, SC 30 November 1864
  Birth: Ipswich, MA

Date of Issue: 18 November 1895
Citation: Under a heavy fire carried his wounded commanding officer from the field.

Evans, Ira H. Rank and Organization: Captain, Company B, 116th U.S.C.T.
  Place and Date: Hatchers Run, VA 2 April 1865
  Entered Service: Barre, VT
  Birth: Piermont, NH
  Date of Issue: 24 June 1892
  Citation: Voluntarily passed; between the lines, under a heavy fire from the enemy, and obtained important information.

Merriam Henry C. Rank and Organization: Lieutenant Colonel, 73d U.S.C.T.
  Place and Date: Fort Blakely, AL 9 April 1865
  Entered Service: Houlton, ME
  Birth: Houlton, ME
  Date of Issue: 28 June 1894
  Citation: Volunteered to attack the enemy's works in advance of orders and, upon permission being given, made a most gallant assault.

Nichols, Henry C. Rank and Organization: Captain, Company E, 73d U.S.C.T.
  Place and Date: Fort Blakely, AL 9 April 1865
  Birth: Brandon, VT
  Date of Issue: 3 August 1897
  Citation: Voluntarily made a reconnaissance in advance of the line held by his regiment and, under heavy fire, obtained information of great value.

Thorn, Walter. Rank and Organization: Second Lieutenant, Company G, 116th U.S.C.T.
  Place and Date: Dutch Gap Canal, VA 1 January 1865
  Birth: New York, NY
  Date of Issue: 8 December 1898
  Citation: After the fuse to the mined bulkhead had been lit, this officer, learning that the picket guard had not been withdrawn, mounted the bulkhead and at great personal peril warned the guard of its danger.

Wright, Albert D. Rank and Organization: Captain, Company G, 43d U.S.C.T.
  Place and Date: Petersburg, VA 30 July 1864
  Birth: Elkland, Tioga County, PA
  Date of Issue: 1 May 1893
  Citation: Advanced beyond the enemy's lines, capturing a stand of colors and its color guard; was severely wounded.

There were 7,122 Officers in the United States Colored Troops; 13 of these officers received the Medal of Honor. This is a higher proportion of officers than in any branch of the military during the Civil War.

## Appendix II

## Executions

The following lists of executions of U.S. Colored Troops are from, "List of U.S. Soldiers Executed by the United States Military Authorities during the late War," A.G.O. 1885.

Fifty-two men in the United States Colored Troops were executed. Below are the offenses that they committed, and the methods of their executions.

| SHOT | OFFENSE | HUNG |
|---|---|---|
| 14 | Mutiny | |
| 6 | Murder | 20 |
| 6 | Rape | 4 |
| 1 | Desertion | |
| | Rape/Murder | 1 |
| Total | | |
| 27 | | 25 |

The first soldier of the U.S. Colored Troops was executed on November 19, 1863. Private Lawson Kemp, Company A, 55th U.S.C.T. was shot for rape; authority was given through a drum-head court martial.

The last soldier of the U.S. Colored Troops executed was Private Lewis Wilson of Company A, 10th Heavy Artillery. He was shot for the offense of murder; authority was given by General Court Martial Order No. 20, Dept. of Louisiana on March 6, 1866.

The following regiments of the U.S. Colored Troops had men executed.

### Cavalry

| Regiment | No. of Men |
|---|---|
| 1st | 1 |
| 6th | 1 |
| | |
| Total | 2 |

### Artillery

| Regiment | No. of Men |
|---|---|
| 1st | 4 |
| 3rd | 1 |
| 5th | 1 |
| 6th | 2 |
| 10th | 1 |
| 11th | 1 |
| 13th | 1 |
| | |
| Total | 11 |

### Infantry

| Regiment | No. of Men | Regiment | No. of Men |
|---|---|---|---|
| 2d | 2 | 55th | 1 |
| 3d | 6 | 57th | 1 |
| 10th | 1 | 66th | 1 |
| 21st | 2 | 69th | 1 |
| 37th | 1 | 79th | 1 |
| 38th | 3 | 96th | 1 |
| 48th | 2 | 104th | 2 |
| 49th | 2 | 116th | 2 |
| 52d | 8 | Unassigned | 1 |
| 53d | 1 | | |

Total 39

## Appendix III

## Corps d'Afrique Regiments Redesignated into the United States Colored Troops

The Corps d'Afrique, United States Volunteers, was a particular branch of the military independent of the United States Colored Troops until it was amalgamated into the U.S.C.T. This list includes those state regiments that were redesignated into the Corps d'Afrique and then further redesignated into the U.S.C.T., as compiled in *A Compendium of the War of the Rebellion* by Frederick H. Dyer, Volume III, pp. 1718-1720.

| Corps d' Afrique | Date(s) of Organization | Unit Redesignation |
|---|---|---|
| *Cavalry* | | |
| 1st Regiment | September 12, 1863 | 4th U.S. Colored Cavalry |
| *Artillery (Heavy)* | | |
| 1st Regiment | November 19, 1863 from 1st Louisiana Colored Heavy Artillery | 10th U.S. Colored Artillery (Heavy) |
| *Engineers* | | |
| 1st Regiment | April 28, 1863 | 95th U.S.C.T. |
| 2nd Regiment | August 15, 1863 | 96th U.S.C.T. |
| 3rd Regiment | August 26, 1863 | 97th U.S.C.T. |
| 4th Regiment | September 3, 1863 | 98th U.S.C.T. |
| 5th Regiment | February 10, 1864, from 15th Infantry Corps d'Afrique | 99th U.S.C.T. |
| *Infantry* | | |
| 1st Regiment | June 6, 1863, from 1st Louisiana Native Guard Infantry | 73rd U.S.C.T. |
| 2nd Regiment | June 6, 1863, from 2nd Louisiana Native Guard Infantry | 74th U.S.C.T. |

| | | |
|---|---|---|
| 3rd Regiment | June 6, 1863, from 3rd Louisiana Native Guard Infantry | 75th U.S.C.T. |
| 4th Regiment | June 6, 1863, from 4th Louisiana Native Guard Infantry | 76th U.S.C.T. |
| 5th Regiment | December 8, 1863 | 77th U.S.C.T. |
| 6th Regiment | June 6, 1863, from 1st Regiment Ullman's Brigade | 78th U.S.C.T. |
| 7th Regiment | June 6, 1863, from 2nd Regiment Ullman's Brigade | 79th (old) U.S.C.T. |
| 8th Regiment | June 6, 1863, from 3rd Regiment Ullman's Brigade | 80th U.S.C.T. |
| 9th Regiment | June 6, 1863, from 4th Regiment Ullman's Brigade | 81st U.S.C.T. |
| 10th Regiment | June 6, 1863, from 5th Regiment Ullman's Brigade | 82nd U.S.C.T. |
| 11th Regiment | August 17, 1863 | 83rd (old) U.S.C.T. |
| 12th Regiment | September 24, 1863 | 84th U.S.C.T. |
| 13th Regiment | September 1863 | 85th U.S.C.T. |
| 14th Regiment | August 12, 1863 | 86th U.S.C.T. |
| 15th Regiment | August 27, 1863 Corps d'Afrique | 5th Engineers |
| 16th Regiment | October 8, 1863 | 87th (old) U.S.C.T. |
| 17th Regiment | September 24, 1863 | 88th (old) U.S.C.T. |
| 18th Regiment | October 9, 1863 | 89th U.S.C.T. |
| 19th Regiment | February 11, 1864 | 90th U.S.C.T. |

| | | |
|---|---|---|
| 20th Regiment | September 11, 1863 | 91st U.S.C.T. |
| 22nd Regiment | September 30, 1863 | 92nd U.S.C.T. |
| 25th Regiment | November 21, 1863 | 93rd U.S.C.T. |

The 15th Regiment Infantry, Corps d'Afrique was redesignated on February 10, 1864; all other regiments were redesignated on April 4, 1864 into the United States Colored Troops.

## Appendix IV

### State Volunteer Regiments Redesignated into U.S.C.T. Regiments

Fifteen states raised Volunteer Regiments that were redesignated into the United States Colored Troops. This does not include those regiments of Corps d'Afrique that were redesignated into the U.S.C.T.

| *State Volunteer Regiment* | *Redesignated U.S.C.T.* |
|---|---|
| **Alabama** | |
| Artillery (African Descent) | |
| 1st Seige | 11th Infantry (new) |
| Infantry (African Descent) | |
| 1st | 55th Infantry |
| 2nd | 110th Infantry |
| 3rd | 111th Infantry |
| 4th | 106th Infantry |
| **Arkansas** | |
| Light Artillery (Colored) | 2nd Light Artillery |
| 1st Battery | Battery H |
| Infantry (African Descent) | |
| 1st | 46th Infantry |
| 2nd | 54th Infantry |
| 3rd | 56th Infantry |
| 4th | 57th Infantry |
| 5th | 112th Infantry |
| 6th | 113th Infantry |
| **Connecticut** | |
| Infantry (Colored) | |
| 30th (Battalion) | 31st Infantry |
| **Indiana** | |
| Infantry (Colored) | |
| 28th | 29th Infantry |
| **Iowa** | |
| Infantry (African Descent) | |
| 1st | 60th Infantry |
| **Kansas** | |
| Infantry (Colored) | |
| 1st | 79th Infantry (new) |
| 2nd | 83rd Infantry (new) |

## Louisiana
### Light Artillery (African Descent)

| | |
|---|---|
| 1st Battery | 2nd Light Artillery Battery C |
| 2nd Battery | 2nd Light Artillery Battery D |
| 3rd Battery | 2nd Light Artillery Battery E |

### Infantry (African Descent)

| | |
|---|---|
| 7th | 64th Infantry |
| 8th | 47th Infantry |
| 9th | 63rd Infantry |
| 9th | 5th Heavy Artillery |
| 10th | 48th Infantry |
| 11th | 49th Infantry |
| 12th | 50th Infantry Michigan |

### Infantry (Colored)

| | |
|---|---|
| 1st | 102nd Infantry |

## Mississippi
### Cavalry (African Descent)

| | |
|---|---|
| 1st | 3rd Cavalry |

### Heavy Artillery (African Descent)

| | |
|---|---|
| 1st | 4th Heavy Artillery to 5th Heavy Artillery |
| 2nd | 6th Heavy Artillery |

### Infantry (African Descent)

| | |
|---|---|
| 1st | 51st Infantry |
| 2nd | 52nd Infantry |
| 3rd | 53rd Infantry |
| 4th | 66th Infantry |
| 6th | 58th Infantry |

## Missouri
### Infantry (African Descent)

| | |
|---|---|
| 1st | 62nd Infantry |
| 2nd | 65th Infantry |
| 3rd | 67th Infantry |
| 4th | 68th Infantry |

## North Carolina
### Heavy Artillery (Colored)

| | |
|---|---|
| 1st | 14th Heavy Artillery |

199

Infantry
    1st                                   35th Infantry
    2nd                                 36th Infantry
    3rd                                 37th Infantry

Ohio
    Infantry
        127th                            5th Infantry

Rhode Island
    Heavy Artillery (Colored)
        14th                     8th then 11th Artillery
                                      (Heavy)

South Carolina
    Infantry (African Descent)
        1st                        33rd Infantry
        2nd                      34th Infantry
        3rd                      21st Infantry
        4th                      21st Infantry

Tennessee
    Heavy Artillery (African Descent)
        1st                     3rd Heavy Artillery
        2nd                    4th Heavy Artillery

    Light Artillery (African Descent)
        Memphis                  Light Artillery
                                   Battery F

    Infantry (African Descent)
        1st                     59th Infantry
        2nd                    61st Infantry

## Appendix V

### State Volunteers

The following states raised black volunteers which maintained their state identifications throughout their periods of service.

Connecticut
   (Colored) Infantry
      29th (3 years)

Kansas
   (Colored) Light Artillery
      Independent Battery (1 year) Infantry
         Leavenworth Militia (20 days)

Louisiana (African Descent)
   Infantry
      6th (60 days)
      7th (60 days)

Massachusetts
   Cavalry
      5th
   Infantry
      54th
      55th

Missouri (Colored)
   Infantry
      2nd Battalion, St. Louis City Guard (37 days)

Pennsylvania (Colored) Infantry
   Independent Company (100 days)

Virginia (Colored) Infantry
   Company A, Unassigned (1 year)

## Appendix VI

### Recruiters of Black Soldiers

Many recruiters of black soldiers were never recorded. The following lists of known recruiters indicate, where possible, the regiment, state or department to which the recruiters were associated.

### *Black Recruiters*

Francis A. Boyd, Chaplain, 109th U.S.C.T. (Appointment Revoked)
William Wells Brown, Massachusetts
Martin R. Delaney, Major, 104th and 105th U.S.C.T. and Massachusetts
Frederick Douglass, Universal in his recruiting
George T. Downing, Massachusetts
Henry Highland Garney, Massachusetts
John Jones, Ohio
John Mercer Langston, Ohio
John S. Rock, Massachusetts
Henry M. Turner, Chaplain, 1st U.S.C.T.
O.S.B. Wall, Captain, appointed and awaiting muster 104th U.S.C.T. and Massachusetts
Garland S. White, Captain, 28th U.S.C.T.

### *White Recruiters*

Governor John A. Andrew, Massachusetts
William Birny, Washington, D.C. and Maryland
Major General Ambrose E. Burnside, Tennessee
Major General Benjamin F. Butler, Louisiana
Brigadier General Augustus Chetlain, Tennessee and Kentucky
Senator James H. Lane, Kansas
Major Reuben D. Musey, Commissioner for black troops Middle and East Tennessee; replaced Major Stearns as Commissioner for Recruiting of Colored Troops
Brigadier General Lorenzo Thomas, Upper Mississippi Valley
Governor David Tod, Ohio
Brigadier General Daniel Ullman, Department of the Gulf
Thomas Webster, Philadelphia, Chairman of the Supervisory Committee for recruiting Colored Troops, Camp William Penn
Brigadier General Edward A. Wild, Massachusetts and North Carolina

## Appendix VII

## Songs of the Black Soldiers

**Song:** Marching Song of the First Arkansas
**Words:** Captain Lindley Miller
**Music:** "John Brown's Body"

Oh, we're the bully soldiers of the "First of Arkansas,"
We are fighting for the Union, we are fighting for the Law,
We can hit a Rebel further than a white man ever saw,
As we go marching on.

Chorus:

Glory, glory hallelujah,
Glory, glory hallelujah,
Glory, glory hallelujah,
As we go marching on.

See, there above the center, where the flag is waving bright,
We are going out of slavery; we're bound for freedom's light;
We mean to show Jeff Davis how the Africans can fight,
As we go marching on!

(Chorus)

We have done with hoeing cotton, we have done with hoeing corn,
We are colored Yankee soldiers, now, as sure as you are born;
When the masters hear us yelling, they'll think it's Gabriel's horn,
As we go marching on.

(Chorus)

They have to pays us wages, the wages of their sin,
They will have to bow their foreheads to their colored kith and kin,
They will have to give us house-room, or the roof shall tumble in!
As we go marching on.

(Chorus)

We heard the Proclamation, master hush it as he will,
The bird he sing it to us, hoppin' on the cotton hill,
And the possum up the gum tree, he couldn't keep it still,
As he went climbing on.

(Chorus)

They said, "Now colored brethren, you shall be forever free.

203

From the first of January, Eighteen hundred sixty-three."
We heard it in the river going rushing to the sea,
As it went sounding on.

(Chorus)

Father Abraham has spoken and the message has been sent,
The prison doors he opened, and out the pris'ners went,
To join the sable army of the "African descent,"
As we go marching on.

(Chorus)

Then fall in, colored brethren, you'd better do it soon,
Don't you hear the drum a-beating the Yankee Doodle tune?
We are with you now this morning, we'll be far away at noon,
As we go marching on.

[On the song sheet of the 1st Arkansas printed and distributed by the Supervisory Committee for the Recruitment of Colored Regiments, there is an additional comment by Captain Miller. It reads: "boys sing the song on dress parade with an effect which can hardly be described," and "while it is not very conservative, it will do to fight with."]


**Song:** The Second Louisiana
**Words:** George H. Boker
**Music:** The Charge of the Light Brigade

Dark as the clouds of even,
Ranked in the Western heaven,
Waiting the breath that lifts
All the dread mass, and drifts
Tempest and falling brand
Over a ruined land;—
So still and orderly,
Arm to arm, knee to knee,
Waiting the great event,
Stands the black regiment.

Down the long dusty line
Teeth gleam and eyeballs shine;
And the bright bayonet,
Bristling and firmly set,
Flashed with a purpose grand,
Long ere the sharp command
Of the fierce rolling drum
Told them their time had come,
Told them what work was sent
For the black regiment.

"Now," the flag-sergeant cried,
"Though death and hell betide,
Let the whole nation see
If we are fit to be
Free in this land: or bound
Down, like the whining hound—
Bound with red stripes of pain
In our old chains again!"
Oh! what a shout there went
From the black regiment!

"Charge!" Trump and drum awoke,
Onward the bondment broke:
Bayonet and sabre-stroke
Vainly opposed their rush.
Through the wild battle's crush,
With but one thought aflush,
Driving their lords like chaff,
In the guns mouths they laugh:

Or at the slippery brands
Leaping with open hands,
Down they tear man and horse,
Down in their awful course:
Trampling with bloody heel
Over the crashing steel,
All their eyes forward bent,
Rushed the black regiment.

"Freedom!" their battle-cry—
"Freedom! or leave to die!"
Ah! and they meant the word,
Not as with us 'tis heard,
Not a mere party-shout:
They gave their spirits out;
Tursted the end to God,
And on the gory sod
Rolled in triumphant blood.
Glad to strike one free blow,
Whether for weal or woe;
Glad to breathe one free breath,
Though on the lips of death.
Praying—alas! in vain!—
That they might fall again,
So they could once more see
That burst to liberty!
This was what "freedom" lent
To the black regiment.

Hundreds on hundreds fell;
But they are resting well;
Scourges and shackles strong
Never shall do them wrong.
O, to the living few,
Soldiers, be just and True!
Hail them as comrades Tried;
Fight with them side by side;
Never, in the field or tent,
Scorn the black regiment.

[This song was also titled "The Black Regiment." It was published and distributed by the Supervisory Committee for Recruiting Colored Soldiers.]

**Song:** Give Us a Flag
**Words:** Unknown member of Company A
**Music:** Hoist up the Flag

Oh, Fremont he told them when the war it first begun,
How to save the Union and the way it should be done,
But Kentucky swore so hard and Old Abe he had his fears,
Till ev'ry hope was lost by the colored volunteers.

Chorus:

Oh, give us a flag all free without a slave:
We'll fight to defend it as our fathers did so brave;
The gallant Comp'ny A will make the Rebels dance,
And we'll stand by the Union if we only have a chance.

McClellan went to Richmond with two hundred thousand brave;
He said, "Keep back the niggers" and the Union he would save.
Little Mac had his way, still the Union is in tears,
NOW they call for the help of the colored volunteers.

(Chorus)

Old Jeff says he'll hang us if we dare to meet him armed,
A very big thing, but we are not at all alarmed;
For he first has to catch us before the way is clear,
And that is "what's the matter" with the colored volunteer.

(Chorus)

So rally, boys, rally, let never mind the past;
We had a hard road to travel, but our day is coming fast;
For God is for the right, and we have no need to fear,
The Union must be saved by the colored volunteer.

(Chorus)

Then here is to the 54th, which has been nobly tried,
They were will, they were ready, with their bayonets by their side,
Colonel Shaw led them on and he had no cause to fear,
About the courage of the colored volunteer.*

(Chorus)

* This verse was added sometime after the battle at Fort Wagner.

[Note the similarity in the words to "Give us a Flag" and the words to "Colored Volunteer" as seen earlier in this book.

**Song:** They Look Like Men of War
**Words:** Men of the 9th U.S.C.T.
**Music:** Unknown

Hark! Listen to the trumpeters,
They call for volunteers,
On Zion's bright and flowery mount—
Behold the officers!

Chorus:

They look like men,
They look like men,
They look like men of war.


**Song:** Captain Fiddler's Come to Town
**Words:** 13 year old drummer boy
**Music:** Yankee Doodle

Captain Fiddler's come to town
With his abolition papers;
He swears he's one of Lincoln's men,
He's cutting almight capers.

Captain Fiddler's come to town
With his abolition triggers;
He swears he's one of Lincoln's men,
"Enlisting all the niggers."

You'll see the rebels on the street,
Their noses like a bee gum;
I don't care what in thunder they say,
I'm fighting for my freedom!
My old massa's come to town,
Cutting a Southern figure;
What's the matter with they man?
Lincoln's got his niggers.

We'll get our colored regiments strung
out in a line of battle;
I'll bet my money agin' the South
The rebels will skedaddle.

## Appendix VIII

## Index of Battles

As compiled in the *Official Army Register of the Volunteer Force of the United States Army, 1861-65*, Part VIII, United States Colored Troops and other black units took part in the following battles and skirmishes during the Civil War.

"ALLIANCE," STEAMER, FLA.
(March 8, 1865)
U.S.C.T.— 99th inf.

AMITE RIVER, LA.
(March 18, 1865)
U.S.C.T.— 77th inf.

APPOMATTOX COURT HOUSE, VA.
(April 9, 1865)
U.S.C.T.— 41st inf.

ARKANSAS RIVER, ARK.
(Dec. 18, 1864)
U.S.C.T.— 54th inf.

ASH BAYOU, LA.
(Nov. 19, 1864)
U.S.C.T.— 93rd inf.

ASHEPOO RIVER, S.C.
(May 16, 1864)
U.S.C.T.— 34th inf.

ASHWOOD, MISS.
(June 25, 1864)
U.S.C.T.— 63rd inf.

ASHWOOD LANDING, LA.
(May 1 and 4, 1864)
U.S.C.T.— 64th inf.

ATHENS, ALA.
(Sept. 24, 1864)
U.S.C.T.— 106th, 110th and 111th inf.

BARRANCAS, FLA.
(July 22, 1864)
U.S.C.T.— 82d inf.

BAXTER'S SPRINGS, KAN.
(Oct. 6, 1863)
U.S.C.T.— 83d (new) inf.

BAYOU BIDELL, LA.
(Oct. 15, 1864)
U.S.C.T.— 52d inf.

BAYOU BOEUF, ARK.
(Dec. 13, 1863)
U.S.C.T.— 3d cav.

BAYOU MASON, MISS.
(July--, 1864)
U.S.C.T.— 66th inf.

BAYOU ST. LOUIS, MISS.
(Nov. 17, 1863)
U.S.C.T.— 91st inf.

BAYOU TENSAS, LA.
(Aug. 10, 1863)
U.S.C.T.— 48th inf.

BAYOU TENSAS, LA.
(July 30 and Aug. 26, 1864)
U.S.C.T.— 66th inf.

BAYOU TUNICA, LA.
(Nov. 9, 1863)
U.S.C.T.— 73d inf.

BERMUDA HUNDRED, VA.
(May 4, 1864)
U.S.C.T.— 4th inf.

BERMUDA HUNDRED, VA.
(May 20, 1864)
U.S.C.T.— 1st cav.

BERMUDA HUNDRED, VA.
(Aug. 24 and 25, 1864)
U.S.C.T.— 7th inf.

BERMUDA HUNDRED, VA.
(Nov. 30 and Dec. 4, 1864)
U.S.C.T.— 19th inf.

BERMUDA HUNDRED, VA.
(Dec. 1, 1864)
U.S.C.T.— 39th inf.

BERMUDA HUNDRED, VA.
(Dec. 13, 1864)
U.S.C.T.— 23d inf.

BERWICK, LA.
(April 26, 1864)
U.S.C.T.— 98th inf.

BIG CREEK, ARK.
(July 26, 1864)
U.S.C.T.— Batt'y E, 2d lt. art., 60th inf.

BIG SPRINGS, KY.
(Jan.--, 1865)
U.S.C.T.— 12th hy. art.

BLACK CREEK, FLA.
(July 27, 1864)
U.S.C.T.— 35th inf.

BLACK RIVER, LA.
(Nov. 1, 1864)
U.S.C.T.— 6th hy. art.

BOGGS' MILLS, ARK.
(Jan. 24, 1865)
U.S.C.T.— 11th (old) inf.

BOYD'S STATION, ALA.
(March 18, 1865)
U.S.C.T.— 101st inf.

BOYKIN'S MILL, S.C.
(April 18, 1865)
U.S.C.T.— 54th (Mass.) inf.

BRADFORD'S SPRINGS, S.C.
(April 18, 1865)
U.S.C.T.— 102d inf.

BRAWLEY FORK, TENN.
(March 25, 1865)
U.S.C.T.— 17th inf.

BRICE'S CROSS ROADS, MISS.
(June 10, 1864)
U.S.C.T.— Batt'y F, 2d lt. art.; 55th & 59th inf.

BRIGGEN CREEK, S.C.
(Feb. 25, 1865)
U.S.C.T.— 55th (Mass.) inf.

BRYANT'S PLANTATION, FLA.
(Oct. 21, 1864)
U.S.C.T.— 3d inf.

CABIN CREEK, C.N.
(July 1 and 2, 1863)
U.S.C.T.— 79th (new) inf.

CABIN CREEK, C.N.
(Nov. 4, 1865)
U.S.C.T.— 54th inf.

CABIN POINT, VA.
(Aug. 5, 1864)
U.S.C.T.— 1st cav.

CAMDEN, ARK.
(April 24, 1864)
U.S.C.T.— 57th inf.

CAMP MARENGO, LA.
(Sept. 14, 1864)
U.S.C.T.— 63d inf.

CEDAR KEYS, FLA.
(Feb. 16, 1865)
U.S.C.T.— 2d inf.

CHAPIN'S FARM, VA.
(Sept. 29 and 30, 1864)
U.S.C.T.— 2d cav.; 1st, 4th, 5th, 6th, 7th, 8th, 9th, 22d, 29th, (Conn.,) 36th, 37th, and 38th inf.

CHAPIN'S FARM, VA.
(Nov. 4, 1864)
U.S.C.T.— 22d inf.

CHATTANOOGA, TENN.
(Feb.--, 1865)
U.S.C.T.— 16th inf.

"CHIPPEWIA," STEAMER, ARK.
(Feb. 17, 1865)
U.S.C.T.— 83d (new) inf.

"CITY BELLE," STEAMER, LA.
(May 3, 1864)
U.S.C.T.— 73d inf.

CITY POINT, VA.
(May 6, 1864)
U.S.C.T.— 5th inf.

CITY POINT, VA.
(June--, 1864)
U.S.C.T.— Batt'y B, 2d lt. art.

CLARKSVILLE, ARK.
(Jan. 18, 1865)
U.S.C.T.— 79th (new) inf.

CLINTON, LA.
(Aug. 25, 1864)
U.S.C.T.— 4th cav.

COLEMAN'S PLANTATION, MISS.
(July 4, 1864)
U.S.C.T.— 52d inf.

COLUMBIA, LA.
(Feb. 4, 1864)
U.S.C.T.— 66th inf.

CONCORDIA BAYOU, LA.
(Aug. 5, 1864)
U.S.C.T.— 6th hy. art.

COW CREEK, KAN.
(Nov. 14, 1864)
U.S.C.T.— 54th inf.

COX'S BRIDGE, N.C.
(March 24, 1865)
U.S.C.T.— 30th inf.

DALLAS, GA.
(May 31, 1864)
U.S.C.T.— 110th inf.

DALTON, GA.
(Aug. 15 and 16, 1864)
U.S.C.T.— 14th inf.

DARBYTOWN ROAD, VA.
(Oct. 13, 1864)
U.S.C.T.— 7th, 8th, 9th & 29th (Conn.) inf.

DAVIS' BEND, LA.
(June 2 and 29, 1864)
U.S.C.T.— 64th inf.

DECATUR, TENN.
(Aug. 18, 1864)
U.S.C.T.— 1st hy. art.

DECATUR, ALA.
(Oct. 28 and 29, 1864)
U.S.C.T.— 14th inf.

DECATUR, ALA.
(Dec. 27 and 28, 1864)
U.S.C.T.— 17th inf.

DEEP BOTTOM, VA.
(Aug. 14 to 18, 1864)
U.S.C.T.— 7th and 9th inf.

DEEP BOTTOM, VA.
(Sept. 2 and 6, 1864)
U.S.C.T.— 2d cav.

DEEP BOTTOM, VA.
(Oct. 1, 1864)
U.S.C.T.— 38th inf.

DEEP BOTTOM, VA.
(Oct. 31, 1864)
U.S.C.T.— 127th inf.

DEVEAUX NECK, S.C.
(Dec. 7, 8, and 9, 1864)
U.S.C.T.— 32d, 34th, 55th (Mass.) and 102d inf.

DRURY'S BLUFF, VA.
(May 10, 16, and 20, 1864)
U.S.C.T.— 2d cav.

DUTCH GAP, VA.
(Aug. 24, 1864)
U.S.C.T.— 22d inf.

DUTCH GAP, VA.
(Sept. 7, 1864)
U.S.C.T.— 4th inf.

DUTCH GAP, VA.
(Nov. 17, 1864)
U.S.C.T.— 36th inf.

EAST PASCAGOULA, MISS.
(April 9, 1863)
U.S.C.T.— Cos. B and C, 74th inf.

EASTPORT, MISS.
(Oct. 10, 1864)
U.S.C.T.— 61st inf.

FAIR OAKS, VA.
(Oct. 27 and 28, 1864)
U.S.C.T.— 1st, 5th, 9th, 22d, 29th (Conn.) and 37th inf.

FEDERAL POINT, N.C.
(Feb. 11, 1865)
U.S.C.T.— 39th inf.

FILLMORE, VA.
(Oct. 4, 1864)
U.S.C.T.— 1st inf.

FLOYD, LA.
(July--, 1864)
U.S.C.T.— 51st inf.

FORT ADAMS, LA.
(Oct. 5, 1864)
U.S.C.T.— 3d cav.

FORT ANDERSON, KY.
(March 25, 1864)
U.S.C.T.— 8th hy. art.

FORT BLAKELY, ALA.
(March 31 to April 9, 1865)
U.S.C.T.— 47th, 48th, 50th, 51st, 68th, 73d, 76th, 82d, and 86th inf.

FORT BRADY, VA.
(Jan. 24, 1865)
U.S.C.T.— 118th inf.

FORT BURNHAM, VA.
(Dec. 10, 1864)
U.S.C.T.— 41st inf.

FORT BURNHAM, VA.
(Jan. 24, 1865)
U.S.C.T.— 7th inf.

FORT DONELSON, TENN.
(Oct. 11, 1864)
U.S.C.T.— 4th hy. art.

FORT GAINES, ALA.
(Aug. 2 to 8, 1864)
U.S.C.T.— 96th inf.

FORT GIBSON, C.N.
(Sept. 16, 1864)
U.S.C.T.— 79th (new) inf.

FORT GIBSON, C.N.
(Sept.--, 1865)
U.S.C.T.— 54th inf.

FORT JONES, KY.
(Feb. 18, 1865)
U.S.C.T.— 12th hy. art.

FORT PILLOW, TENN.
(April 12, 1864)
U.S.C.T.— Batt'y F, 2d lt. art.; 11th (new) inf.

FORT POCAHONTAS, VA.
(Aug.--, 1864)
U.S.C.T.— 1st cav.

FORT SMITH, ARK.
(Aug. 24, 1864)
U.S.C.T.— 11th (old) inf.

FORT SMITH, ARK.
(Dec. 24, 1864)
U.S.C.T.— 83d (new) inf.

FORT TAYLOR, FLA.
(Aug. 21, 1864)
U.S.C.T.— 2d inf.

FORT WAGNER, S.C.
(July 18 and Sept. 6, 1863)
U.S.C.T.— 54th (Mass.) inf.

FORT WAGNER, S.C.
(Aug. 26, 1863)
U.S.C.T.— 3d inf.

FRANKLIN, MISS.
(Jan. 2, 1865)
U.S.C.T.— 3d cav.

GHENT, KY.
(Aug. 29, 1864)
U.S.C.T.— 117th inf.

GLASGOW, MO.
(Oct. 15, 1864)
U.S.C.T.— 62d inf.

GLASGOW, KY.
(March 25, 1863)
U.S.C.T.— 119th inf.

GOODRICH'S LANDING, LA.
(March 24 and July 16, 1864)
U.S.C.T.— 66th inf.

GRAND GULF, MISS.
(July 16, 1864)
U.S.C.T.— 53d inf.

GREGORY'S FARM, S.C.
(Dec. 5 and 9, 1864)
U.S.C.T.— 26th inf.

HALL ISLAND, S.C.
(Nov. 24, 1863)
U.S.C.T.— 33d inf.

HARRODSBURG, KY.
(Oct. 21, 1864)
U.S.C.T.— 5th cav.

HATCHER'S RUN, VA.
(Oct. 27 and 28, 1864)
U.S.C.T.— 27th, 39th, 41st, 43d and 45th
inf.

HAYNES' BLUFF, MISS.
(Feb. 3, 1864)
U.S.C.T.— 53d inf.

HAYNES' BLUFF, MISS.
(April--, 1864)
U.S.C.T.— 3d cav.

HELENA, ARK.
(Aug. 2, 1864)
U.S.C.T.— 64th inf.

HENDERSON, KY.
(Sept. 25, 1864)
U.S.C.T.— 118th inf.

HOLLY SPRINGS, MISS.
(Aug. 28, 1864)
U.S.C.T.— 11th (new) inf.

HONEY HILL, S.C.
(Nov. 30, 1864)
U.S.C.T.— 32d, 35th, 54th and 55th
(Mass.,) and 102nd inf.

HONEY SPRING, I.T.
(July 17, 1863)
U.S.C.T.— 79th (new) inf.

HOPKINSVILLE, VA.
(Dec. 12, 1864)
U.S.C.T.— 5th cav.

HORSE-HEAD CREEK, ARK.
(Feb. 17, 1864)
U.S.C.T.— 79th (new) inf.

INDIAN BAY, ARK.
(April 13, 1864)
U.S.C.T.— 56th inf.

INDIANTOWN, N.C.
(Dec. 18, 1863)
U.S.C.T.— 36th inf.

INDIAN VILLAGE, LA.
(Aug. 6, 1864)
U.S.C.T.— 11th hy. art.

ISLAND MOUND, MO.
(Oct. 27 and 29, 1862)
U.S.C.T.— 79th (new) inf.

ISLAND NO. 76, MISS.
(Jan. 20, 1864)
U.S.C.T.— Batt'y E, 2d lt. art.

ISSEQUENA COUNTY, MISS.
(July 10 and Aug. 17, 1864)
U.S.C.T.— 66th inf.

JACKSON, LA.
(Aug. 3, 1863)
U.S.C.T.— 73d, 75th, and 78th inf.

JACKSON, MISS.
(July 5, 1864)
U.S.C.T.— 3d cav.

JACKSONVILLE, FLA.
(March 29, 1863)
U.S.C.T.— 33d inf.

JACKSONVILLE, FLA.
(May 1 and 28, 1864)
U.S.C.T.— 7th inf.

JACKSONVILLE, FLA.
(April 4, 1865)
U.S.C.T.— 3d inf.

JAMES ISLAND, S.C.
(July 16, 1863)
U.S.C.T.— 54th (Mass.) inf.

JAMES ISLAND, S.C.
(May 21, 1864)
U.S.C.T.— 55th (Mass.) inf.

JAMES ISLAND, S.C.
(July 1 and 2, 1864)
U.S.C.T.— 33d, and 55th (Mass.) inf.

JAMES ISLAND, S.C.
(July 5 and 7, 1864)
U.S.C.T.— 7th inf.

JAMES ISLAND, S.C.
(Feb. 10, 1865)
U.S.C.T.— 55th (Mass.) inf.

JENKINS' FERRY, ARK.
(April 30, 1864)
U.S.C.T.— 79th (new) and 83d (new) inf.

JENKINS' FERRY, ARK.
(May 4, 1864)
U.S.C.T.— 83d (new) inf.

JOHN'S ISLAND, S.C.
(July 5 and 7, 1864)
U.S.C.T.— 26th inf.

JOHN'S ISLAND, S.C.
(July 9, 1864)
U.S.C.T.— 7th and 34th inf.

JOHNSONVILLE, TENN.
(Sept. 25, 1864)
U.S.C.T.— 13th inf.

JONES' BRIDGE, VA.
(June 23, 1864)
U.S.C.T.— 28th inf.

JOY'S FORD, ARK.
(Jan. 8, 1865)
U.S.C.T.— 79th (new) inf.

LAKE PROVIDENCE, LA.
(May 27, 1863)
U.S.C.T.— 47th inf.

LAWRENCE, KAN.
(July 27, 1863)
U.S.C.T.— 79th (new) inf.

LITTLE ROCK, ARK.
(April 26 and May 28, 1864)
U.S.C.T.— 57th inf.

LIVERPOOL HEIGHTS, MISS.
(Feb. 3, 1864)
U.S.C.T.— 47th inf.

"LOTUS" STEAMER, ARK.
(Jan. 17, 1865)
U.S.C.T.— 83d (new) inf.

MADISON STATION, ALA.
(Nov. 26, 1864)
U.S.C.T.— 101st inf.

MAGNOLIA, TENN.
(Jan. 7, 1865)
U.S.C.T.— 15th inf.

MARIANA, FLA.
(Sept. 27, 1864)
U.S.C.T.— 82nd inf.

MARION, VA.
(Dec. 18, 1864)
U.S.C.T.— 6th cav.

MARION COUNTY, FLA.
(March 10, 1865)
U.S.C.T.— 3d inf.

McKAY'S POINT, S.C.
(Dec. 22, 1864)
U.S.C.T.— 26th inf.

MEFFLETON LODGE, ARK.
(June 29, 1864)
U.S.C.T.— 56th inf.

MEMPHIS, TENN.
(Aug. 21, 1864)
U.S.C.T.— 61st inf.

MILLIKEN'S BEND, LA.
(June 5,6, and 7, 1863)
U.S.C.T.— 5th hy. art.; 49th and 51st inf.

MILLTOWN BLUFF, S.C.
(July 10, 1863)
U.S.C.T.— 33d inf.

MITCHELL'S CREEK, FLA.
(Dec. 17, 1864)
U.S.C.T.— 82d inf.

MORGANZIA, LA.
(May 18, 1864)
U.S.C.T.— 73d inf.

MORGANZIA, LA.
(Nov. 23, 1864)
U.S.C.T.— 84th inf.

MOSCOW, TENN.
(June 15, 1864)
U.S.C.T.— 55th inf.

MOSCOW STATION, TENN.
(Dec. 4, 1863)
U.S.C.T.— 61st inf.

MOUND PLANTATION, LA.
(June 29, 1863)
U.S.C.T.— 46th inf.

MOUNT PLEASANT LANDING, LA.
(May 15, 1864)
U.S.C.T.— 67th inf.

MUD CREEK, ALA.
(Jan. 5, 1865)
U.S.C.T.— 106th inf.

MURFREESBORO, TENN.
(Dec. 24, 1864)
U.S.C.T.— 12th inf.

N. AND N. W. R.R., TENN.
(Sept. 4, 1864)
U.S.C.T.— 100th inf.

NASHVILLE, TENN.
(May 24, 1864)
U.S.C.T.— 15th inf.

NASHVILLE, TENN.
(Dec. 2 and 21, 1864)
U.S.C.T.— 44th inf.

NASHVILLE, TENN.
(Dec. 7, 1864)
U.S.C.T.— 18th inf.

NASHVILLE, TENN.
(Dec. 15 and 16, 1864)
U.S.C.T.— 12th, 13th, 14th, 17th, 18th and
100th inf.

NATCHEZ, MISS.
(Nov. 11, 1863)
U.S.C.T.— 58th inf.

NATCHEZ, MISS.
(April 25, 1864)
U.S.C.T.— 98th inf.

NATURAL BRIDGE, FLA.
(March 6, 1865)
U.S.C.T.— 2d and 99th inf.

NEW KENT COURT HOUSE, VA.
(March 2, 1864)
U.S.C.T.— 5th inf.

NEW MARKET HEIGHTS, VA.
(June 24, 1864)
U.S.C.T.— 22d inf.

OLUSTEE, FLA.
(Feb. 20, 1864)
U.S.C.T.— 8th and 35th, and 54th (Mass.)
inf.

OWENSBORO, KY.
(Aug. 27, 1864)
U.S.C.T.— 108th inf.

PALMETTO RANCH, TEXAS
(May 15, 1865)
U.S.C.T.— 62d inf.

PASS MANCHAS, LA.
(March 20, 1864)
U.S.C.T.— 10th hy. art.

PETERSBURG, VA.
(June 15, 1864 to April 2, 1865)
U.S.C.T.— 5th (Mass.) cav.; 1st, 4th, 5th,
6th, 7th, 10th, 19th, 22d, 23d, 27th, 28th,
29th, 29th (Conn.,) 30th, 31st, 36th, 39th,
41st, 43d, 45th, and 116th inf.

PIERSON'S FARM, VA.
(June 16, 1864)
U.S.C.T.— 36th inf.

PINE BARREN CREEK, ALA.
(Dec. 17, 18, and 19, 1864)
U.S.C.T.— 97th inf.

PINE BARREN FORD, FLA.
(Dec. 17 and 18, 1864)
U.S.C.T.— 82d inf.

PINE BLUFF, ARK.
(July 2, 1864)
U.S.C.T.— 64th inf.

PLEASANT HILL, LA.
(April 9, 1864)
U.S.C.T.— 75th inf.

PLYMOUTH, N.C.
(Nov. 26, 1863 and April 18, 1864)
U.S.C.T.— 10th inf.

PLYMOUTH, N.C.
(April 1, 1864)
U.S.C.T.— 37th inf.

POINT LOOKOUT, VA.
(May 13, 1864)
U.S.C.T.— 36th inf.

POINT OF ROCKS, MD.
(June 9, 1864)
U.S.C.T.— 2d cav.

POINT PLEASANT, LA.
(June 25, 1864)
U.S.C.T.— 64th inf.

POISON SPRINGS, ARK.
(April 18, 1864)
U.S.C.T.— 79th (new) inf.

PORT HUDSON, LA.
(May 22 to July 8, 1863)
U.S.C.T.— 73d, 75th, 78th, 79th (old)
80th, 81st, 82d, and 95th inf.

POWHATAN, VA.
(Jan. 25, 1865)
U.S.C.T.— 1st cav.

PRAIRIE D'ANN, ARK.
(April 13, 1864)
U.S.C.T.— 79th (new) and 83d (new) inf.

PULASKI, TENN.
(May 13, 1864)
U.S.C.T.— 111th inf.

RALEIGH, N.C.
(April 7, 1865)
U.S.C.T.— 5th inf.

RECTOR'S FARM, ARK.
(Dec. 19, 1864)
U.S.C.T.— 83d (new) inf.

RED RIVER EXPEDITION, LA.
(May--, 1864)
U.S.C.T.— 92d inf.

RICHLAND, TENN.
(Sept. 26, 1864)
U.S.C.T.— 111th inf.

RICHMOND, VA.
(Oct. 28 and 29, 1864)
U.S.C.T.— 2d cav.; 7th inf.

RIPLEY, MISS.
(June 7, 1864)
U.S.C.T.— 55th inf.

ROACHE'S PLANTATION, MISS.
(March 31, 1864)
U.S.C.T.— 3d cav.

ROLLING FORK, MISS.
(Nov. 22, 1864)
U.S.C.T.— 3d cav.

ROSEVILLE CREEK, ARK.
(March 20, 1864)
U.S.C.T.— 79th (new) inf.

ROSS' LANDING, ARK.
(Feb. 14, 1864)
U.S.C.T.— 51st inf.

ST. JOHN'S RIVER, S.C.
(May 23, 1864)
U.S.C.T.— 35th inf.

ST. STEPHEN'S S.C.
(March 1, 1865)
U.S.C.T.— 55th (Mass.) inf.

SALINE RIVER, ARK.
(May 4, 1864)
U.S.C.T.— 83d (new) inf.

SALINE RIVER, ARK.
(May--, 1865)
U.S.C.T.— 54th inf.

SALKEHATCHIE, S.C.
(Feb. 9, 1865)
U.S.C.T.— 102d inf.

SALTVILLE, VA.
(Oct. 2, 1864)
U.S.C.T.— 5th and 6th cav.

SALTVILLE, VA.
(Dec. 20, 1864)
U.S.C.T.— 5th cav.

SAND MOUNTAIN, TENN.
(Jan. 27, 1865)
U.S.C.T.— 18th inf.

SANDY SWAMP, N.C.
(Dec. 18, 1863)
U.S.C.T.— 5th inf.

SCOTTSBORO, ALA.
(Jan. 8, 1865)
U.S.C.T.— 101st inf.

SECTION 37, N. AND N.W.R.R., TENN.
(Nov. 24, 1864)
U.S.C.T.— 12th inf.

SHERWOOD,MO.
(May 18, 1863)
U.S.C.T.— 79th (new) inf.

SIMPSONVILLE, KY.
(Jan. 25, 1865)
U.S.C.T.— 5th cav.

SMITHFIELD, VA.
(Aug. 30, 1864)
U.S.C.T.— 1st cav.

SMITHFIELD, KY.
(Jan. 5, 1865)
U.S.C.T.— 6th cav.

SOUTH TUNNEL, TENN.
(Oct. 10, 1864)
U.S.C.T.— 40th inf.

SPANISH FORT, ALA.
(March 27 to April 8, 1865)
U.S.C.T.— 68th inf.

SUFFOLK, VA.
(March 9, 1864)
U.S.C.T.— 2d cav.

SUGAR LOAF HILL, N.C.
(Jan. 19, 1865)
U.S.C.T.— 6th inf.

SUGAR LOAF HILL, N.C.
(Feb. 11, 1865)
U.S.C.T.— 4th, 6th, and 30th inf.

SULPHUR BRANCH TRESTLE, ALA.
(Sept. 25, 1864)
U.S.C.T.— 111th inf.

SWIFT'S CREEK, S.C.
(April 19, 1865)
U.S.C.T.— 102d inf.

TAYLORSVILLE, KY.
(April 18, 1865)
U.S.C.T.— 119th inf.

TIMBER HILL, C.N.
(Nov. 19, 1864)
U.S.C.T.— 79th (new) inf.

TOWN CREEK, N.C.
(Feb. 20, 1865)
U.S.C.T.— 1st inf.

TOWNSHIP, FLA.
(Jan. 26, 1863)
U.S.C.T.— 33d inf.

TUPELO, MISS.
(July 13, 14, and 15, 1864)
U.S.C.T.— 59th, 61st, and 68th inf.

VICKSBURG, MISS.
(Aug. 27, 1863)
U.S.C.T.— 5th hy. art.

VICKSBURG, MISS.
(Feb. 13, 1864)
U.S.C.T.— 52d inf.

VICKSBURG, MISS.
(June 4, 1864)
U.S.C.T.— 3d cav.

VICKSBURG, MISS.
(July 4, 1864)
U.S.C.T.— 48th inf.

VIDALIA, LA.
(July 22, 1864)
U.S.C.T.— 6th hy. art.

WALLACE'S FERRY, ARK.
(July 26, 1864)
U.S.C.T.— 56th inf.

WARSAW, N.C.
(April 6, 1865)
U.S.C.T.— 1st inf.

WATERFORD, MISS.
(Aug. 16 and 17, 1864)
U.S.C.T.— 55th and 61st inf.

WATERLOO, LA.
(Oct. 20, 1864)
U.S.C.T.— 75th inf.

WATERPROOF, LA.
(Feb. 14, 1864)
U.S.C.T.— 49th inf.

WATERPROOF, LA.
(April 20, 1864)
U.S.C.T. — 63d inf.

WHITE OAK ROAD, VA.
(March 31, 1865)
U.S.C.T.— 29th inf.

WHITE RIVER, ARK.
(Oct. 22, 1864)
U.S.C.T.— 53d inf.

WILLIAMSBURG, VA.
(March 4, 1864)
U.S.C.T.— 6th inf.

WILMINGTON, N.C.
(Feb. 22, 1865)
U.S.C.T.— 1st inf.

WILSON'S LANDING, VA.
(June 11, 1864)
U.S.C.T.— 1st cav.

WILSON'S WHARF, VA.
(May 24, 1864)
U.S.C.T.— Batt'y B, 2d lt. art.; 1st and
10th inf.

YAZOO CITY, MISS.
(March 5, 1864)
U.S.C.T.— 3d cav.; 47th inf.

YAZOO CITY, MISS.
(May 13, 1864)
U.S.C.T.— 3d cav.

YAZOO CITY, MISS.
(March 15, 1865)
U.S.C.T.— 3d cav.

YAZOO EXPEDITION, MISS.
(Feb. 28, 1864)
U.S.C.T.— 3d cav.

# Appendix IX

## U.S. Colored Troops Dates of Organization and Muster-Out, States Furnishing Men, and Armament

As compiled in the *Official Army Register of the Volunteer Force of the United States Army, 1861-65*, a list of all black regiments with dates of organization and muster-out is presented below. All of these units were enlisted for a term of service of 3 years, except the 38th, 41st, 45th, 122nd, 123rd and 127th Infantry which had enlistments of 1, 2 and 3 years. A few other exceptions are noted.

The years listed under the "Armament" heading indicate the year in which a specific weapon was issued to the particular regiment. Several sources provided this information.

| Unit | Date or Period of Organization | Date of Muster-Out | States Furnishing Men | Armament* |
|---|---|---|---|---|
| 1st Cav. | Dec. 22, 1863 | Feb. 4, 1866 | VA | |
| 2d Cav. | Dec. 22, 1863-Jan. 8, 1864 | Feb. 12, 1866 | VA | |
| 3d Cav. | Oct. 9, 1863-Mar. 1, 1864, as 1st Miss. Cav. (A.D.) | Jan. 26, 1866 | MS | |
| 4th Cav. | Sept. 12, 1863-July 19, 1864, as 1st Cav., C. d'Afr. | Mar. 20, 1866 | LA | 1863: Remington .44 M1840 sabre |
| 5th Cav. | Oct. 24-30, 1864 | Mar. 16, 1866 | KY | |
| 6th Cav. | Nov. 1, 1864-June 21, 1865 | Apr. 15, 1866 | KY | |
| 5th Mass. Colored Cav. | Jan. 9-May 5, 1864 | Oct. 31, 1865 | MA | |
| 1st Hv. Arty. | Feb. 20-Nov. 12, 1864 | Mar. 31, 1866 | TN | 1864: Springfield .58 |
| 3d Hv. Arty. | June 5-Dec. 22, 1863, as 1st Tenn. Hv. Arty. (A.D.) | Apr. 30, 1866 | TN | 1863: M1842 rifled .69 1864: Springfield .58 |
| 4th Hv. Arty. | June 16, 1863-Apr. 19, 1864, as 2d Tenn. Hv. Arty. (A.D.) | Feb. 25, 1866 | MS | |
| 5th Hv. Arty. | Aug. 7, 1863-Jan. 17, 1864, as 9th La. Volunteers (A.D.) | May 20, 1866 | MS | 1863: Austrian .54 1864: Springfield .58 |
| 6th Hv. Arty. | Sept. 12, 1863-Jan. 21, 1864, as 2d Miss. Hv. Arty. (A.D.) | May 13, 1866 | MS | 1863: Austrian .54 1864: Enfield .577 & Springfield |
| 8th Hv. Arty. | Apr. 26-Oct. 13, 1864 | Feb. 10, 1866 | KY & RI | 1864: Enfield .577 |
| 9th Hv. Arty. | Oct. 8-Nov. 1, 1864 | Broken up May 5, 1865 | TN | 1864: Enfield .577 |
| 10th Hv. Arty | Nov. 29, 1862-Nov. 8, 1864, as 1st Regt., La. Hv. Arty. (A.D.) | Feb. 22, 1867 | LA | 1864: Enfield .577, M1863 rm |
| 11th Hv. Arty. | Aug. 28, 1863-Jan. 25, 1864, as 14th R.I. Colored Hv. Arty. | Oct. 2, 1865 | RI | Austrian .54 |
| 12th Hv. Arty. | July 15, 1864-July 15, 1865 | Apr. 24, 1866 | KY | 1864: Enfield .577 |
| 13th Hv. Arty. | June 23, 1865 | Nov. 18, 1865 | KY | 1864: Belgian or French rm |
| 14th Hv. Arty. | Mar. 14, 1864-Apr. 30, 1865, as 1st N.C. Hv. Arty. (Colored) | Dec. 11, 1865 | NC | 1864: Enfield .577 |
| 2d Lt. Arty. Btry. A | April 30, 1864 | Jan. 13, 1866 | TN | |
| Btry. B | Jan. 8-Feb. 27, 1864 | Mar. 17, 1866 | VA | |

| | | | | |
|---|---|---|---|---|
| Btry. C | Nov. 6, 1863, as 1st Btry., La. Lt. Arty. (A.D.) | Dec. 28, 1865 | LA | |
| Btry. D | Dec. 21, 1863, as 2d Btry., La. Lt. Arty. (A.D.) | Dec. 28, 1865 | LA | |
| Btry. E | Dec. 1, 1863, as 3d Btry., La. Lt. Arty. (A.D.) | Sept. 26, 1865 | LA | |
| Btry. F | Nov. 23, 1863, as Memphis Lt. Btry. (A.D.) | Dec. 28, 1865 | TN | |
| Btry. G | May 24, 1864 | Aug. 12, 1865 | SC | |
| Btry H. | June 4, 1864, as 1st Ark. Colored Btry. | Sept. 15, 1865 | AR | |
| Btry. I | Apr. 19, 1864 | Jan. 10, 1866 | TN | |
| Independent Btry. | Dec. 23, 1864 | July 22, 1865 | KS | |
| 1st Inf. | May 19-June 30, 1863 | Sept. 29, 1865 | DC | 1863: M1842 smoothbore .69<br>1864: Springfield .58 |
| 2d Inf. | June 23-Nov. 11, 1863 | Jan. 5, 1866 | VA | 1863: M1842 smoothbore .69<br>1864: Springfield & Enfield |
| 3d Inf. | Aug. 3-10, 1863 | Oct. 31, 1865 | PA | 1863: Springfield .58 |
| 4th Inf. | July 15-Sept. 1, 1863 | May 4, 1866 | MD | 1863: Enfield & Springfield |
| 5th Inf. | Aug. 6, 1863-Jan. 15, 1864, as 127th Ohio Inf. | Sept. 20, 1865 | OH | 1863: Springfield .58 |
| 6th Inf. | July 28-Sept. 12, 1863 | Sept. 20, 1865 | PA | 1863: Springfield .58 |
| 7th Inf. | Sept. 26-Nov. 12, 1863 | Oct. 13, 1866 | MD | 1863: Springfield & Enfield |
| 8th Inf. | Sept. 22-Dec. 4, 1863 | Nov. 10, 1865 | PA | 1863: Springfield .58 |
| 9th Inf. | Nov. 11-30, 1863 | Nov. 26, 1866 | MD | 1863: Enfield & Springfield |
| 10th Inf. | Nov. 18, 1863-Sept. 23, 1864 | May 17, 1866 | VA | 1863: Enfield .577 |
| 11th Inf. (old) | Dec. 19, 1863-Sept. 23, 1864 | Consolidated with 113th Regt., Apr. 22, 1865 | AR | 1864: Springfield & Enfield |
| 11th Inf. (new) | June 20, 1863-Apr. 2, 1864, as 1st Ala. Siege Arty. (A.D.) | Jan. 12, 1866 | AL | 1864: Springfield .58 |
| 12th Inf. | July 24-Aug. 14, 1863 | Jan. 16, 1866 | TN | 1863: M1842 rifled .69<br>1864: Enfield .577 |
| 13th Inf. | Nov. 19, 1863 | Jan. 10, 1866 | TN | 1863: altered muskets<br>1864: Enfield .577 |
| 14th Inf. | Nov. 16, 1863-Jan. 8, 1864 | Mar. 26, 1866 | TN | 1863: altered muskets<br>1864: Enfield .577 |
| 15th Inf. | Dec. 2, 1863-Mar. 11, 1864 | Apr. 7, 1866 | TN | 1863: altered muskets |
| 16th Inf. | Dec. 4, 1863-Feb. 13, 1864 | Apr. 30, 1866 | TN | 1863: M1842 rifled .69 |
| 17th Inf. | Dec. 12-21, 1863 | Apr. 25, 1866 | TN | 1863: M1842 rifled .69 |
| 18th Inf. | Feb. 1-Sept. 28, 1864 | Feb. 21, 1866 | MO | 1864: Enfield .577 |
| 19th Inf. | Dec. 25, 1863-Jan. 16, 1864 | Jan. 15, 1867 | MD | 1864: Enfield & Springfield |
| 20th Inf. | Feb. 9, 1864 | Oct. 7, 1865 | NY | 1864: Enfield .577 |
| 21st Inf. | June 19, 1863-Oct. 1, 1864, as 3d & 4th S.C. | Apr. 25, 1866 | SC | 1864: Springfield .58 |
| 22d Inf. | Jan. 10-29, 1864 | Oct. 16, 1865 | PA | 1863: Springfield .58 |
| 23d Inf. | Nov. 23, 1863-June 30, 1864 | Nov. 30, 1865 | VA | 1863: Enfield .577<br>1864: Springfield .58 |
| 24th Inf. | Jan. 30-Mar. 30, 1865 | Oct. 1, 1865 | PA | |
| 25th Inf. | Jan. 13-Feb. 12, 1864 | Dec. 6, 1865 | PA | 1864: Enfield .577 |

| | | | | |
|---|---|---|---|---|
| 26th Inf. | Feb. 27, 1864 | Aug. 28, 1865 | NY | 1864: Enfield .577 |
| 27th Inf. | Jan. 16-Aug. 6, 1864 | Sept. 21, 1865 | OH | 1864: Springfield & Enfield |
| 28th Inf. | Dec. 24, 1863-Mar. 31, 1864 | Nov. 8, 1865 | IN | 1864: Springfield .58 |
| 29th Inf. | 6 companies organized Apr. 24, 1864; 4 companies organized Oct. 23, 1864-Jan. 1, 1865 | Nov. 6, 1865 | IL | 1864: Springfield .58 |
| 30th Inf. | Feb. 12-Mar. 18, 1864 | Dec. 10, 1865 | MD | 1864: Enfield & Springfield |
| 31st Inf. | Apr. 29-Nov. 14, 1864, as 30th Conn. Colored Volunteers | Nov. 7, 1865 | NY | 1864: Springfield .58 |
| 32d Inf. | Feb. 17-Mar. 7, 1864 | Aug. 22, 1865 | PA | 1864: Enfield & Springfield |
| 33d Inf. | Jan. 31, 1863, as 1st S.C. Volunteers (A.D.) | Jan. 31, 1866 | SC | 1863: Austrian & Prussian rm 1864: Belgian & French rm |
| 34th Inf. | May 22, 1863-Dec. 31, 1864, as 2d S.C. Colored Volunteers | Feb. 28, 1866 | SC | 1863: foreign smoothbores 1864: Enfield .577 |
| 35th Inf. | June 30, 1863, as 1st N.C. Volunteers | June 1, 1866 | NC | 1863: Enfield .577 1864: M1863 rifled musket .58 |
| 36th Inf. | Oct. 28, 1863, as 2d N.C. Colored Volunteers | Oct. 28, 1866 | NC | 1864: Enfield .577 |
| 37th Inf. | Jan. 30-Sept. 19, 1864, as 3d N.C. Volunteers | Feb. 11, 1867 | NC | 1863: Enfield .577 1864: M1863 rifled musket .58 |
| 38th Inf. | Jan. 23, 1864-Mar. 30, 1865 | Jan. 25, 1867 | VA | |
| 39th Inf. | Mar. 22-31, 1864 | Dec. 4, 1865 | MD | 1864: Springfield .58 |
| 40th Inf. | Feb. 29, 1864-May 6, 1865 | Apr. 25, 1866 | TN | 1864: Enfield .577, M1842 rifled and smoothbore .69 |
| 41st Inf. (Bn. of ) | Sept. 30-Dec. 7, 1864 | Dec. 10, 1865 | PA | 1864: Springfield .58 |
| 42d Inf. | April 20, 1864-July 6, 1865 | Jan. 31, 1866 | TN | 1864: Enfield .577 |
| 43d Inf. | Mar. 12-June 3, 1864 | Oct. 20, 1865 | PA | 1864: Springfield .58 |
| 44th Inf. | Apr. 7-Sept. 16, 1864 | Apr. 30, 1866 | GA | 1864: Springfield .58 |
| 45th Inf. | June 13-Aug. 19, 1864 | Nov. 4, 1865 | PA | 1864: Springfield .58 |
| 46th Inf. | May 1, 1863, as 1st Ark. Volunteers (A.D.) | Jan. 30, 1866 | AR | 1863: Austrian .54 |
| 47th Inf. | May 5, 1863, as 8th La. Volunteers (A.D.) | Jan. 5, 1866 | LA | 1863: Austrian .58 1864: M1863 rifled musket .58 |
| 48th Inf. | May 6-Aug. 8, 1863, as 10th La. Volunteers (A.D.) | Jan. 4, 1866 | LA | 1863: Austrian .54 1864: M1863 rifled musket .58 |
| 49th Inf. | May 23-Aug. 22, 1863, as 11th La. Volunteers (A.D.) | Mar. 22, 1866 | LA | 1863: Austrian .54 1864: M1863 rifled musket .58 |
| 50th Inf. | July 11-27, 1863, as 12th La. Volunteers (A.D.) | Mar. 20, 1866 | LA | 1863: Enfield .577 1864: M1863 rifled musket .58 |
| 51st Inf. | May 16, 1863-Mar. 7, 1864, as 1st Miss. Volunteers (A.D.) | June 16, 1866 | MS | 1863: Austrian .54 1864: Springfield .58 |
| 52d Inf. | July 27-Dec. 22, 1863, as 2d Miss. Volunteers (A.D.) | May 5, 1866 | MS | 1863: Enfield .577 1864: Springfield .58 |
| 53d Inf. | May 19, 1863, as 3d Miss. Volunteers (A.D.) | Mar. 8, 1866 | MS | |
| 54th Inf. | Sept. 4-Dec. 25, 1863, as 2d Ark. Volunteers (A.D.) | Dec. 31, 1866 | AR | 1863: M1840 rifle & .69 smooth 1864: Springfield, Enfield & foriegn rifled muskets |
| 55th Inf. | May 21, 1863, as 1st Ala. Volunteers (A.D.) | Dec. 31, 1866 | AL | 1863: Enfield .577 1864: Springfield .58 |

| | | | | |
|---|---|---|---|---|
| 56th Inf. | Aug. 12-Sept. 29, 1863, as 3d Ark. Volunteers (A.D.) | Sept. 15, 1866 | AR | 1864: Enfield .577 |
| 57th Inf. | Dec. 2, 1863-Mar. 1, 1864, as 4th Ark. Volunteers (A.D.) | Dec. 13, 1866 | AR | 1864: Enfield .577 |
| 58th Inf. | Aug. 27, 1863, as 6th Miss. Volunteers (A.D.) | Apr. 30, 1866 | MS | 1863: Enfield .577<br>1864: Springfield .58 |
| 59th Inf. | June 6-27, 1863, as 1st Tenn. Volunteers (A.D.) | Jan. 31, 1866 | TN | 1863: Enfield & Springfield |
| 60th Inf. | Oct. 15-Dec. 4, 1863, as 1st Iowa Volunteers (A.D.) | Oct. 15, 1865 | IA | 1863: Enfield .577 |
| 61st Inf. | June 30-Aug. 8, 1863, as 2d Tenn. Volunteers (A.D.) | Dec. 30, 1865 | TN | 1863: Enfield .577 |
| 62d Inf. | Dec. 7-14, 1863, as 1st Mo. Volunteers (A.D.) | Mar. 31, 1866 | MO | 1864: Enfield .577 |
| 63d Inf. | Nov. 19-Dec. 14, 1863, as 9th La. Volunteers (A.D.) | Jan. 9, 1866 | LA | 1863: Enfield .577 & Austrian .54<br>1864: M1863 rifled musket |
| 64th Inf. | Dec. 1, 1863-Feb. 1, 1864 as 7th La. Volunteers (A.D.) | Mar. 13, 1866 | LA | 1864: Enfield .577 |
| 65th Inf. | Dec. 18, 1863-Jan. 16, 1864, as 2d Mo. Volunteers (A.D.) | Jan. 8, 1867 | MO | 1864: Enfield .577 |
| 66th Inf. | Dec. 11, 1863-Jan. 11, 1864, as 4th Miss. Volunteers (A.D.) | Mar. 20, 1866 | MS | 1863: Springfield & Enfield |
| 67th Inf. | Jan. 19-Feb. 13, 1864, 3d Mo. Volunteers (A.D.) | July 12, 1865 | MO | 1864: Enfield .577 |
| 68th Inf. | Mar. 8-Apr. 23, 1864, as 4th Mo. Volunteers (A.D.) | Feb. 5, 1866 | MO | 1864: Enfield .577 |
| 69th Inf. | Dec. 14, 1864-Mar. 17, 1865 | Discontinued September 20, 1865 | AR | 1864: Enfield .577 |
| 70th Inf. | Apr. 23-Oct. 1, 1864 | Mar. 7, 1866 | MS | 1864: Enfield .577 |
| 71st Inf. | Mar. 3-Aug. 13, 1864 | Nov. 8, 1864 | MS | |
| 72d Inf. | Apr. 18-22, 1865 | Discontinued May 3, 1865 | KY | |
| 73d Inf. | Sept. 27, 1862, as 1st La. Native Guards (A.D.) | Mustered-out when terms of service expired | LA | 1862: Enfield .577<br>1864: M1863 rifled musket |
| 74th Inf. | Oct. 12, 1862, as 2d La. Native Guards (A.D.) | Oct. 11, 1865 | LA | 1862: Enfield .577 & M1842 smoothbore .69 |
| 75th Inf. | Nov. 24, 1862, as 3d La. Native Guards (A.D.) | Nov. 25, 1865 | LA | 1862: Austrian .54<br>1864: M1863 rifled musket |
| 76th Inf. | Feb. 10-Mar. 6, 1863, as 4th La. Native Guards (A.D.) | Dec. 31, 1865 | LA | |
| 77th Inf. | Dec. 8, 1863, as 5th Inf., C. d'Afr. | Consolidated with 10th U.S. Colored Hv.Arty., Oct. 1, 1865 | LA | 1863: Austrian .54 |
| 78th Inf. | Sept. 4, 1863, as 6th Inf., C. d'Afr. | Jan. 6, 1866 | LA | 1863: M1842 smoothbore .69 |
| 79th Inf. (old) | Aug. 31, 1863, as 7th Inf. C. d'Afr. | Broken up July 28, 1864 | LA | |
| 79th Inf. (new) | Jan. 13-May 2, 1863, as 1st Kans. Colored Volunteers | Oct. 1, 1865 | KS | 1863: converted muskets |
| 80th Inf. | Sept. 1, 1863, 8th Inf. C. d'Afr. | Mar. 1, 1867 | LA | 1863: M1842 smoothbore .69<br>1864: Enfield .577 |

216

| | | | | |
|---|---|---|---|---|
| 81st Inf. | Sept. 2, 1863, as 9th Inf. C. d'Afr. | Nov. 30, 1866 | LA | 1863: M1842 smoothbore .69<br>1864: Enfield .577 |
| 82d Inf. | Sept. 1, 1863, as 10th Inf. C. d'Afr. | Sept. 10, 1866 | LA | 1863: M1842 smoothbore .69 |
| 83d Inf. (old) | Aug. 17, 1863, as 11th Inf. C. d'Afr. | Broken up July 28, 1864 | LA | 1863: M1842 smooth & Springfield .58<br>1864: Enfield .577 |
| 83d Inf. (new) | Aug. 11-Oct. 17, 1863, as 2d Kans. Colored Volunteers | Oct. 9, 1865 | KS | 1863: Enfield .577 |
| 84th Inf. | Sept. 24-Oct. 16, 1863, as 12th Inf., C. d'Afr. | Mar. 14, 1866 | LA | 1863: Austrian .54 |
| 85th Inf. | Mar. 11, 1864, as 13th Inf. C. d'Afr. | Consolidated with 77th U.S. Colored Inf., May 24, 1864 | LA | |
| 86th Inf. | Aug. 12-Sept. 3, 1863, as 14th Inf., C. d'Afr. | Apr. 10, 1866 | LA | 1863: converted muskets<br>1864: M1863 rifled musket & Enfield .577 |
| 87th Inf. (old) | Oct. 8-16, 1863, as 16th Inf., C. d'Afr. | Subsequently changed to 87th U.S. Colored Inf. (new), Dec. 19, 1864 | LA | 1863: converted muskets<br>1864: Enfield .577 |
| 87th Inf. (new) | Nov. 26, 1864, as 81st U.S. Colored Inf. (new)' designated 87th U.S. Colored Inf. (new) on Dec. 19, 1864 | Consolidated with 84th U.S. Colored Inf., Aug. 14, 1865 | LA | 1863: converted muskets<br>1864: Enfield .577 |
| 88th Inf. (old) | Sept. 24, 1863, as 17th Inf., C. d'Afr. | Broken up July 28, 1864 | LA | 1863: M1842 smoothbore .69 |
| 88th Inf. (new) | Feb. 20-Aug. 10, 1865 | Consolidated with 3d U.S. Colored Hv. Arty., Dec. 16, 1865 | TN | |
| 89th Inf | Oct. 9-Nov. 8, 1863, as 18th Inf., C. d'Afr. | Broken up July 28, 1864 | LA | 1863: M1842 smoothbore .69<br>& Enfield .577 |
| 90th Inf. | Feb. 11, 1864, as 19th Inf., C. d'Afr. | Broken up July 28, 1864 | LA | 1863: Enfield .577 |
| 91st Inf. | Sept. 1, 1863, as 20th Inf., C. d'Afr. | Consolidated with 74th U.S. Colored Inf., July 7, 1864 | LA | 1863: Enfield .577 |
| 92d Inf. | Sept. 30-Oct. 24, 1863, as 22d Inf., C. d'Afr. | Dec. 31, 1865 | LA | 1863: converted muskets<br>1864: M1863 rifled musket |
| 93d Inf. | Nov. 21, 1863, as 25th Inf., C. d'Afr. | Broken up June 23, 1865 | LA | 1863: converted muskets<br>1864: M1863 rifled musket |
| 95th Inf. | Apr. 28, 1863, as 1st Engineers, C. d'Afr. | Consolidated with 87th U.S. Colored Inf. to form 81st U.S. Colored Inf., Nov. 26, 1864 | LA | 1863: Belgian & French rifled musket |
| 96th Inf. | Aug. 15, 1863, as 2d Engineers, C. d'Afr. | Jan. 29, 1866 | LA | 1863: converted muskets |
| 97th Inf. | Aug. 26, 1863, as 3d Engineers, C.d'Afr. | Apr. 6, 1866 | LA | 1863: Belgian & French rm<br>1864: M1863 rifled musket |
| 98th Inf. | Sept. 3, 1863-Mar. 3, 1864, as 4th Engineers, C. d'Afr. | Consolidated with 78th Regt., Aug. 26, 1865 | LA | 1863: converted muskets<br>1864: M1863 rifled musket |
| 99th Inf. (Bn. of) | Aug. 27, 1863, as 15th Inf., C. d'Afr. | Apr. 23, 1866 | LA | 1863: converted muskets<br>1864: M1863 rifled musket |

| | | | | |
|---|---|---|---|---|
| 100th Inf. | May 3-June 1, 1864 | Dec. 26, 1865 | KY | 1864: Enfield .577 |
| 101st Inf. | Sept. 16, 1864-Aug. 5, 1865 | Jan. 21, 1866 | TN | 1864: altered muskets |
| 102d Inf. | Feb. 17, 1864, as 1st Mich. Colored Volunteers | Sept. 30, 1865 | MI | Austrian .58, later M1863 rifled musket |
| 103d Inf. | Mar. 10, 1865 | Apr. 15-20, 1866 | SC | |
| 104th Inf. | Apr. 28-June 25, 1865 | Feb. 5, 1866 | SC | |
| 106th Inf. | Mar. 31-Aug. 10, 1864, as 4th Ala. Inf. (A.D.) | Condolidated with 40th U.S.Colored Inf., Nov. 7, 1865 | AL | 1864: Springfield .58 |
| 107th Inf. | May 3-Sept. 15, 1864 | Nov. 22, 1866 | KY | 1864: Springfield .58 |
| 108th Inf. | June 20-Aug. 22, 1864 | Mar. 21, 1866 | KY | 1864: Enfield .577 |
| 109th Inf. | July 5, 1864 | Feb. 6, 1866 | KY | 1864: Enfield .577 |
| 110th Inf. | Nov. 20, 1863-Jan. 14, 1864, as 2d Ala. Volunteers (A.D.) | Feb. 6, 1866 | AL | 1864: Enfield .577 |
| 111th Inf. | Jan. 13-Apr. 5, 1864, as 3d Regt., Ala. Volunteers (A.D.) | Apr. 30, 1866 | AL | 1864: M1842 rifled .69 |
| 112th Inf. | Apr. 23-Nov. 8, 1864 | Consolidated with 11th U.S. Colored Inf. (old) to form 113th U.S. Colored Inf. (new), Apr. 1, 1865 | AR | 1864: Enfield .577 |
| 113th Inf. (old) | Mar. 1-June 20, 1864, as 6th Ark. Volunteers (A.D.) | Consolidated with 11th U.S. Colored Inf. and 112th U.S. Colored Inf. to form 113th U.S. Colored Inf. (new) on April 1, 1865 | AR | |
| 113th Inf. (new) | Apr. 1, 1865, by consolidation of the 11th (old), 112th, and 113th (old) U.S. Colored Infantries | Apr. 9, 1866 | AR | 1864: Enfield .577 |
| 114th Inf. | July 4, 1864 | Apr. 2, 1867 | KY | 1864: Enfield .577 |
| 115th Inf. | July 15-Oct. 21, 1864 | Feb. 10, 1866 | KY | 1864: Enfield .577 |
| 116th Inf. | June 6-July 12, 1864 | Jan. 17, 1867 | KY | 1864: Enfield .577 |
| 117th Inf. | July 18-Sept. 27, 1864 | Aug. 10, 1867 | KY | 1864: Enfield .577 |
| 118th Inf. | Oct. 19, 1864 | Feb. 6, 1866 | KY | 1864: Enfield .577 |
| 119th Inf. | Jan. 18-May 16, 1865 | Apr. 27, 1866 | KY | 1864: Enfield .577 |
| 120th Inf. | Nov. 1864-June 1865 | Discontinued June 21, 1865 | KY | 1864: Enfield .577 |
| 121st Inf. | Oct. 8, 1864-May 31, 1865 | Discontinued June 30, 1865 | KY | 1864: Enfield .577 |
| 122d Inf. (Bn. of) | Dec. 31, 1864 | Feb. 8, 1866 | KY | 1864: Enfield .577 |
| 123d Inf. | Dec. 2, 1864 | Oct. 16, 1865 | KY | 1864: Enfield .577 |
| 124th Inf. | Jan. 1-Apr. 27, 1865 | Oct. 24, 1865 | KY | |
| 125th Inf. | Feb. 13-June 2, 1865 | Oct. 31, 1867- Dec. 20, 1867 | KY | |
| 127th Inf. (Bn.) | Aug. 23-Sept. 10, 1864 | Oct. 20, 1865 | PA | 1864: Springfield .58 |
| 128th Inf. | Apr. 23-29, 1865 | Oct. 10, 1866 | SC | |
| 135th Inf. | Mar. 28, 1865 | Oct. 23, 1865 | NC | |
| 136th Inf. | July 15, 1865 | Jan. 4, 1866 | GA | |

| | | | | |
|---|---|---|---|---|
| 137th Inf. | Enrolled Apr. 8, 1865; mustered into U.S. service June 1, 1865 | Jan. 15, 1866 | GA | |
| 138th Inf. | July 15, 1865 | Jan. 6, 1866 | GA | |
| 54th Mass. Colored Inf. | Mar. 30-May 13, 1863 | Aug. 20, 1865 | MA | 1863: Enfield .577 |
| 55th Mass. Colored Inf. | May 31-June 22, 1863 | Aug. 29, 1865 | MA | 1863: Enfield .577 |
| 29th Conn. Colored Inf. | Mar. 8, 1864 | Oct. 24, 1865 | CT | 1864: Enfield .577 |
| 6th La. Colored Inf. (60 days) | July 4, 1863 | Aug. 13, 1863 | LA | |
| 7th La. Colored Inf. | July 10, 1863 | Aug. 6, 1863 | LA | |
| Company A, unassigned (1 year) | Sept. 28, 1864 | July 29, 1865 | VA | |
| Independent Company A (100 days) | July 20, 1864 | Nov. 14, 1864 | PA | |

*To conserve space, certain abbreviations have been used:

Enfield or Enfield .577 = Enfield rifles or rifled muskets .577 cal.. P1853

Springfield or Springfield .58 = M1855 or M1861 Harpers Ferry or Springfield rifled muskets or other regulation US rifled muskets .58 cal.

M1863 rm or M1863 rifled musket = M1863 Springfield rifled muskets .58 cal.

Austrian .54 = Austrian rifled muskets .54 or .55 cal.

M1842 rifled .69 = M1842 Springfield or other regulation US rifled muskets .69 cal.

M1842 smoothbore .69 = M1842 Springfield smoothbore muskets .69 cal.

altered or converted muskets = generally, .69 cal. smoothbore muskets that may have been originally flintlock weapons.

Remington .44 = M1861 Remington Army revolver .44 cal.

rm = rifled musket

# Bibliography

Andrew, C.C. *History of the Campaign of Mobile; Including the Cooperative Operations of Gen. Wilson's Cavalry in Alabama*. New York: D. Van Nostrand, 1889.

Bahney, Robert Stanley. *Generals and Negroes: Education of Negroes by the Union Army, 1861-1865*. Ann Arbor, MI: University Microfilms; unpublished dissertation, University of Michigan, 1965.

Baird, George W. *The 32d Regiment, U.S.C.T. at the Battle of Honey Hill.* n.p. [1889].

Bangs, I.S. *The Ullman Brigade.* Warpapers, State of Maine, MOLLUS, vol. II, 1902.

Bates, Samuel P. *History of Pennsylvania Volunteers 1861-1865.* 5 vols. Harrisburg, 1869-1871.

Beatty, John. *The Citizen-Soldier; or, Memoirs of a Volunteer*. Cincinnati: Wilstach, Baldwin and Co., 1879.

Berlin, Ira, et al, Editors. *Freedom: A Documentary History of Emancipation, 1861-1867, Series II, The Black Military Experience.* London: Cambridge University Press, 1982.

Berry, Mary Frances. *Military Necessity and Civil Rights Policy: Black Citizenship and the Constitution, 1861-1868.* Port Washington, NY: Kennikat Press, 1977.

Binder, Frederick M. "Pennsylvania Negro Regiments in the Civil War," *Journal of Negro History.* vol. 37, October 1952.

Blassingame, John W. "The Freedom Fighters," *Negro History Bulletin.* vol. 28, February 1965.

—. "Negro Chaplains in the Civil War," *Negro History Bulletin.* vol. 27, October 1963.

—. "The Organization and Use of Negro Troops in the Union Army, 1863-1865." Unpublished Master's Thesis, Howard University, 1961.

—. "The Recruitment of Colored Troops in Kentucky, Maryland and Missouri, 1863-1865," *The Historian.* 1967.

—. "The Selection of Officers and Non-Commissioned Officers of Negro Troops in the Union Army, 1863-1865," *Negro History Bulletin.* vol. 30, January 1967.

—. "The Union Army as an Educational Institution for Negroes, 1862-1865," *Journal of Negro Education.* vol. 34, Spring 1965.

Brewer, James H. *The Confederate Negro: Virginia's Craftsmen and Military Laborers, 1861-1865.* Durham, NC Duke University Press, 1969.

Brown, William Wells. *The Negro in the American Rebellion, His Heroism and His Fidelity.* Boston: Lee and Shepard, 1867.

Browne, Frederick W. *My Service in the U.S. Colored Cavalry.* Cincinnati: Ohio Commandery of the Loyal Legion, 1908.

Burchard, Peter. *One Gallant Rush: Robert Gould Shaw and His Brave Black Regiment*. New York: St. Martin's Press, 1965.

Butler, Benjamin F. *Butler's Book*. Boston: A.M. Thayer and Co., 1892.

[Califf, J.M.] *Record of the Services of the Seventh Regiment, U.S. Colored Troops, from September, 1863, to November, 1866*. Providence, RI: E.L. Freeman and Co., 1878.

Chase, Salmon P. *Inside Lincoln's Cabinet*. Edited by David Donald. New York: Longmans, Green and Co., 1954.

Chenery, William H. *The Fourteenth Regiment Rhode Island Heavy Artillery (Colored) in the War to Preserve the Union, 1861-1865*. Providence RI: Snow and Farnham, 1898.

Clark, Peter H. *The Black Brigade of Cincinnati: Being a Report of its Labors and a Muster-Roll of its Members*. Cincinnati: Joseph B. Boyd, printer, 1864.

Cochrane, John. *Arming the Slaves in the War for the Union*. New York: Rogers and Sherwood, 1875.

Coffet, W.A. and J.M. Moris. *The Military and Civil History of Connecticut During the War of 1861-1865*. Ledyard Bill, NY, 1869.

Confederate States of America. Congress. *Journal of the Congress of the Confederate States of America, 1861-1865*. 7 vols., Washington, DC: GPO, 1904.

Cornish, Dudley Taylor. *The Sable Arm: Negro Troops in the Union Army, 1861-1865*. New York: Longmans, Green and Co., 1956.

Cowden, Robert. *A Brief Sketch of the Organization and Services of the Fifty-Ninth Regiment of United States Colored Infantry, and Biographical Sketches*. Dayton, OH: United Brethren Publishing House, 1883.

Dennett, George M. *History of the Ninth U.S.C. Troops*. Philadelphia: King and Baird, 1866.

Drinkard, Dorothy Lee. *A Regiment History of the Twenty-Ninth Infantry, United States Colored Regiments, 1864-1865*. Washington, DC: Howard University, 1963.

Dyer, Frederick H. *A Compendium of the War of the Rebellion*. Dayton, OH: Morningside Bookshop, 1978.

Emilio, Luis F. *The Assault on Fort Wagner, July 18, 1863: The Memorable Charge of the Fifty-Fourth Regiment of Massachusetts Volunteers*. Boston: Rand Avery Co., 1887.

—. *A Brave Black Regiment: History of the Fifty-Fourth Regiment of Massachusetts Volunteer Infantry, 1863-1865*. New York: Arno Press, 1969; originally published 1894.

—. *History of the Fifty-Fourth Regiment of Massachusetts Volunteer Infantry, 1863-1865*. Boston: Boston Book Co., 1894.

Fleetwood, Christian A. *The Negro As A Soldier*. Washington, DC: Howard University Press, 1895.

*Forty-Fourth Regiment U.S. Colored Troops*. Gettysburg, PA: J.E. Wible, 1866.

Frassanito, William A. *Grant and Lee, The Virginia Campaign*. NY: Charles Scribner's Sons.

Friends' Association of Philadelphia. *Statistics of the Operations of the Executive Board of Friends' Association of Philadelphia, and its Vicinity, for the Relief of Colored Freedmen*. 19 January 1864. Philadelphia: Inquirer Printing Office [1864].

Glatthaar, Joseph T. *Forged in Battle*. New York: Free Press, 1990.

Hallowell, Norwood P. *The Negro as a Soldier in the War of the Rebellion*. Boston: Little, Brown and Co., 1897.

Headly, P.C. *Massachusetts in the Rebellion*. Boston: Walker, Fuller, and Co., 1866.

Heitman, F. *Historical Register and Dictionary of the U.S. Army*. vol. 1, GPO, 1903.

Higginson, Thomas Wentworth. *Army Life in a Black Regiment*. Boston: Fields, Osgood, and Co., 1870.

Hill, Isaac J. *A Sketch of the 29th Regiment of Connecticut Colored Troops*. Baltimore: Daugherty, Maguire and Co., 1870.

Hunter, David. *Report of the Military Services of Gen. David Hunter, U.S.A*. New York: D. Van Nostrand, 1873.

Johnson, Robert, and Clarence Buel, eds. *Battles and Leaders of the Civil War*. 4 vols. New York: The Century Co., 1887-1888.

Kautz, August V. *Reminiscences of the Civil War*. Typed manuscript, July 1936.

Kireker, Charles. *History of the 116th Regiment U.S.C. Infantry*. Philadelphia: King and Baird, 1866.

Knox, Thomas W. *Camp-Fire and Cotton-Field*. New York: Blelock and Co., 1865.

Lawrence, Catherine S. *Sketch of Life and Labors of Miss Catherine S. Lawrence*. Revised edition, Albany, NY: James B. Lyon, 1896.

Lord, Francis A. *Civil War Sutlers and Their Wares*. A.S. Barnes and Co., 1969.

Main, Edwin M. (compiler). *The Story of the Marches, Battles and Incidents of the Third United States Colored Cavalry, a Fighting Regiment in the War of the Rebellion, 1861-1865. With Official Orders and Reports Relating Thereto, Compiled from the Rebellion Records*. Louisville, KY: Globe Printing Co., 1908.

Matson, Dan. "The Colored Man in the Civil War," *Sketches and Incidents*. vol. 2, Des Moines, IA: The Kenyon Press, 1898.

McConnell, Roland C. Negro *Troops of Antebellum Louisiana: A History of the Battalion of Free Men of Color*. Baton Rouge, LA: Louisiana State University Press, 1968.

McPherson, James M. *Marching Toward Freedom: The Negro in the Civil War, 1861-1865*. New York: Alfred A. Knopf, 1967.

—. *The Negro's Civil War*. New York: Pantheon Books, 1965.

Meyer, Howard N. *Colonel of the Black Regiment: The Life of Thomas Wentworth Higginson*.

Michigan. Adjutant General's Office. *Record of Service of Michigan Volunteers in the Civil War 1861-1865: First Colored Infantry*. Kalamazoo, MI: Michigan Legislature, n.d.

Mickley, Jeremiah Marion. *The Forty-Third Regiment United States Colored Troops*. Gettysburg, PA: J.E. Wible, 1866.

Moore, Frank, ed. *The Rebellion Record: A Diary of American Events*. 11 vols. New York: D. Van Nostrand, 1861-1868.

Newton, Alexander Herritage. *Out of the Briars: An Autobiography and Sketch of the Twenty-Ninth Regiment Connecticut Volunteers*. Philadelphia: A.M.E. Book Concern, 1910.

Norton, Henry Allyn. "Colored Troops in the War of the Rebellion," *Glimpse of the Nation's Struggle*. St. Paul, MN: Review Publishing Co., 1903.

Parton, James. *General Butler in New Orleans: History of the Administration of the Department of the Gulf in the Year 1862*. New York: Mason Bros., 1864.

Phisterer, Frederick. *Statistical Record of the Armies of the United States*. Charles Scribner's Sons, 1883.

Rollin, Frank A. *Life and Public Services of Martin R. Delany*. Boston: Lee and Shepard, 1868.

Sauers, Richard A. *Advance the Colors*. Capitol Preservation Committee, 1987.

Seraile, William. "New York's Black Regiments During the Civil War." Unpublished Doctoral Dissertation, City University of New York, 1977.

Taylor, Frank H. *Philadelphia in the Civil War 1861-1865*. Philadelphia, 1913.

Taylor, Susie King. *Reminiscences of My Life in Camp*. New York: Arno Press, 1968; originally published 1902.

Thomas, Henry Goddard. "The Colored Troops at Petersburg," *Century Illustrated Monthly*. September 1887, vol. 34.

Todd, Frederick P. *American Military Equipage 1851-1872*. vol. II, State Forces. Chatham Square Press, 1983.

Trowbridge, Charles Tyler. "Six Months in the Freedmen's Bureau with a Colored Regiment," *Glimpses of the Nation's Struggle*, vol. 6. Minneapolis, MN: Aug. Davis, Publisher, 1909.

U.S. Army War College. Historical Section. *The Colored Soldier in the United States Army*.

U.S. Congress. Joint Committee on the Conduct of the War. Report. 38th Congress, 1st session. Sen. Rep. Com. No. 63 and 68. Washington, DC: n.p. 1864.

—. *Report of the Committee...on the Attack on Petersburg, on the 30th Day of July, 1864*. 38th Congress, 2d session, Sen. Rep. Com. No. 114. Washington, DC: GPO, 1865.

United States Senate. Committee on Veterans' Affairs. "Medal of Honor Recipients, 1863-1978." Washington, DC: GPO, 1979.

U.S. War Department. *Official Army Register of the Volunteer Force of the United States Army, 1861-1865*. Part VIII, Washington, DC, 1867.

—. *U.S. Infantry Tactics...for the Use of the Colored Troops of the United States Infantry*. New York: D. Van Nostrand, 1863.

—. *The War of the Rebellion: A Compilation of the Official Records of the Union and Confederate Armies*. 128 vols. Washington, DC: GPO, 1880-1901.

Urwin, Gregory J.W. "I Want You to Prove Yourself Men," *Civil War Times Illustrated*. Nov./Dec. 1989.

Voegeli, V. Jacque. *Free But Not Equal: The Midwest and the Negro During the Civil War*. Chicago: University of Chicago Press, 1967.

# Index

227